Redcoats Along the Hudson
The Struggle for North America, 1754–63

The Death of General Wolfe. Edward Penny. *Ashmolean Museum, University of Oxford.*

Noel St John Williams is a former regular Army officer who served with the Sherwood Foresters (45th Foot) and was attached to the Intelligence Corps as a Japanese Interrogator during the Second World War. He later served as the last Chief Education Officer in the Far East. As a civilian, he served as Assistant Director of Education on the Cheshire County Council and as District Education Officer in Chester. He is a graduate of King's College London, where he studied History, English and French Literature.

Colonel Williams is the author of *Judy O'Grady and the Colonel's Lady: The Army Wife and Camp Follower Since 1600* and *Redcoats and Courtesans: The Birth of the British Army 1660–90*, both published by Brassey's, and of *Tommy Atkins' Children: 300 Years of Army Children's Education.*

REDCOATS
ALONG THE
HUDSON

The Struggle for North America 1754-63

NOEL ST JOHN WILLIAMS

First English Edition 1997
First Paperback Edition 1998

UK editorial offices:
Brassey's, 33 John Street, London WC1N 2AT
Tel. 0171 753 7777 Fax. 0171 753 7794
E-mail: brasseys@dial.pipex.com
Website: http://www.brasseys.com
UK orders: Marston Book Services, PO Box 269, Abingdon, OX14 4SD

North American orders: Brassey's Inc., PO Box 960,
Herndon, VA 22070, USA

Noel St John Williams has asserted his moral right to be identified as
the author of this work.

Library of Congress Cataloging in Publication Data
available

British Library Cataloguing in Publication Data
A catalogue record for this book is available from the British Library

ISBN 1 85753 224 4 Paperback

Typeset by Harold, Martin and Redman Ltd
Printed in Great Britain by Biddles Ltd, Guildford, Surrey

For my wife, Christina,
for a lifetime's support

CONTENTS

PREFACE

On 29 May 1993 the London *Daily Telegraph* published an article entitled *'Redcoats of the Hudson Valley to be buried with full military honours in America'*. Bones of British soldiers and their women and children had been found in a mass grave in 1952 when Fort William Henry – the setting for James Fenimore Cooper's famous novel and the film *The Last of the Mohicans* – was rebuilt as a tourist attraction. Thousands of artefacts (cannons, musket balls, coins, rifles, belts and buckles, and so on), including human and animal skeletons, were unearthed by the archaeologists. They were put on display in the museum's restored buildings, including the bones: to honour the remains of a British soldier, let alone his women and children was unthinkable. For 200 years, since the War of American Independence, the redcoat had been the symbol of a colonial yoke, and an object of dislike for every true American.

But by the 1990s the American people had come to believe that time and a mature nation should heal old wounds, dispel mythology, and kindle an interest in part of their historical past. One obvious result has been the authentic reconstruction in Canada and America of many of the forts and battle sites mentioned in this book, which today attract thousands of visitors. And another result was that the bones of the British soldiers were to be given a public burial, televised nationwide, with all the ceremonial of a military funeral.

William Henry, and the nearby Fort Edward, were two strategic bases built by the British during the long British–French struggle for mastery of the Champlain Valley–Hudson River route connecting the American colonies with Canada. During the 1750s, in the conflict known in Europe as the Seven Years' War (1756–63) and in America as the French and Indian War, thousands of British and provincial soldiers and their families occupied these forts. In the summer of 1757, after a merciless pounding by French artillery, the small group of British and colonial defenders in Fort William Henry were forced to surrender to the Marquis de Montcalm and his 10,000-strong army of French and Indians. The terms of the capitulation were broken, and many British and colonial men, women and children were massacred by the bloodthirsty Indians. The 1936 movie version of this event, *The Last of the Mohicans*, is shown hourly at Fort William Henry, together with video and live enactments of military life at the fort.

In 1755 the neighbouring Fort Edward was built at the 'Great Carrying Place', with barracks, blockhouses, guardrooms and stores, and a hospital to house British regular and provincial soldiers. Robert Rogers and some 400 of his famous Rangers camped there. In 1759 General Amherst assembled his army at the fort for the attack on

Ticonderoga. Fort Edward has also been reconstructed, and its exhibits displayed to the public.

The story of the French and Indian War is rich in dramatic situations and colourful characters, and is certainly not overshadowed by the later American War of Independence, though strangely neglected by comparison. The names of Washington, Wolfe and Montcalm may stir a few school memories; their deeds may be recorded in military textbooks; but their significant contributions in shaping the English-speaking world is too often forgotten. The British still feel a national pride in General Wolfe, the French in the Marquis de Montcalm, the Americans in General Washington and Canada in its governor, the Marquis de Vaudreuil. However, each nation tends to shade its accounts of the conflict, in accordance with its own national, political or religious preferences. I, for instance, am a former British army officer, whose regiment the 45 Foot (the Sherwood Foresters) features in the story. I hope that my army and regimental pride show but do not prejudice the story I tell.

The central part of the story is well known – the midnight climb of the precipitous cliffs to assault the nigh-impregnable fortress of Quebec, the brief clash of arms, and the deaths of the two opposing commanders in the moment of victory and defeat. These stirring events still capture people's imaginations after 250 years. It was 'the most pregnant single event in all American History, since Columbus discovered the New World,' wrote the Canadian historian William Wood.[1] Another wrote[2] that the rise and fall of New France is the most dramatic chapter in that story. The French and Indian War also has an important political and social setting, in which women, both high and low, played a meaningful role. I hope readers will feel I have done justice to such a story!

ACKNOWLEDGEMENTS

This book owes much to the printed sources listed in the references and to those who have kindly given permission to reproduce copyright material. As always, Brassey's (UK) Ltd have been the most courteous and helpful of publishers. I received invaluable help from Mrs JoAnne Fuller of Fort Edward and Michael J Palumbo, Curator of Fort William Henry. I would also like to acknowledge my debt to Mr Angus Madders and the staff of the Chester Public Library; Mr Tim Ward, Librarian, The Prince Consort's Library; The Director, National Army Museum; Mrs Heather Gillis (Photo Archives) and Mr Eric Krause, Historical Records Supervisor, Fortress of Louisbourg National Historic Site; Colonel J M A Tillett, Curator, Regimental Museum (Oxford), The Royal Green Jackets; Adrian Bristow, Diane and Brian Dodwell for historical material; Lesley Armstrong for her helpful suggestions and excellent word-processing; Cherry Ekins, who once again has given valuable help in the editing and processing of this book; and to the following for permission to reproduce copyright material.

Ian K Steele, *Betrayals: Fort William Henry and the Massacre*, Oxford University Press, New York, 1990. Margaret T Trouncer, *The Pompadour*, Hutchinson, 1936. Dorothy Marshall, *18th Century England*, Longman, 1989 Group Ltd. The Master and Fellows of Massey College, University of Toronto. Charles P Stacey, *Quebec 1759*, Macmillan, 1959. Arthur R M Lower, *Colony to Nation: A History of Canada,* Longman Group Ltd. G E Mingay, *English Landed Society in the 18th Century*, Routledge and Kegan Paul, 1963. International Thomson Publishing. James A Williamson, *A Short History of British Expansion (The Old Colonial Empire),* Macmillan Ltd, 1947. William Wood, *The Fight for Canada*, Constable Publishers, 1905. Beckles Willson, *The Life and Letters of James Wolfe*, Heinemann, 1909. Reed Consumer Books. R H Mahon, *The Life of General James Murray*, John Murray. Jacques Levron, *Pompadour,* Allen and Unwin, HarperCollins 1963. H Noel Williams, *Madame de Pompadour*, Harper, 1925. HarperCollins Publishers Ltd. *English Historical Documents Vol IX.*, Eye & Spottiswoode, reprinted by permission of Reed Books. J O Lindsay (ed.), *The New Cambridge Modern History Vol 7*, Cambridge University Press, 1979, The Colonel Commandant, officers and men of the Royal Green Jackets for Lewis Butler, *The Annals of The King's Royal Rifle Corps. Vol I: The Royal Americans (60 Foot),* 1913. The Colonel Commandant, officers and men of the 22 Foot. The Cheshire Regiment for Bernard Rigby, *Ever Glorious: The History of the Cheshire Regiment,* 1994. Roy Porter, *The Penguin Social History of Britain: English Society in the 18th Century*, Allen Lane, 1982; revised edition, Penguin Books, 1980. The Fortress of Louisbourg Parks Canada, for colour slides representing military life at the fortress during the 18th century.

LIST OF ILLUSTRATIONS

LIST OF MAPS

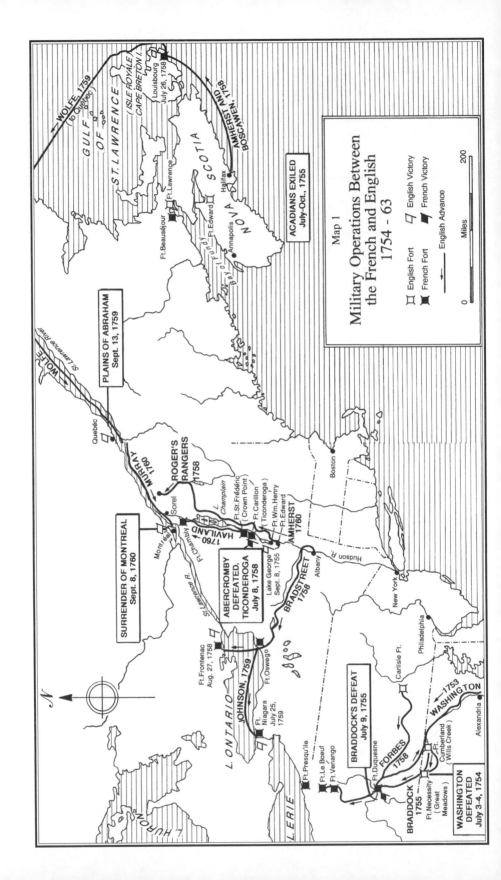

Map 1

Military Operations Between
the French and English
1754 - 63

1

EARLY SETTLERS,
IN NORTH AMERICA

The English claim to North America dates from the reign of Henry VII. In 1497 John Cabot, a mariner from Genoa, 'bravely set forth' from Bristol under Henry's patronage with an English crew of 18, 'to set up our banner on any new found land'. Three months later, Cabot returned with the exciting news that he had found land on the other side of the Atlantic.[1] To the king's disappointment, Cabot had discovered 'banks of teeming fish but not the rich spices, jewels and silks of the Orient' he was seeking. Thus Newfoundland with its rich fishing grounds became the oldest of the British dominions; Cabot explored the coasts of Maine and Massachusetts, and Britain entered the struggle for trade and sovereignty in the New World.

England's rivals were France, Holland, Spain and Portugal, also pursuing trade and settlement. Their early explorers, fired by a spirit of adventure and the promise of rich rewards, would claim for king and country the lands they strove to reach.[2] In 1492, for instance, Christopher Columbus, sailing under the banner of Ferdinand and Isabella, landed in the Bahamas and later in Haiti. Followed by the soldier-adventurer Hernando Cortes, he opened up for Spain the gold and silver of Mexico and Peru.

Although England claimed to have discovered the North American continent (named after the Florentine Amerigo Vespucci), France, too, was exploring these waters. As early as 1534, Jacques Cartier, a master pilot of St Malo, having heard mass and written his last will and testament, had sailed to Newfoundland and, hugging the coastline, planted the Catholic cross beside the great waterway of the St Lawrence. Then he lodged the French *fleurs de lis* on the Bay of Gaspé, claiming the land for his Catholic master, François I. In a second voyage the following year, 'this Columbus of French Canada' reached Mont Réal, the hill on which Montreal now stands, although Montreal island had been inhabited by Mohawk Indians of the Iroquois nation long before. To support his territorial claims, Cartier took two native Americans and some animal furs to show his king.[3] But the king was at war and Cartier had found no gold; soon Cartier and Canada disappeared from view.

Earlier still, the fishermen of Normandy and Brittany had been active around the coast of Newfoundland, naming Cape Breton after their homeland.

Each spring Basque, Portuguese, English and French fishermen netted huge hauls of cod in these waters, to supply over 100 days of abstinence from meat each year in Catholic Europe. In 1523–4 the Florentine Verrazzano, in the employ of the King of France, had landed in what is now North Carolina. He visited today's New York and Newport, and sailed along the coast of New England to Acadia (modern Nova Scotia), giving France some claim to these territories.

In 1605 the great French explorer Samuel de Champlain founded Port Royal in Acadia (later named Annapolis Royal by the British). Port Royal became the first French settlement in the New World. There, in 1610, Jean de Poutrincourt, a nobleman and military officer, employed a priest called Flesché to baptise the old Micmac chief Membertou, 'the first step in that great task of Christianising the New World, which marked the first years of France's imperial policy'.[4] Membertou's squaws, children, grandchildren and entire tribe were next converted, and renamed after the French royal family, court nobles and ladies of rank. Membertou became Henri, his chief squaw Marie, and a son of the old chief was called Louis in honour of the heir to the French throne. For Poutrincourt it was also a symbol of friendship, which helped to ensure the survival of the settlers.

In 1608, Champlain founded Quebec. He explored the lake which bears his name, as far as the two headlands, which feature prominently in our story – Crown Point (Fort St Frédéric) and Ticonderoga (Fort Carillon).[5] He took the warpath with the Hurons against the mighty Iroquois to the south of Lake Oneida, pushing westward to the Great Lakes. Like Sir Walter Raleigh, who founded Virginia and named the colony after his 'Virgin Queen', Elizabeth I, Champlain carried a vision of empire and of a New France established in America.[6]

These early 17th century adventurers found a land unexplored but by no means uninhabited. Indians had crossed from Siberia and the Bering Straits, then a bridge of glacial ice, at least 10,000 years earlier, and spread over the length and breadth of America. The tribes had different cultures and customs, spoke over 600 different languages, and ranged from the highly civilised Mayas, Aztecs and Incas in the south to the more primitive tribes in the north.[7]

During the reigns of the Tudors, Mary and Elizabeth, England was blessed with domestic peace and growing prosperity. She sent expeditions to the four corners of the globe, and English 'sea-dogs' began to attack Spanish naval power. John Hawkins systematically raided Spain's Caribbean ports, while supplying their mines and sugar plantations with slaves from Africa. His young cousin Francis Drake sacked Spanish towns all over the Americas, before returning home in 1580 in the *Golden Hind* 'very richly fraught with gold, silver, silk, pearls and precious stones'.[8] Elizabeth debated whether to clap him into prison as a pirate or reward him for rendering good service to the

State. She knighted him! With the defeat of the Spanish Armada in 1588, the power and prestige of Spain began to decline, leaving the British to dominate the colonial scene. Martin Frobisher explored northeast Canada in search of a 'Northwest Passage', and in 1585 Sir Walter Raleigh settled briefly in Roanoke Island, which proved unsuitable for a permanent military base. Henry Hudson, also seeking the wealth of Asia, sailed into New York harbour in 1609, and proceeded up the majestic river named after him.

In 1607 the English made their first permanent settlement at James Town in Virginia, chosen for its fine anchorage and potential as a fort. (Traces of the original fort, as well as the remains of one of the first English settlers, i.e. person and helmet and breastplate, English coins dated 1560–1603 and native jewellery were recently discovered, according to a report of 13 September 1996 in *The Independent*.) They survived epidemics, constant raids by the native Indians, internal disputes and famine, thanks to their strong Puritan faith and the rigid military discipline imposed by their High Marshal, Thomas Dale, who had seen military service in the Netherlands. He punished 'Idleness, Gambling, Drunkenness and excess in Apparel with hanging, burning, whipping and breaking on the wheel'. To keep peace between the Indians and the settlers, he kidnapped Pocahontas, the chief's attractive daughter, and kept her hostage at James Town. There she met and married (1614) John Rolfe, a prominent planter, who successfully raised tobacco and cured it to give the colony a new lease of life. Dale wanted to marry Pocahontas's younger sister, a request her father wisely refused, especially as Dale already had a wife in England.

The first settlers in Virginia were chiefly single men, 'who had not the encumbrance of wives and children in England, and, if they had, they did not expose them to the fatigue and hazard of so long a voyage, until they saw how it should fare with themselves'. When they had settled comfortably in Virginia, 'they grew sensible of the misfortune of wanting wives; and such as had left wives in England sent for them'. Unwilling to marry Indian women because they were pagans (although some informal liaisons had taken place), the single men hoped that 'the plenty in which they lived might invite modest and well-behaved women of small fortunes to go over thither from England'. Women of good character but without fortune might also marry very well. In fact, 'the first planters were so far from expecting money with a woman, that it was a common thing for them to buy a deserving wife [from the Joint Stock Company] at the price of 100 pound of best tobacco leaf, and make themselves believe they had a hopeful bargain'. Women immigrants thus came to the colony, with Mrs Forrest and her maid, Anne Burras, becoming the first women settlers in North America.[9]

In 1620 the Pilgrim Fathers landed in the *Mayflower* at Plymouth Rock in Massachusetts, bringing another wave of immigrants: 102 men, women and children, with William Bradford, the destined leader of the colony.

More than a century had now elapsed since Cabot's discovery of the American continent. Neither England nor France had made much progress in extending their dominion in the New World. The famous historian Francis Parkman wrote:

> On the banks of the James River was a nest of woebegone Englishmen, a handful of Dutch fur traders at the mouth of the Hudson, and a few shivering Frenchmen among the snowdrifts of Acadia: while deep within the wild monotony of desolation on the icy verge of the great St Lawrence river, the hand of Champlain upheld the *fleur de lis* on the rocks of Quebec.[10]

The balance of future settlement, however, lay with France, since the St Lawrence formed a highway into the Canadian interior, promising access to regions unknown to the English colonists.[11]

During the 17th century the pace of exploration and settlement quickened. In 1621, James I gave a Scottish nobleman, Sir William Alexander, a grant of land, which he called Nova Scotia after his native country. He planted a colony there. In 1627, during a war with France, London merchants funded an expedition up the St Lawrence, captured Quebec, and established settlements in Cape Breton. But Charles I, always short of money, especially as only half of the dowry of his queen, Henrietta Maria, sister of King Louis XIII of France, had been paid, sold these conquests back to France (1632) for the paltry sum of £50.000.[12] By 1630, the Massachusetts Bay Company had founded Boston and ten other Puritan settlements in the neighbourhood with over 1,000 inhabitants.

In 1660, Montreal was the outpost of New France, a fort with about 40 houses clustered round the church, protecting 150 Frenchmen and their families. It was constantly under threat from the hostile Iroquois Indians, who prowled around their houses, seized their womenfolk, and forced the men to carry weapons wherever they went. In answer to their petitions for help, Louis XIV sent a regiment of 1,200 seasoned regulars (the Carignan-Salières Regiment) to the St Lawrence to protect the scattered hamlets. The soldiers built Forts Chambly and St Jean in the Richelieu valley, and marched against the Mohawk villages. Losing its way, the regiment arrived at Albany, recently ceded to Britain. After obtaining provisions they withdrew – the first time regular troops from New France had stood on the frontiers of the British colonies.

Henry Hudson, an Englishman, had explored New York, Albany and the Hudson river in the name of the Dutch East India Company. The Dutch Republic, quick to appreciate the opportunities for fur trading, claimed the Hudson region for themselves. Finding this trade more profitable than plundering treasure-laden Spanish galleons sailing from Spanish ports in the West Indies or South America, Dutch merchants soon established and owned a large part of the carrying trade between the New World and the Old. Trading posts were built from Fort Orange (Albany) to Fort Nassau (near modern Philadelphia) on the Delaware river and at Fort Amsterdam on Manhattan Island.[13] In 1626 they bought the island from the Manhattan Indians for 60 guilders. They surrounded Fort Amsterdam with a wall (New York's Wall Street) to keep the Indians out and straying settlers in, and restored the old Indian hunting track, which they called the Broad Way.[14]

In 1664, Colonel Richard Nicolls, appointed by the Duke of York to claim New Netherlands for the British crown, appeared with a fleet and a body of New England volunteers before Fort Amsterdam and demanded its surrender. Peter Stuyvesant, the governor, was forced to capitulate. Fort Amsterdam was renamed New York, and the Dutch New Netherlands, an obstacle to a continuous Anglo-Saxon seaboard, was removed. In 1667 the Treaty of Breda confirmed the British acquisition in exchange for Surinam in the Dutch East Indies, and at the same time New Sweden became New Jersey and Delaware.[15]

In 1678 Robert de la Sale, a young Frenchman of good family with a passion for exploration, discovered the Niagara Falls. Recognising their strategic importance, he built a fort there. He then embarked at Lake Michigan and paddled down the Mississippi, until he reached the Gulf of Mexico. He called its shores Louisiana, in honour of Louis XIV. De la Sale had travelled 5,000 miles, and claimed for France the vast territory between the Alleghenies and the Rocky Mountains through which he had passed. Thus France began the settlement of both extremes of the Mississippi. Enthusiastically, de la Sale made great plans for colonisation and commerce between Europe and the Mississippi. Twice he visited France, and tried unsuccessfully to interest Colbert, France's minister for industry, commerce and naval affairs, in his schemes.[16] In 1687 this romantic figure, the greatest of all French explorers, was treacherously slain by one of his own men.

In order to protect their territorial claims and monopoly of the lucrative Indian fur trade, the French built an arc of fortified stockades, mission stations and trading posts, which usually consisted of three or four log buildings surrounded by a palisade. These stretched from the mouth of the St Lawrence to the mouth of the Mississippi – in the territory now covered by the states of Wisconsin, Minnesota, Michigan and Illinois. Count Frontenac, one of the greatest governors of New France, built the strategic fort which bears his name (modern Kingston) at the outlet of Lake Ontario, the key to the colony's west, deep in Iroquois territory. In 1718, New Orleans was founded as the capital of the infant province of French Louisiana.[17]

When Charles II was restored to his throne in 1660, he inherited a very varied collection of American 'plantations'. Virginia had become a royal colony (1625), prospering by hard work, tobacco, and slaves imported from African

Guinea in ships trading from Liverpool and Bristol. Its aristocracy supported the Stuarts but the common people, dissatisfied with poor tobacco prices and tax burdens, revolted. The governor, William Berkeley, personified in his dress, bearing and views the court of Charles II, and was the natural leader of Virginian Cavalier society. Berkeley suppressed the rebellion cruelly, hanging 37 of the leaders and fining, banishing and imprisoning many more. Charles II replaced him, but supported the autocratic rule of his successors. The majority of the population were under 30 years of age, the men outnumbering the women by three to one.

By now, 'the advantages of the climate and the fruitfulness of the soil were well known, and all the dangers incident to infant settlement were over'. Gone, too, were the days 'when parents disburdened themselves of lascivious sons, masters of bad servants, and wives of ill-husbands, who would rather starve than lay their hands to labour.' So people of better condition began to settle in the colony 'with their families, either to increase their estates, or else to avoid religious or political persecution'. For example, Roundheads for the most part went to New England, and Cavaliers to Virginia, 'because that country was famous for holding out the longest for the [Stuart] royal family of any of the English dominions'.[18] This helped to balance the sexes and increase the population.

A charter for the establishment of the colony of Maryland had been issued in 1632 to the Catholic George Calvert, created Baron Baltimore by Charles I, after whose queen, Henrietta Maria, the colony was named. The colony established in 1634 by the second Lord Baltimore prospered, thanks to the healthiness of the location and the friendliness of the Indians. Here, too, single males predominated – many of them indentured servants – who were needed for the heavy work on the land. For the women this meant earlier marriage, a choice of suitors and remarriage on the death of their partner. It had been intended to establish the colony as a refuge for persecuted English Catholics but, to attract settlers, Lord Baltimore opened up the colony to penalised Protestants, many from neighbouring Virginia. To assist the governor and council, the people were allowed to elect a representative assembly, similar to Virginia's House of Burgesses. But for years Maryland was really the Baltimore's family property, until it was placed under the crown in 1691.

Charles II found the four New England colonies (Massachusetts, Connecticut, Rhode Island and New Hampshire) were in the hands of the Puritans, who had beheaded his father. During the Great Migration (1630–43), 20,000 hungry workers and religious dissenters had settled in 'New' England to lay the foundations of Anglo-Saxon North America. Another 45,000 settled in the southern colonies and in the West Indies. By 1650 the total population of the colonies was 52,000, but during the next 50 years it would rise rapidly to 250,000, aided by a vigorous colonisation policy, which offered 100 acres of land to free men and women who transported themselves to the plantations. A promotional tract for the Carolina proprietors, for instance, published in London in 1666, promised:

> If any maid or single woman have a desire to go over [to Carolina], they will think themselves in the Golden Age, when men paid a dowry for their wives. For if they be but civil, and under 50 years of age, some honest man or other will purchase them for their wives.[19]

Edicts of Charles II authorised the transportation to the English plantations in North America and the West Indies of such 'rogues, vagabonds and sturdy beggars as should be duly convicted or adjudged incorrigible'. To supply the great lack of servants there, parliament enacted on 21 March 1718 that:

> Those liable to be whipt or burnt in the hand or ordered to a workhouse could contract themselves to be transported for seven years.[20]

As a result of this Transportation of Convicts Act some 30,000 felons were shipped to America during the first half of the 18th century, though felony often included minor misdemeanours.

To reward his Cavalier friends and court favourites, and to pay off the huge debts incurred in regaining his throne, Charles II in 1663 gave large tracts of land in New York, New Jersey, the Carolinas, Delaware and Pennsylvania to eight proprietary stockholders.[21] They are remembered in many of the geographical names in the area. In 1670 he granted land and a charter to the Hudson Bay Company. In 1680 New Hampshire became a royal colony: the following year William Penn was granted a charter to establish Pennsylvania and in 1682 Philadelphia was founded. Commercial profit and religious freedom became the driving forces for the rapid expansion and prosperity of the 'plantations'. Within the space of 25 years there was a continuous line of 13 English colonies, with no political tie save a common allegiance to the English crown, extending along the North Atlantic seaboard from Maine to Spanish Florida. When the Duke of York was crowned James II in 1685, New York too became a royal colony.

In 1689 Louis XIV declared war on England: King William's War, which would drag on for 24 years, until ended by the Treaty of Utrecht in 1713. In America, Count Frontenac, the able but arrogant governor of New France and a handsome Gascon soldier of commanding presence, whose life had been spent amid the ceremony and gaiety of Versailles and the hardships of the European battlefield under Turenne, prepared to march on Albany and New York, via Lake George and Lake Champlain. His Indian allies swept down with fire and tomahawk on the defenceless frontiers of New York, Maine and

Massachusetts.[22] The 13 self-governing colonies showed neither unity nor zeal for the common cause. Each local governor, representing the crown, had to consult his elected assembly. Each refused to provide the troops[23] required by the English commander in chief, who had been sent out at the request of Massachusetts; and each colony haggled over the necessary supplies and transport. Fortunately, Frontenac's appeal to Louis XIV to send a French fleet to capture New York fell on deaf ears, and New York was spared. Otherwise, the story of Canada and of the United States might have been very different.[24]

The methods of colonisation adopted by Catholic France and Protestant Britain were fundamentally different, and proved one of the chief factors in deciding the conflict between them. The French, following the St Lawrence river and the Great Lakes, traded with the Indians for beaver furs, moose hides and deer skins, which were hunted and trapped by the Indian men and processed by their women. These wandering traders (*coureurs de bois),* often men of good birth, despised the French *habitants* as mere peasants and scorned marriage with their daughters. Instead, they chose an Indian wife or concubine, produced a brood of children, and in a few generations scarcely a native American tribe of the west was free from an infusion of French blood. With profit not settlement as their motive, the French debauched the Indians by selling them brandy, and debased their morals with their licentiousness. The Jesuits protested against these practices, but regarded their marriages to Indian girls as a method of disseminating the Catholic faith. Missionaries and soldiers followed the trade routes and French traders into Indian territory, made friends with the Indians, tried to convert and civilise them, and settled down in their native villages, intermarrying and living with them in peaceful co-existence.[25] But they did not dispossess them of their land, and at least outwardly respected their traditional rights.

The Jesuits led the way as soldiers of the Cross in French North America. The first Jesuit arrived in 1611, followed by a definite mission in 1625. The Society of Jesus was Spanish in origin and policy, not French, but its aim was to convert rather than exterminate the savage Indians. Many Jesuits travelled with Indian bands, slept and fed in their tents, and mastered their many dialects. Their missionary zeal earned for many a martyr's crown, and a record of unselfish heroism which constitutes one of Canada's proudest traditions.[26] Nuns, too, came to New France – the Ursulines to teach, the Hospitalières to heal, the Carmelites to pray, the Franciscans to serve the sick and poor. Many died in the service of God and France; their orders still survive in Montreal and Quebec in convents and hospitals.

Yet few new French immigrants were willing to settle in Canada and till its unrewarding soil, and investors saw only limited opportunities for economic development. France could produce daring soldiers, seamen and explorers in profusion, but never sufficient sober, hardworking cultivators of the New

England and Maryland type.[27] In 1664 the French government forbade agricultural settlement up-country from Montreal, and in 1716 refused to grant seigneuries (manors) in the region. Furthermore, by refusing French Huguenots the right to settle on the banks of the Mississippi, Louis XV checked the growth of the colony. 'The King has not driven Protestants from France to make a republic for them in America' they were told, when they petitioned to be allowed to settle with freedom of conscience.[28]

In 1674 New France became a royal colony and was given the constitution of a French province. While New England governed itself, New France was always under the hand of Old France and dependent on it. New France was given a governor, appointed by the French King, to whom he was responsible. Inside Canada he carried out the king's policies and directives, assisted by subordinate governors in Montreal and Three Rivers, and post commandants in the interior. The governor, domiciled in Quebec, commanded military operations and Indian affairs. In peacetime the man with the real power was the intendant and his subordinates, who were responsible for local administration, justice, police and finance, with great opportunities for fraud and corruption. Both governor and intendant were responsible to, and corresponded separately with, the minister of marine in Paris, who was charged with responsibility for colonial administration. Completing the governing trinity was the Catholic bishop, who controlled religious matters and church property. This system of government was cheap and swift, and with French law the basis of the land tenure, was founded on France's centralised feudalism[29] – with one important difference. The Canadian tenants (*habitants*) were virtually free of the feudal services and taxes, which ground down the peasants of the homeland.

To increase the number of settlers in New France, Louis XIV through his chief minister, Jean Baptiste Colbert, offered inducements to immigrants in 1674. Disbanded officers and soldiers of the Carignan regiment were given grants of land to settle and farm both sides of the St Lawrence and along the River Richelieu. Social life centred around the manor house (*seigneurie*) and the village church and priest. Here, army officers who had settled in Canada, government officials, and successful middle-class merchants, locally enrolled but despised by the French *noblesse*, hired out their land to *habitants*.[30] To help populate these new settlements, Colbert sent out shiploads of single men and 'assorted consignments of nubile but dowerless wenches, willing to marry anyone in a position to provide them with a home'.[31] In France a dowry was an essential prerequisite for marriage; and dowerless and illegitimate girls were sent to convents or faced a bleak economic future as low-paid servants, textile workers or worse.

It is estimated that between 1665 and 1673 Colbert sent 1,000 *filles de roi*, orphans or maidens without resources, to Canada and provided them with dowries and marriage bonuses. During Louis XIV's long reign some 20,000 such girls emigrated from France to be married – *'les demoiselles bien choisies'* for the officers, the humbler majority for the soldier and peasant settlers. In this market, according to one commentator,[32] the willing bridegrooms

> singled out their Brides, just as a Butcher does an Ewe from amongst a Flock of Sheep, with as much variety of size and shape and colour and change of Diet as could satisfy the most whimsical of appetites.

Colbert desired the young men to marry at 18 or 19, the girls at 14 or 15. There was no time for courtship; most were married in a fortnight. But, despite these measures, the French population could not keep pace with the continual influx of settlers in the English colonies, augmenting the natural population increase of those already settled. In 1663, for instance, the French inhabitants of New France numbered a mere 2,500, compared with a white population of over 80,000 in the American colonies. The 1666 census gave 3,215, of whom 2,034 were males. Quebec had a population of 547. One hundred years later, the Canadian census of 1754 gave a population of 55,000, and 7,000 in Louisiana, to the English colonial population of over one and a half million.[33] 'The English countered the French trader and priest with the settler,' wrote one historian,[34] 'whose slow, steady onward march dismayed the French, who had no answer for it but wilderness forts.'

Land hunger drove the British colonials westward, expanding over the Allegheny Mountains into the vast Indian hunting grounds, and, for commercial reasons, turning them into prosperous settlements. They built roads, along which their lumbering wagons could carry heavier loads than the light canoes of the French. They built houses, founded villages, tilled the soil, and bred children. The next group penetrated a little farther. As farmers and town-dwellers they concentrated in ever expanding groups and rapidly out-populated the French. By 1760 the population of the American colonies was approaching 1,700,000.[35] This was 'a population and wealth that New France could never hope to rival,' wrote Lower[36] – factors which would be decisive in the coming struggle!

The 'Thirteen Colonies' cultivated the friendship of the five (later six) nations of the Iroquois Indians (Mohawk, Oneida, Onondaga, Cajuga, Seneca and Tuscaroras, whose eagle and arrows feature on the American shield, living for the most part in New York state and northeast Pennsylvania), who numbered around 15,000. In 1701 the Iroquois, 'the best fighting savages in North America', ceded to King William III 'the territory north of the Ohio, stretching from Lake Erie as far as Ottawa, in return for the protection of the Crown of England'.[37] During the period 1714–50, this powerful Indian confederacy would act as a shield to the New York frontier and guard the highway to the west along the

Mohawk river. But the English never tried to understand the Indians, as the French did. 'The gayer nature of the French people,' wrote a contemporary,[38] 'led them to drink, dance and intermarry with the natives, even to dress in their war-paint and feathers, as the Governor, Count Frontenac (appointed in 1672), once did.' The Puritan Briton thought such practices shameful and classed them, along with the ritual of Popery and the Jesuits found so appealing by the Indians, as 'monkey tricks'.[39]

The French were careful to spread the belief that they only wished to hunt and trade, using the Indians as allies and commercial agents on terms favourable to both parties. The English, they declared, were enemies of the Indians, destroying their hunting grounds and driving away their game in order to establish crops and farmsteads. Although the English could undersell the French in trade goods – hatchets, tools, weapons and clothing – and their rum was cheaper than French brandy, they never gained the help of the Indians as the French did. In the early years of the struggle, the French would use considerable numbers of Indian 'braves' to supplement their regular forces.

Nevertheless, America's original inhabitants were doomed to decimation by warfare, disease, and the destruction and loss of their traditional hunting grounds. Over half their number would fall victim to malaria, typhoid, yellow fever, smallpox and dysentery brought by the European and African immigrants. During the 18th century, the Micmacs would be dispossessed in Acadia; the French and British would dispute the Ohio Valley with the Iroquois, and in the south the Cherokees would be threatened by the conflicting ambitions of Britain, France and Spain.[40]

The native Americans would make an important contribution to their European and colonial conquerors. They would teach them how to grow crops like maize and tobacco, to build and use the birch canoe and snowshoes, and how to use woodcraft in warfare. Above all, they would provide a consumer market for their manufactured goods, in exchange for native furs, hides and food.[41] But, commented Lower:[42]

> Whether the white man came to the Indian with Roman Catholicism or rum, bible or brandy, good intentions or bad, native habits and the structure of tribal life were shattered for ever by the unaccustomed, complex civilisation of the European.

Map 2

New France and
The British Colonies
in 1750

Scale of Miles

0   100   200   300   400

2

THE AMERICAN COLONIES

The Treaty of Utrecht (1713) ended France's bid to dominate Europe. It enhanced the prestige of Britain, especially in North America, and established her supremacy at sea. French military and diplomatic efforts, coupled with the Indian raids, had delayed the spread of English settlements and damaged New England's trade and fisheries. But the losses would be repaired, and trade and territory continue to expand in the colonies.[1]

The treaty successfully prevented the union of the French and Spanish crowns, and confirmed Britain's acquisition of Port Mahon in Minorca and the capture of Gibraltar (1704). The Asiento clause gave English merchants for 30 years the exclusive right to supply the Spanish colonies with 4,800 African slaves, and to send one British ship each year to Portobello to exchange manufactured goods for silver, indigo, and dyewoods. Despite Louis XIV's reluctance to surrender Acadia (Nova Scotia) 'according to its ancient boundaries', Newfoundland and all the French ports in Hudson Bay were ceded to Britain. The vagueness of the boundaries in Acadia would be a source of future conflict, but these concessions would especially benefit the New England colonists.

To compensate for the loss of Acadia, the French in 1720 began to build at enormous expense the fortress of Louisbourg on Cape Breton Island (Isle Royale). Louisbourg would command access through the mouth of the St Lawrence to the heart of Canada. The French also recognised the old claim that the Iroquois Indians were subjects of the English king. But with the assistance of their Jesuit priests, the French used their own Indian allies to harass the English settlers and stir up discontent among the Acadians. They built forts at Beauséjour in Nova Scotia, a massive stone fort at Crown Point, and others at Niagara and Chambly to protect Montreal from any attack from Lake Champlain. Detroit was built to exclude the English from the fur trade among the Indian nations of the west.

For the American colonies the period 1713 to 1763 was an era of rapid expansion and prosperity. The population grew from 360,000 to nearly 1,700,000 whites from Maine to Georgia, and this 'explosion' would continue. The 18th century immigrants were the aggrieved middle classes and the poor, who came to America, voluntarily or involuntarily, as freemen with some capital, indentured servants, or transported convicts. The nobles, the wealthy, the established and the contented, stayed at home. Population begat wealth; wealth was the offspring of trade; all three would lay the foundation of power. Travel and social life improved, as the pioneers steadily pushed back the frontiers, established towns and new settlements, laid out farms and plantations, reared their families and expanded their trade.

Before 1713 there was no real town between Philadelphia and Charles Town (Charleston). Boston, made the capital of Massachusetts in 1632, with its 20,000 inhabitants had become the largest and most important town in the colonies. With New York, it was nearly half a century old when Philadelphia was founded in 1681, and over 100 years old when Baltimore was settled in 1730. By 1760, Virginia had the largest population among the 13 colonies. Massachusetts Bay took second place, Pennsylvania third. New York had to yield sixth place to North Carolina.[2] The five most important towns were Philadelphia (23,000), New York (18,000), Boston (16,000), Charleston (8,000) and Newport (7,500).

Under the Hanoverians, the four New England colonies were nearly all of English descent. Their towns were compact little communities, centred around the meeting house, school and chapel. Their interests were agricultural and commercial, and because of their good harbours, seafaring, fishing, lumbering and shipbuilding prospered. They exported pickled beef and port, distilled West Indian sugar and molasses into rum, sent their best grades of fish to the Catholic countries of southern Europe and their 'refuse grades' to feed the West Indian slaves. Timber, pitch and tar were supplied to the British navy in exchange for clothing and manufactured goods. Rum was shipped to the Guinea coast in trade for ivory and African slaves to work the southern and West Indian plantations, with whose planter society they had little in common.[3] Such varied activities required skilled personnel – smiths, tanners, shipwrights, clerks – from the local population.

Boston, for long a thriving port, sent its merchant ships to ply the coastal, transatlantic, West Indian and Mediterranean sea routes. Connected to New York by a main highway, Boston resembled a bustling English town of some 3,000 houses. Thanks to the rich resources of Massachusetts and the industry of its inhabitants, the wealthy Boston merchants were able to build brick houses in excellent architectural taste, fronted by streets paved with stone. They would fill them with expensive furniture and silver plate, import an English coach and horses, and 'enjoy smuggled French and Spanish wines. Their wives could visit, drink tea and neglect the affairs of their families with as good a grace as the finest ladies in London.' Framed family portraits and engravings by Hogarth decorated their walls, English china their sideboards, and four-poster beds, adorned with silk, damask or chintz curtains, their bedrooms. Men and women not only wore foreign fabrics but deliberately copied foreign fashions, and depended on the English merchant for fit, style and colour. Despite Puritan and Quaker complaints about finery and adornments, the ladies wore damask silk and calico dresses with bows and sashes, silk and cotton stockings, calfskin, kid or morocco high-heeled shoes. With silk or straw hats, 'borrowed' hair and looped skirts, 'resembling the dome of St Paul's, they startled the men and fretted their souls' with their vain extravagances. But the men, too, wore velvet, satin, lace and wigs.[4]

Dr Alexander of Annapolis, visiting Boston in 1744, found that despite its Puritan roots:

> The assemblies of the gayer sort are frequent here: the gentlemen and ladies meeting almost every week at concerts of music and balls. This place abounds with pretty women, elegantly dressed, who are, for the most part, free and affable, as well as pretty. I saw not one prude, while I was there.[5]

For the men, the taverns provided resorts for billiards, cards, gambling, smoking and much hard drinking. The Puritan Sunday was strictly observed, and the theatre under a ban. But amateur theatricals were popular throughout the colonies, nearly all the plays being of English origin. Boston, being a seaport, was always full of sailors on leave, who attracted the inevitable loose women, a brothel and a well-populated, if not very secure jail.[6] Thanksgiving Day, the time-honoured New England institution originated by the Pilgrim Fathers in 1621, was celebrated annually in November as a holiday with church gatherings and home feasting.

The middle colonies, New York, New Jersey and Pennsylvania, though similar to New England in climate and staple products, differed considerably from that Puritan world in population and topography. Agriculture, especially wheat-growing, was the most important occupation in the villages and countryside; commerce was developing in the urban centres, especially in Philadelphia and New York. Philadelphia, founded in 1682 on the navigable portion of the Delaware River and connected with good roads to the prosperous farms of the hinterland, grew rapidly to become the largest and most important of the American cities, with spacious public and private buildings, quays and docks, and a variety of places of worship. By 1750 it was comparable in size to Bristol, Manchester and Norwich. New York, with two or three thousand buildings and some 16–17,000 people in 1760, grew less rapidly. Many of its houses were built in the old Dutch style, and its streets were crooked and narrow. Its cosmopolitan population of Dutch, English, Germans, Swiss, Irish, French and Jews thrived as merchants, shopkeepers and tradesmen. A visiting British naval officer wrote in 1756:

> Every man of industry and integrity has it in his power to live well: many are
> the instances of persons, who came here distressed by their poverty, who
> now enjoy ease and plentiful fortunes.[7]

With a shortage of labour and skills of all kinds, indentured servants from
Europe filled the gap. Women, too, had a part to play in the general prosperity
of the community.

In none of the colonies was the Englishman, whose military or official
duty had brought him to America, so much at home in tastes, habits and
culture as in New York. English models were closely followed in dress and
social practices, although London fashions were somewhat out of date by the
time they were adopted in New York.[8] As in England, wealthy landed gentry
intermarried among their own class, spent their summers on their large estates,
farming and trading in timber and furs, and their winters among the city's
many entertainments. Although its broad interior, drained by the Hudson and
Mohawk Rivers, offered boundless promise for the future, the province of
New York was small in area, much of it mountainous, and exposed to Indian
attacks. Consequently, it was backward and given to factional quarrelling.
Though not so lighthearted or cultured as their Boston neighbours, nevertheless
New Yorkers enjoyed a high standard of living.[9]

Albany, today's state capital of New York, was the second oldest permanent
settlement in the 13 original colonies. Fort Amsterdam, constructed on the
lower end of Manhattan Island, became the capital of the Dutch New
Netherlands. Offering an easier route to Canada, via the Hudson waterway,
than that along the ice-strewn and dangerous St Lawrence, Albany grew in
importance as a British garrison and army headquarters for many of the
campaigns of the French and Indian War. In 1700 the governor, the Earl of
Bellomont, reported that the 400-strong garrison had been halved by death
and desertion; the survivors were in a miserable condition, almost naked, and
about to perish because their pay was so much in arrears. So tattered were
their uniforms 'that those parts of them, which modesty forbids me to name,
are exposed to view, and the women are forced to cover their eyes, as often as
they pass'.[10] Fifty years later, Albany's 330 families would be forced to house
15,000 troops and their womenfolk, and Lord Loudoun, the British commander
in chief, with his military administration.

Pennsylvania attracted more foreigners than any other colony, but the
British predominated. In 1692 it became a royal colony. Thanks to the strong
Quaker faith and liberal traditions of its founder, William Penn, it was perhaps
the most diverse, dynamic and prosperous of the colonies. Pennsylvania was
'a heaven for farmers, a paradise for artisans and women, a purgatory for men,
and hell for officials, preachers, and horses', noted the Reverend Gottlieb
Mittelberger, who made the terrible 'Atlantic Crossing' to America in 1750, and

wrote of his experiences. By 1760 one-third of its population of 300,000 were of German origin. The Scots-Irish immigrants provided some 30 per cent of the citizens, seeking religious freedom and economic opportunities. Its Quaker pacifism would often be at odds with its patriotism in the coming war, and a source of conflict with its neighbours and the British government. In Benjamin Franklin, Pennsylvania would possess the most outstanding public figure in colonial history.[11] In his youth he moved from Boston to edit and own the *Pennsylvania Gazette*, the best of an increasing number of weekly papers in English America. He would play an important part in combating the colony's pacifist tendencies during the French and Indian War, and in supporting its military plans.

The climate, geography and industries of the southern colonies made them very different from those of the north. Agricultural villages were largely replaced by mansions surrounded by the wood cabins of the slave gangs, toiling under the whips of overseers on the tobacco plantations of Virginia and Maryland. The broken coastline and navigable estuaries prevented the formation of any large seaport: instead, every tobacco estate has its own landing stage and wharf. The heat and fertility of the soil favoured slave labour, mostly supplied by Britain, which, after the Spanish Asiento concessions in the Utrecht Treaty, became the dominant slaving nation. Slaves were cheap to purchase, house and feed. Virginian planters tended to breed their own slaves, unlike the Caribbean sugar planters, who replaced their overworked and overpunished labour force by importing fresh slaves every seven years.

Labour throughout all the colonies was in short supply, and depended on the indentured servant, the apprentice, the convict and the slave. There were, of course, free hired labourers, paid considerably higher wages than in the mother country, but never enough for the growing colonial economy. Indentured servitude arose from the English poor, lured, seduced or forced to emigrate to America for almost 200 years. The indentured servant covenanted himself, or herself, for a term of years in order to pay off a debt. Most, hoping for a better life, came from the England of Defoe and Hogarth, or from the Continent, binding themselves to the captain of the ship on which they sailed. The captain paid the emigrant's passage, provided clothing, food and drink during the voyage, and then sold his time and labour on the ship's arrival in port.

Thousands of indentured servants aged from ten to 40, many from Ireland, were to be found in every colony. In Virginia, for instance, there were in 1680 3,000 slaves and 15,000 indentured servants; 18,000 came to Maryland between 1718 and 1760. Labourers, artisans, tradesmen and members of the professions were bought and sold at auctions in Boston or Charleston for a period of four to seven years. Bonded servants were the chattels of their masters, and subject to his corporal punishments. If they ran away, they were deemed felons, whipped and had their time extended; unclaimed runaways were auctioned. Marriage without the master's consent was illegal: the crimes of fornication and bastardy were punished by ceremonial floggings. Should a female servant have a child, especially with a Negro father, she was whipped 'on the bare back until the blood came', compelled to pay 2,000 pounds of tobacco to her master or serve an extra two years of indenture, and the child 'bound out' until aged 30.

Persons transported for religious or political reasons were fewer in number than the thousands of 'king's prisoners' or convict 'transports' from Newgate, Marshalsea and other British prisons sent to serve seven or 14 years, some for life, in the colonies. Sold like indentured servants, they worked alongside them and the Negroes on farm or plantation.

In 1718 an Act of Parliament provided that all persons convicted of offences such as burglary, robbery, perjury, forgery and theft, after being sentenced to death, might, if their crimes did not seem too heinous, 'at the discretion of the court, be transported to America for at least seven years'. They remained punishable with death without further trial, if they returned before the expiration of their sentences. Between 1720–30, 2,138 convicts were so transported, 'not a few being female'. By 1760 the total reached 30,000, convicts being the cheapest kind of hired labour. Most were sent to Virginia or Maryland, where they were readily snapped up by the poorer planters.

Though the servant's loss of liberty was temporary, that of the Negro, the mainstay of labour on the southern plantations, was permanent. In 1700 the Negro population in all 13 colonies was about 2,800. By 1715 there were 23,000 Negroes in Virginia out of a population of 95,000; in Maryland 30 per cent of the 35,000 population were Negroes. In South Carolina and the West Indies, the blacks outnumbered the whites ten or 20 to one. By 1760, when colonial black slavery was nearing its peak, about 284,000 Negroes lived in the southern colonies alone, from Maryland to Georgia.[12]

Charles Town, capital of South Carolina, became the entrepôt of all the colony's trade and its political and social centre. It was also the principal residence of its wealthy planters, who left overseers to run their estates, while they divided their time between the colony and the mother country. But as the Negroes began to multiply rapidly, many colonial leaders recognised the inherent social and moral dangers to the white population of miscegenation, concubinage and rape.

Commerce and land speculation were the principal sources of wealth in all the southern colonies. Every year new families climbed into the gentry class up this financial ladder. Virginian society, led by the governor at the capital, Williamsburg, 'now became established as the traditional Virginia of brave gallants and fair women, horse-races and fox-hunting, six horse coaches and ten-gallon punch bowls'.

The planters built fine brick houses with detached servants' quarters, and furnished them with furniture, silver, china and rich fabrics purchased from England. They connected their estates with good roads and by water, so that families could socialise. They sent their sons to English public schools and universities, read English books and periodicals, discussed court news and English politics in tavern and club, and frequented dancing assembly, circulating library and musical society.

Between the dominant and flamboyant wealthy upper crust of planters and the lowest level of a modest number of poor whites and the mass of blacks, stood a broad class of moderately prosperous, or at least comfortable, white farmers. Many owned their own slaves, and all felt the decisive bond of whiteness in a society rapidly growing blacker.[13]

The family was the foundation on which colonial society rested. American family institutions, courtship and marriage customs were profoundly influenced by religion, economic circumstances, social traditions, and the proportion of young men to women of marriageable age. There were marked regional differences between north and south, and variations between the home country and the New World in social and moral ethos.

In New England the strict doctrines of the founding Puritans still influenced every aspect of public and private life, though by the middle of the 18th century attitudes were softening. These demanded observance of the Sabbath, paternal authority, the subordination of women, an abundance of children, and discipline and modesty in dress and behaviour. A husband could legally chastise his wife and children, and many did so. Increasingly, the decision about whom to marry was made by the contracting parties themselves, care being taken about character as well as material considerations. Marriage was for life, for the creation of children: a girl's place in society was that of a caring mother and keeper of a frugal home. 'She was good, not brilliant, useful not ornamental, and the mother of 15 children', proudly proclaimed a Washington epitaph.[14]

Early marriages and large families were demanded by a pioneering and enterprising society. In New England, men married on average at 26, the women at 22, couples usually marrying two years earlier than in England. A healthier climate and a better diet than in Europe ensured a greater life expectancy and a lower infant mortality. Bachelors were scarce; spinsters were despised, for 'any husband was better than none'. Widows and widowers remarried after only brief periods of mourning. Ten or 12 children in a family were very common: if a man married more than once, 20 to 25 children were far from rare. 'Happy is the man who has his quiver full of them,' says the Bible.[15]

The bride's dowry was a matter for careful negotiation, for most Puritan parents agreed with the saying 'there belongeth more to marriage than two payre of bare leggs'. The man had to maintain a home, the bride to furnish it with money or goods. In the absence of balls, dancing and card-playing, and with the high death and infant mortality rates, baptisms, weddings and funerals formed a large part of social occasions. There was a more liberal separation policy than in England, especially when based on a civil contract, and separations were frequently granted for desertion, cruelty or breach of vows. When granted, the wife, unlike in England, could remarry if she were the innocent party. In New England the strange custom of 'bundling' or 'courtship in bed' was practised, where unmarried couples were permitted during courtship to sleep in the same bed without taking off their clothes. 'An understandable custom in places and houses with inadequate facilities and warmth for courting!'[16]

In the middle colonies there was diversity in population, nationality and religion. New York and New Jersey, for example, were under early Dutch influence, and Pennsylvania was mainly Quaker. Family life was less rigid, and subject to less regulation. In New York, husband and wife were equal in the eyes of the law and usually inherited possessions 'absolutely' from each other. But in church they sat apart. The marriage ceremony normally took place in the home of the bride's parents, with civil contracts, parental consent and banns normal practices. Dutch law required consummation of the marriage within a month of the banns; and couples usually found their partners within the community. Twenty five was the average age of marriage for Quaker women. Bachelors were held in low esteem. The wife was head of the household, distinguished from maidens by her dress:

> They stayed at home, read their Bibles and managed their families, with becoming parsimony, good providence and singular neatness.

Other women were active in New York as shopkeepers, merchants and Indian traders. They carried on the business after the death of their husband, and managed his estate. There were double standards for adultery, and a woman with an illegitimate child was penalised by whippings and public humiliation. Divorce, with the right of remarriage, was available only in New England, and was rare even there.[17]

In the royal colony of Virginia a different set of values and practices prevailed. These were partly caused by traditional and economic ties with the old country, and partly by geography and the development of the plantation system. The ceremonial of the Church of England was prescribed by law, and marriages were performed by clergy, seldom by a magistrate. The church ceremony was followed by lavish feasting, carousing and much 'horse-play'. The aristocratic families were mostly interrelated by marriage, and the wealthy planters of Virginia took a more relaxed view of life than the merchants of

New England or the settlers of Massachusetts.

On 3 November 1619, the Virginia Company had recorded the need to start a policy of sending 'maids young and uncorrupt to make wives to the inhabitants, and by that means to make the men there more settled'. One hundred years later, Moll Flanders, Defoe's notorious heroine, noted: 'Virginia did not yield any great plenty of wives'. So the marriage market favoured southern women, usually to their economic and social advantage – as Moll Flanders found. 'Born in Newgate Prison, 12 years a Whore, eight years a transported Felon to Virginia, and five times a Wife'.[18]

The age of marriage was lower than in the northern colonies and in England; and the colonial maiden entered southern society and married with astonishing precocity. Chief Justice Marshall of Virginia met and fell in love with his wife when she was 14, and married her at 16. Servants arriving in Maryland 'were courted as soon as they landed and besieged with offers of matrimony'. Lady Elizabeth Berkeley, married to the greatest of the Virginian governors, wedded three colonial governors in succession. Betty Hansford, aged 15, wooed a wealthy planter old enough to be her grandfather, and Jane Sparrow buried her husband on a Tuesday and married a merchant the following Sunday. The meats baked for the funeral furnished the marriage table!'[19] Young and attractive widows had no need to remain forlorn for long in a country with a preponderance of males, especially if their feminine charms were supplemented by a fine plantation.[20] Moll Flanders 'grew rich and died a Penitent', owner of a nice little plantation on the York River.

The slave economy and plantation life encouraged Virginian women to indulge in luxury and indolence, though 'their miserable sisters of toil' – the poor, the servants and the slaves – were not so fortunate. They allowed their menfolk to show them off as beautiful adornments, while the men sought fresh fields for extra-marital adventures.[21] Southern 'belles' grew to accept that their husbands and sons would take Negresses and indentured maid servants as concubines on their estates, although they themselves would not knowingly mix socially with persons of Negro or Indian blood. They found little in common, however, with the French in neighbouring Louisiana, where concubinage with Creole, Negro and mulatto women was more common than marriage.[22]

The French hoped that Louisiana would become, like Georgia, a prosperous part of the French empire overseas. But, despite some success with indigo production, the province proved a continuing drain on French resources. It also proved difficult to attract suitable settlers. There were constant appeals to Louis XIV to send girls for wives. In 1713 the commissary general complained that the imported girls were 'too ugly and could not find husbands: more attention should be paid to beauty than virtue'. The governor, Antoine Cadillac, complained that the settlers lived:

In vice with Indian women, whom they prefer to French girls: the soldiers all have Indian wives, who cook for them and wait on them. The government takes criminals, vagabonds, foundlings and prostitutes and ships them to America by force. But transplanting the refuse of prisons to the New World will not change them into good wives and mothers.[23]

His successor, Jean Baptiste Bienville, who founded New Orleans in 1718, called the colonists from France thieves, knaves, drunkards, gamblers and blasphemers, who preferred to marry squaws than the French girls sent from France. Many behaved so badly that they were severely punished by making them ride the 'wooden horse' or by a whipping from the regiment of soldiers that guarded the town. By 1731, however, the colony had become more firmly established, and a new generation of Canadian women had grown up ready for matrimony. The colony was now taken over by Louis XV from the Louisiana Company, to whom it had been leased. Thus New Orleans was added to Quebec in a fortified line stretching over 1,000 miles, which France was determined to hold against both Spain and Britain.

In 1733 James Oglethorpe, an English soldier and philanthropist, founded Georgia, the last of the mainland American colonies. The first settlement was Savannah, which was laid out in a series of squares, like an army camp. Georgia, named after George II, was to be a frontier garrison, manned by soldier-farmers, and a haven for England's debtor prisoners seeking a new start in life. Its charter stated it was founded for:

The relief of the King's poor subjects, [who might] not only gain a comfortable subsistence for themselves and families, but also strengthen our colonies and increase the trade, navigation and wealth.[24]

Like a Roman military colony planted to defend the empire, Georgia would become a bulwark against the Spaniards in Florida, the French in Louisiana, and the southern Indian Cherokees. Negro slaves and Catholics were prohibited, since both were considered military liabilities in case of war with the Spaniards or French. In 1752 Georgia became a royal colony with a governor, council and assembly.

'Geography is three-quarters of military science,' wrote Field Marshal von Moltke, who modernised the Prussian Army – and the French and Indian War demonstrates the truth of this military dictum! The natural features of the vast American continent dictated the strategy and campaign plans of both combatants.[25] The Appalachians, running up parallel to the coast through New England and between the St Lawrence River and the Atlantic, end up at the sea in Gaspé. These mountains formed a strong barrier between the St Lawrence basin and the English colonies. The only opening through them was up the

Hudson River from New York to Lake George and Lake Champlain, and thence down the Richelieu River. It was up and down this natural highway that our campaigns were to rage. Here stood the famous forts – Ticonderoga, Edward, Crown Point (Frédéric) and William Henry. The second inland route was formed by the Mohawk, a tributary of the Hudson, which enters near Albany and emerges on Lake Ontario at Fort Oswego (founded 1723). The route then continued to Montreal.

Lines of communication and supply were long and costly, and the enemy difficult to locate. Never, wrote Parkman,[26] was the problem of moving troops, encumbered with baggage, stores and artillery, more difficult than through the savage forests, mountains and marsh lands, where thoroughfares of lakes and rivers were often choked with fallen trees and obstructed by cataracts. The question was less how to fight the enemy than how to get at him. The British had to use waterways as highways, build roads to waterways, find wagons and animals, and build boats (bateaux) to convey stores and provisions.[27] If a few good roads had criss-crossed this vast wilderness, the war would have been shortened, and its character changed.

The French were outnumbered 15 to one by the English colonial population in America. But only part of this numerical superiority could be used by the British in offensive operations. The rest of their forces were required to garrison the many static forts and blockhouses, and to protect a frontier, isolated farms, settlements and supply dumps, stretching from Nova Scotia in the north to southern Georgia. Fighting a largely defensive war, the French forced the British and Americans to penetrate hundreds of miles of trackless country. Using interior lines, the French and Canadians could select time, weather and target, and compel Britain and the colonies to keep thousands of men on constant alert against a few hundred marauding savages. Because the French could concentrate their forces so easily and quickly, and base their operations on the continuous waterway between Louisbourg and Niagara, they enjoyed local superiority, numerically, in five out of the ten major encounters. They would gain victories at Oswego, Fort William Henry, Montmorency and Ste Foy (Quebec), and over Braddock on the Monongahela River.

Perhaps the most important single advantage enjoyed by France was its unified command, when compared with the internal jealousies and dissension among the colonies. This advantage would be, however, offset to some extent by the personal rivalries and quarrels of Vaudreuil and Montcalm. The small population of New France was homogeneous, militarily efficient, and at the sole disposal of its governor.[28] From 1669 the entire male population between the ages of 15 and 60 were liable, on the orders of the French king, to serve in the militia, without pay, maintain themselves without charges, and march without stores and baggage – a big advantage compared with English colonial practices! They were regularly exercised and officered by Canadians of the seigneurial class. All together, the French military organisation was larger than the British, and more successful in forming alliances with the Indians.[29]

The English colonial militias, on the other hand, were divided among a dozen uncoordinated governments, and seldom called out except in emergency. They were accustomed to finding fault with their orders from the king's representatives, and to treating their own officers with democratic familiarity.[30] These 'uncoordinated governments' had been founded separately and at different times: their constitutions and economic frameworks varied according to historical and geographical circumstances. They owed allegiance to the British crown, which allowed them to make their own laws, raise their own taxes, and mostly left them to their own devices, save for the king's representative, appointed from London. He was head of the executive, approved all appointments and summoned or dismissed the local assembly, elected by the freemen. As commander-in-chief of the local forces, he was responsible for the defence of the province. But for all colonials, the baiting and thwarting of the royal governor was an established pastime![31]

3

FRANCE AND PETTICOAT GOVERNMENT

'The man who lets himself be ruled by a woman is a fool'. Napoleon

In 1715 Louis XIV died, leaving to his great-grandson, an ailing child of five, his magnificent palace at Versailles and a bankrupt nation. During his 72-year reign, France had dominated Europe but Louis had had little interest in his overseas possessions. He had an army of 200,000 men and a fleet of 100 warships to maintain, and New France only drained his resources. War and economic distress had reduced France's population to some 19 million: now, like England, she desperately needed a period of peace to ensure her stability and security.[1] So France and England concluded a triple alliance with Holland, which saved Europe from another war for the next 25 years.

Louis XIV built the Palace of Versailles to show off his power and dazzle Europe with his magnificent court. With its State dignitaries, royal mistresses and elaborate ceremonial, it provided the ornamental setting for the Sun King, who ruled by divine right. He attracted to his court the French nobility, in order to subdue it. He never forgot the humiliations of his boyhood, when his mother was hunted from Paris, the royal army fired at from the Bastille, and the monarchy almost destroyed by a rebellious nobility in league with France's enemy, Spain.[2] He determined that what France needed was the strong hand of an absolute monarch, namely himself. *L'état, c'est moi!*

During his long reign, Louis allowed no minister and no favourite, male or female, to govern. He reduced the greatest families in France to mere adornments of his court, instead of rivals to his throne. The provincial nobility, bereft of royal favour, sank into political obscurity. The court nobility, far from their estates and cut off socially from the rest of France, were compelled to live in splendour and idleness, surrounded by etiquette, snobbery and intrigue. With no political influence or power, they watched with envy the roles played by English aristocrats and squires in the affairs of parliament and county. At Versailles the nobles could hunt and gamble, enjoy the ballet and theatre, the balls and fireworks, and pursue their extra-marital intrigues, conducted according to the rules of their aristocratic society. Once the legitimacy of the male heir to the family title and estates had been assured, the husband was permitted his mistress, the wife her lover.[3] Prince de Soubise kept himself out of the way in

Paris, whilst his wife occupied the king's bed at Versailles. He ended up as *duc et pair* (duke and peer of the realm), with a palace (Hôtel Guise), and his family supported from the royal coffers.

Since the Middle Ages, French nobles had been members of the *noblesse de l'épée* who placed their swords at the service of the king in war: in peace, they helped him rule the country. They justified their exalted positions and special privileges by the medieval maxim that society consisted of three estates – the first, who prayed (the clergy), the second, who fought (the nobility), and those who worked (the serfs or peasants). The first two estates paid no taxes. That burden fell on the third estate, who were socially and politically unimportant.

In more recent times, a new and wealthy class of nobles had been created from a rising middle class, the *noblesse de la robe*. These ennobled commoners had been granted hereditary titles to serve the crown in the highest posts in the army, the law and the church, as ministers of state and government administrators (*intendants*).

Both the 'sword' and 'robe' nobility were looked down upon by the *noblesse de la cour*, the court nobility, composed of the most ancient families of France. They alone had direct access to the monarch at Versailles and were able to receive his grace and favour, with the right to court privileges – high offices in the royal households, presentation to the king, access to his carriages, and joining him in the hunt. Able to produce patents or 'proofs' of nobility going back to 1400, they claimed such ancient privileges as the right to wear a sword, trial by special courts, a family pew in the village church, and to have the female members of the family presented to the queen. The family was exempt from billeting, and the men from military service.

The French nobility was thus not a homogeneous group but a hierarchy of different levels of status. Within it the 'high' nobility would never mix its blood with the 'petty' nobility. It was far easier, for example, for the daughter of an ennobled commoner to marry a man of high birth than for a country squire to win the hand of a great house. Marriages were made with an eye to pedigree; family alliances in which compatibility and love were usually secondary to social and economic interests. Monsieur de la Bedoyère was sued by his own family for marrying Agathe Sticoti, a showgirl. But during the 18th century marriages of convenience, based on wealth, education and power, were becoming as fashionable as marriages between equals in dignity – and the happiness of the contracting couple was increasingly an important consideration.

The nobility represented a goal for the aspiring middle class, the bourgeoisie. Not all the nobles were wealthy, but most of the wealthy would end up noble. Merchants, financiers and professional men were keen to gain admission to the ranks of the aristocracy, as soon as they had made their fortunes. Louis XV ennobled many during his reign, on account of their wealth or service. Their daughters and nieces were married into the *noblesse*, or aspired even higher – like Madame de Prie or Madame de Pompadour. The former became the dominating mistress of the Duc de Bourbon, prince of the royal line, the latter *maîtresse en titre* of Louis XV.

There was a great gulf of wealth, education and status between the poor provincial gentry (*les seigneurs*), with impeccable lineages but empty purses, and the court *élite*, able to obtain for themselves, and their friends and relations, the appointments, honours and pensions, which only court influence and proximity to the king could secure. The former, 'too poor to serve in the Army with prospects, and too ill-educated for the church, could not even hope for a slender benefice'. For the latter, a military career (proof of about 100 years' nobility was required for the army) was the most appealing, since rank was obtained by favour and money rather than by merit:

> Whilst upstart stripling colonels enjoyed rapid and brilliant careers, petty nobles without wealth, unknown at Court and unsupported, were forced to limit their dreams of glory to a lieutenant's or captain's commission, won with great effort, after ten, 15 or 25 years of service – and the reward of their devotion, a pension of a few hundred *livres*.[4]

A career in the judiciary was closed to such men, because it was costly to buy an office, and a university education was demanded. The great majority of the nobility, however, lived between these two extremes.

In France, unlike in England, titles and the status of nobility descended from the father to all his children. The result was that in the early 18th century the aristocracy numbered about one per cent of the population. The nobility owned about a quarter to one-third of the land, and most of the feudal rights over the rest. Under Louis XV, the French nobility increased its hold over all the important posts in the State. They commanded the fleets, officered the armies, and filled the higher posts in the civil service and church.[5]

The clergy, too, followed the same pattern. The higher posts in the Church hierarchy were monopolised by the great noble families, who left the more modest and lower-paid positions to men of bourgeois or peasant origins. The Catholic Church was immensely wealthy, supported by a tithe (one-tenth) of every person's livelihood, and paying no taxes. Every year the clergy negotiated its free gift (*don gratuit*) with the crown. The Church drew its rents from its land, and, exactly like the nobility, exercised feudal rights and dues over the peasants. In return, it controlled almost all education, poor relief and hospital provision.

In England, the alliance of the Anglican squire and the country parson was a keystone of national life. In France, Church and State were usually at loggerheads over dogma and temporal control of the Church. There was a widening gulf, too, between the poor parish priest of humble origins and the wealthy hierarchy over the Church's assets and opportunities for promotion. But whatever the problems, the Catholic Church and its clergy maintained a powerful hold over the nation, especially the poorer classes.

At the base of the pyramid of French society were the peasants, urban shopkeepers and craftsmen. Eighty per cent of the French population were peasants, only a small number of whom actually owned the land they farmed. Just under a quarter were tenant farmers: about half had to give half the produce of the land to their lord. The remainder were wage-earners and serfs. In England all classes were taxed alike. In France, the peasants bore the largest burden of the State tax system – the *taille* (land tax), *gabelle* (salt tax), *vingtième* and *capitation*.

Almost without exception, the peasants were subject to the lord of the manor (*seigneur*), and to his various feudal dues. He had the monopoly of the mill, wine-press and oven, and controlled the weights and measures. The peasants owed him so many days' work each week, and had to maintain the roads. In general, since taxes varied from district to district, after paying the rents, seigneurial dues, Church tithes and State taxes, the peasants were left with barely one-third of the income they earned from their labour. Compared with them, the English poorer class appeared well-off, well-clothed and well-shod, and ate white bread rather than the black variety customary in France. Living at subsistence level, the French peasant farmers were totally dependent on the labour of women and children to survive. A bad harvest brought debt or starvation. Since the registration of births, deaths and marriages was taxed, 'the poor baptised their children themselves, and married in secret by mutual consent,' wrote the Duc de Saint-Simon.[6]

Louis XV continued to maintain Versailles, the court and the absolute monarchy he had inherited. In his youth, the people called him '*le Bien-aimé* ' (the Well-beloved): by the end of his long reign of 59 years, they detested him. He would reign but never rule. He claimed absolute power and legislative authority: in practice, he possessed neither.[7] He did not have Louis XIV's administrative ability, nor his prodigious industry, but he clung stubbornly to his great-grandfather's royal prerogatives.

Louis XV's greatest asset was his magnificent presence. He was strikingly handsome and intelligent, but shy, lazy and easily bored with affairs of State and his royal duties. 'Surrounded by crowds of courtiers he hardly knew, moving daily through the fixed routine of Court ceremonies, stared at from morning to night, he was the principal boy in a perpetual pantomime.' At a time when France needed strong government and decisive policies, he turned to his two great passions to avoid making decisions – hunting and women, with a long procession of royal mistresses, among whom only de Pompadour and du Barry 'knew more than a transient favour'.[8] 'He pays not the least attention to what is passing in his kingdom, and signs anything that is put before him,' wrote Cardinal de Tencin, Archbishop of Lyons under Cardinal Fleury.[9]

During Louis's infancy, Philippe, Duc d'Orléans, acted as regent (1715–23). A distinguished general, he was married to one of the legitimate daughters of Louis XIV and Madame de Montespan. He had been installed by the *Parlement* of Paris, which had annulled the will of Louis XIV. The Regency period is identified with frivolity and a laxity of morals, best portrayed by fashionable painters like Watteau and Lancret. Like his great-grandfather, Henri IV, the duke was a *roué*, 'perpetually in the company of loose, aristocratic women', and the model for society to follow.[10] His first task was to dispose of the rival claims of the royal bastards, and free himself from the control of the Council established by Louis XIV. He maintained his position by controlling patronage and gave back to the *Parlement* its powers to remonstrate against royal edicts, but failed to deal with France's most pressing problems – tax reforms and financial stability. He died in 1723 of a stroke, in the arms of his mistress.

When Louis came of age, he appointed in 1726 his old tutor, the 73-year-old Cardinal Fleury, to run his government for him, leaving himself free to enjoy the pleasures of the court. Fleury's main achievement was that, by abstaining from continental commitments, like his contemporary Robert Walpole, he managed to give his country a spell of peace. But from his death in 1745 until Choiseul's appointment in 1758, there was a political vacuum. With the King leaving the direction of affairs for much of the time to others, there was no firm hand to maintain the unity and tradition of the French monarchy.

During this critical period, vital to our story, there was no chief minister in France but a number of secretaries of State, responsible for foreign affairs, war, the navy and colonies, finance and internal affairs. Each was an individual servant of the King, chosen and dismissed by him, with no power of his own and no collective responsibility. Jealous of each other and totally reliant on the king's favour, they cultivated the royal favourites who happened to be dominant at the moment – the Marquise de Pompadour, Cardinal de Bernis, the entourage of the Queen or the Dauphin, who in turn competed for influence over the King. With a natural flair for backstairs intrigue, Louis XV played off one minister against another, while 'women made and unmade the alliances of Court factions'.[11] Life at court, where 'only fools were honest, loyal or chaste', was 'an endless pursuit of advantage, status, pensions, offices and perquisites from those whom royal favour endowed with power to bestow them'.[12] And the choice of measures to govern the country were too often taken in a mistress's bedroom – a council chamber unlikely to encourage clarity of judgement or national interest.[13]

Sexually precocious, Louis was married in 1725 at the age of 15. His health was poor and France needed an heir. Louis had been affianced to his cousin, the Infanta, but France could not wait for the maturity of a little Spanish princess and she was unceremoniously returned to Spain. Instead, the Regent selected Marie Leczinska, the penniless daughter of the dethroned king of Poland, who was a pensioner of France and lived in Strasbourg. Marie was seven years older than Louis. She was intelligent, pious and good-natured, plain and dull but, above all, healthy. '*Toujours coucher, toujours grossesse, toujours accoucher*' (continually bedded, pregnant and giving birth),[14] she presented him with ten children in as many years. Despite this, she had little physical appeal to her sensual husband. Among his numerous infidelities, Louis successively took as his mistress three[15] (or possibly four) of the five attractive daughters of the dissolute Marquis de Neslé, one of the greatest names in France, whose wife was lady-in-waiting to the Queen.

The position of *maîtresse en titre* (official concubine) was well understood in French society, and all the aristocratic ladies of Versailles coveted this favoured and powerful post. Louis XIV had had four – Vallière, Montespan, Fontanges and Maintenon – but they were all of noble birth, and none had been allowed any political influence. A monarch, wrote Louis XIV in his *Memoirs*,[16] should separate the endearments of a lover from the resolution of the sovereign. On the other hand, the lascivious and pleasure-loving Louis XV would allow his mistresses to use 'the infallible route to power and influence' over government policies, court factions and royal appointments.

The most powerful and intelligent of his courtesans, and the one most pertinent to our story, was Jeanne Poisson (1721–64), created marquise (later duchess) by her lover. She was the daughter of an army food contractor (*commissaire aux Vivres*), and had been taught all the accomplishments considered necessary for a young lady to be successful in fashionable French society. From the time the king made her his fourth official *maîtresse en titre* (1745) to her death in 1764, she retained her influence over him and effectively ruled France.

At 20 Jeanne had been married to the nephew of a wealthy tax-farmer, so she belonged not to the court aristocracy but to the bourgeois world of finance (especially of the four powerful Pâris brothers, who made their money, helped by Pompadour, by provisioning the armies of Louis XV). With a town house in Paris and a country seat close to the royal chateau of Choisy, she became one of the most attractive hostesses in middle-class Parisian society. Her salon drew the rich and famous, including Voltaire, Montesquieu and Marivaux.

Her beauty of face and figure, her charm, vivacity and intelligence, together with her artistic talents, 'all conspired to excite desires', reported the contemporary *London Magazine*.[17] 'Every man would have wished to make her his mistress, and she put the prettiest of women in the shade,' wrote the

Count de Cheverny.[18] Soon her fame and beauty (captured for posterity on the canvasses of François Boucher and Maurice de la Tour) were reported to the king. He fell in love with her at first sight, dressed as Diana, goddess of the chase, at a masked ball to celebrate the marriage of the 16-year-old Dauphin to the Spanish Infanta, Maria Theresa. Within days Louis had installed her at Versailles in the apartments of the late Mailly (Neslé) sisters, above his own and reached by a private staircase. There, wrote Nancy Mitford, he overcame his attacks of boredom with his radiant mistress – and made himself ill with too much food, wine and sex.[19] Court circles resented her elevation to the illustrious position of the king's official mistress, which they regarded as a perquisite of the wives and daughters of the aristocracy.

From that time onwards, Louis happily delegated to Jeanne (created Madame de Pompadour) the cares of government, so long as she continued to amuse and entertain him, and dispel the dreadful boredom *(ennui)*, which plagued him throughout his life. She studied to please him, and for fear of losing him made herself available to his every whim, eventually ruining her health in ministering to his pleasures.[20] She danced and sang, disguised herself in a variety of costumes, played a number of instruments, arranged hunts, concerts, ballets and private theatricals,[21] building projects, tours to visit his other palaces, and intimate supper parties, 'a constant succession of new pleasures and recreations and opportunities for intimate dalliance – anything, in short, to distract the royal mind'.[22] 'She has so many talents for pleasing, for inventing new diversions and imparting novelty to old, that all the posts and places in the kingdom were at her disposal,' concluded the *London Magazine.*[23]

Her many detractors at court had other views. 'This Minister of appointments and dismissals … sells everything, even regiments. She makes and unmakes ministers and ambassadors, appoints and removes generals. She fills the Bastille with her enemies, and great questions of policy are at the mercy of her caprices'.[24] 'She was a party to almost every grace the King granted, so that her court was as important as that of a prime minister,"'[25] wrote in his *Memoirs* the Duc de Croÿ, a respected soldier and courtier who had been conspicuous at the battle of Fontenoy.[26] The ministerial council condescended to assemble in her boudoir, commented Beckles Willson. All the great departments of state – army, navy, war, foreign affairs, justice and finance – changed hands regularly, according to her whims and fancies:[27] 'while the King treats her carnally better than ever,' and stinted her in nothing.[28]

Pompadour's political role has been exaggerated by some historians, for decisions in foreign and military affairs mostly belonged to her royal lover. But she certainly had a considerable influence on public affairs through her part in ministerial intrigues, and in the manipulation of the conflicting court factions. Her personal relationships often played a decisive part in policy-making. She made and unmade ministers: she was instrumental in the dismissal of Comte de Maurepas, Minister of Marine and the Colonies (1749); Controller-General Comte d'Orry (1745); Jean Machault, Finance Minister (1745–54) and Minister of Marine (1754–7); and Marquis d'Argenson, the Foreign and War Minister. She promoted the careers of Bernis, Marigny, Machault and Choiseul, and Marshal of France Prince de Soubise was her nomination for an army command against Frederick of Prussia. The brilliant Foreign Minister, the Duc de Choiseul, earned her patronage for revealing to her an amorous intrigue between the King and his cousin, Madame de Choiseul-Romanet. Choiseul dominated Louis XV through the Marquise, and gradually gained control of foreign affairs, the army and navy. He replaced the Abbé de Bernis, Pompadour's friend and protégé, who as Foreign Minister vigorously supported her at the beginning of the Seven Years' War; at the end Bernis condemned her in his *Memoirs* – perhaps in an attempt to excuse his own failings.

> Our army, though large, is inefficient and insubordinate: no agreement in Council: open war between the Navy and Army ministers: the men in office unfit for their work and the public have no confidence in them: scandalous extravagance at Court: the people in a state of misery: no patriotism. Madame de Pompadour controls the government with the caprices of an infant, while the King looks blandly on, undisturbed by our worries, and indifferent to public embarrassments.[29]

Parkman,[30] in his well-known study of Wolfe and Montcalm during the French and Indian War, attributed much of the blame for the loss of Canada to Louis XV and Pompadour. She aspired, he argued, to a share in the conduct of the war. 'Posing as a Roman matron in her perfumed boudoir,' wrote another historian, she affected a greatness of soul in misfortune and defeat... Canada is lost, Louisbourg is in English hands, and above all the treasury is empty.'[31] Though doubtless unable to decide policy herself, wrote Princess Michael of Kent,[32] she was often able to determine who would decide it, and she was the intermediary to the King. Acting as his secretary, she controlled every approach to him. Her sitting-room became the military 'operations centre', where in her presence the King discussed every document and detail of the war with his ministers and generals. She discussed campaigns and battles with them; marking the battle positions with patches from her make-up box, while they listened to her prating with obsequious respect.

When she interfered with the Count de Clermont's military operations around Krefeld in 1758, he exploded in anger:

> Set your mind at rest, Madam. An army is not led as easily, as you draw your finger across a map. The Commander in Chief has no patience with strategists in skirts, nor with Headquarters 200 leagues from the scene of operations.[33]

The chief criticism levelled by historians against Louis and his mistress is that they changed the traditional policy of France, as followed by Francis I, Henri IV, Richelieu, Mazarin and Louis XIV. Louis XV had a taste for *secret* diplomacy. The secretaries of State were committed to the Prussian alliance, but the King and Pompadour allied themselves with France's traditional enemy, Austria. For two-and-a -half centuries opposition to the House of Habsburg had brought France security, territory and prestige. The brilliant young Austrian diplomat Kaunitz used an indirect approach through Pompadour to negotiate with her master. 'I have had a long talk with Mme. de Pompadour and told her a lot of things, which I hope she will pass on to the King.'[34] In what is known as 'the reversal of alliances', (*Le Renversement des Alliances*), France signed a secret treaty with Austria, the *Family Compact*, which plunged France needlessly into the Seven Years War (see Chapter 10), when Frederick II of Prussia invaded Saxony in August 1756. The treaty was signed in Pompadour's lovely and luxurious Chateau Bellevue,[35] the perfect setting for the intrigue, 'where the vanity of a courtesan helped to dispose of the fate of Europe'.[36]

Pompadour received congratulations for her part in the Diplomatic Revolution from Maria Theresa, the Austrian empress, who sent her a miniature framed in brilliants as a token of her appreciation.[37] 'All that has been concluded up to the present time between the two courts is entirely due to your zeal and sagacity, which ought to deserve the approbation of posterity,' wrote Prince von Kaunitz,[38] Maria Theresa's chief negotiator for the Treaty of Versailles, signed with France in May 1756. In reply, the Austrian envoy at Versailles wrote: 'Madame de Pompadour is delighted with the conclusion, of what she looks upon as her own work.'[39]

So France embarked on a policy of European aggression, the conquest of the Netherlands and an advance to the Rhine, instead of turning all her might from the beginning against England and in defence of her colonies. She developed her army at the expense of her navy. Despite her financial weakness, corrupt officials, and an inefficient system of tax collection, the disasters that overtook her might have been averted. This story of the loss of Canada, of the development of the United States, and of the French king and his mistress, might have been very different. But King and Pompadour had little knowledge of, and less interest in, the fate or well-being of New France. Their dreams were of European conquest, captured cities, subjugated provinces, the aggrandisement of France, and the glory of her monarch. They would be compelled to pay the price for their policies in the Treaty of Paris in 1763.[40]

Like most foreign wives and mistresses of France's kings, Pompadour was blamed for all the nation's ills. Posterity, too, has laid on her graceful shoulders the ruin of mid-century France. However influential she may have been for France's entry into the Seven Years' War, she was certainly not responsible for the chronicle of French defeats and disasters during it. The fault lay with the

King. If she required luxury at the cost of any overtaxed people, so had Mazarin, Richelieu and Colbert. The real causes of France's empty treasury were wars and a ruinous mediaeval tax system. Typical of France's attitude to Pompadour was the lampoon published by Horace Walpole:

> *O France, le sexe femelle*
> *Fit toujours ton destin.*
> *Ton bonheur vint d'une Pucelle;*
> *Ton malheur vient d'une catin.*
> (O France, the female sex
> Has always determined your destiny.
> You were saved by the Maid of Orleans;
> And undone by a Whore.)[41]

Pompadour found it increasingly difficult to respond to her royal lover's insatiable appetites (*les fatigues de l'amour sans plaisir*).[42] He was a typical Bourbon, passionate and sexually demanding. She tried aphrodisiacs, and closed her eyes to his numerous infidelities, fearful of losing him and her position at court. But they remained firm friends, and she his confidante, until her death in 1764. Louis finally settled down with his fifth, and last, official concubine, the voluptuous Madame du Barry, 33 years his junior. She was destined to end her career on the guillotine during the French Revolution.[43]

Pompadour's 20-year reign (1745–64) marked the peak of French taste and refinement. She will always be remembered for her patronage (gifts and pensions) of writers and dramatists like Rousseau and Marivaux, of painters like Fragonard and Boucher, whose salacious canvasses of Venus, Diana and Aurora adorned her apartments, and of craftsmen and sculptors like Falconet and Clodion. If her houses and their contents had survived the Revolution, France would have been the richer for her marvellous treasures. She helped to found the Sèvres porcelain factory to rival that of Meissen, and supported the Gobelins and Aubusson tapestries. With her brother Abel, the Marquis de Marigny and Louis XV's Director of Royal Buildings, she planned the Place Louis XV (de la Concorde) with its equestrian statue of the King. It is surrounded by four allegorical figures, known irreverently as his four mistresses, Mailly, Vintimille, Châteauroux and Pompadour. She helped to plan the Champs Elysées, the Madeleine, many of the palaces of the Faubourg St Germain, and the Petit Trianon at Versailles.[44] She owned the Elysée Palace in the Rue St Honoré, where today's president of the French Republic lives; she inspired, and helped to finance by the sale of her diamonds, the École Militaire, opened in 1760 for the education of 500 sons of impoverished officers, which produced Napoleon Buonaparte (1784–5). With her lover Louis Quinze and his court, she represented the elegance and sophistication of all that was best in 18th century French civilisation.

4

HANOVERIAN
ENGLAND

In 1713, despite Louis XIV's humiliations at the peace table, France was still the dominant influence in Europe, and second only to Spain as a colonial power. France enjoyed the prestige of the court of Versailles, a highly centralised government, considerable natural resources, and a population more than three times greater than that of England. The War of the Spanish Succession (1702–13), called in America Queen Anne's War, had emptied her treasury: but the House of Bourbon held the thrones of France, Spain and Naples.

The Treaty of Utrecht (1713) gave Europe 25 years of peace – a rare event in its troubled history – and provided Britain with the stability she needed to consolidate and prosper after a century of war and turbulence.[1] Puritan Roundhead had fought Royalist Cavalier. Charles II had regained his throne, and James II had lost it after an army revolt. William III came from Holland to receive the English crown and gave England a constitutional government. The Declaration of Rights made it illegal 'to raise and keep a Standing Army in time of peace without consent of Parliament'. Queen Anne's military genius, the Duke of Marlborough, ended Louis XIV's dream of European conquest. The Act of Settlement (1701) confirmed that anyone who was a Catholic or married to a Catholic was 'forever uncapable to inherit, possess or enjoy the crown and government of this realm'. It enabled parliament to offer the throne to the Protestant House of Hanover and change the dynasty without the bloodshed which would shake France at the end of the century; and England had strengthened her domestic position immensely by her union with Scotland in 1707.[2]

The English revolution of 1688, giving England religious tolerance, freedom of the press and parliamentary government based on the theory that civil government is founded on the consent of the governed, was the admiration of Europe, and of France in particular. The United Kingdom would become richer and stronger than ever, increasing her naval power as Holland's declined, and gain supremacy at sea. For Britain, maritime and colonial interests would always come first. France and Spain would neglect the sea for the land.

George I landed at Greenwich in 1714, at the age of 54, to claim 'the throne of his ancestors' under the Act of Settlement, despite 50 Catholic relatives whose claims were better. Almost as licentious as Louis XV, he gave no political power to his mistresses. He left domestic affairs and State appointments largely to Sir Robert Walpole, who with William Pitt, Earl of Chatham, would end the reigns of the first two Hanoverian monarchs in a blaze of glory, giving Britain an empire and a position unrivalled in world affairs.[3] 'Walpole,' Dr Johnson remarked, 'was a Minister given by the Crown to the people. Pitt was a Minister given by the people to the Crown.'

George II (1683–1760) succeeded his father on the English throne in 1727, at the age of 44. In 1705 he had married at Herrenhausen, near Hanover, Caroline of Brandenburg-Anspach. The young couple soon produced an heir to cement a marriage, which remained happy throughout the queen's life, despite her husband's numerous conjugal lapses. Having accomplished his marital duty, George felt free to indulge his military aspirations at Oudenarde (1707) under Marlborough, and at Dettingen (1743), where he was the last English king to lead his troops personally into battle.[4] He jealously guarded the royal prerogative of supreme command over all the military forces of the crown. During his reign he ordered 15 regular regiments to raise second battalions, and added the 40 to 72 Foot to the military establishment.[5]

Queen Caroline, a woman of great charm, wit and intelligence, surrounded herself with the most accomplished of the younger Whig nobility and 'a bevy of fair and fashionable ladies'. Two of these were Mary Lepell, a maid of honour, and Lord John Hervey, whose *Memoirs* provide a detailed picture of court life and intrigue. They fell in love and married. Mary's father, a brigadier-general, raised a regiment and made her a cornet in it as soon as she was born. George I commuted her commission for a pension, 'it being too ridiculous to continue her any longer an officer in the Army'. Hervey, 'whose wit and charm made him a special favourite of women', was on intimate terms of friendship with Queen Caroline, and thus had a great influence at court. It was mainly owing to this influence that 'Walpole governed the Queen, and through her the King'.[6]

Every queen had her attendants – ladies-in-waiting, ladies of the bedchamber and maids of honour. They were not highly paid but they enjoyed positions of prestige and influence. One such was Mrs Henrietta Howard, the Queen's mistress of the robes. She became George II's official mistress, and was promoted Lady Suffolk. George's grandmother, the Electress Sophia, approved the liaison; 'at least she will improve his English,' she said. He lodged her in St James's Palace, and paid off her husband with a handsome annuity. Henrietta, like most royal concubines, indulged in 'pillow talk' to influence the king's appointments. The Queen, too, was 'at all times active in influencing appointments'; wisely accepting the inevitable, Caroline was the controlling influence, certainly in political matters, over the King. Would the new king retain Walpole as his first leader of the House of Commons? The

Opposition courted George's mistresses. Spencer Compton, Speaker of the House, relied for support on Henrietta. Walpole relied on Caroline, and won. 'I got the right sow by the ear,' Walpole said, in his characteristically vulgar and agricultural English.[7]

In fact, Caroline played a more significant role in the affairs of State than any other English queen consort since the Middle Ages. Although the king had an important part to play in the English constitution, George II had little personal political importance and was indifferent towards England, its parliament and ministers. 'The King was so completely swayed by her in affairs of State, that he may be said to have been merged in the Queen'. As a contemporary put it:

> You may strut dapper George but 'tis all in vain,
> We know 'tis Caroline, not you, that reign.[8]

Perhaps Caroline's greatest influence over English political affairs was her unfaltering support of Walpole during his long and wise administration (1721–42), covering the years of peace. As first Lord of the Treasury and Chancellor of the Exchequer, and by extensive use of patronage and preferment, he was able to 'manage' the entire government administration. 'With the King in one pocket and the Commons in the other, he was virtually unassailable'. He consolidated the Whig party, confirmed the authority of the cabinet in relation to king and parliament, and established the position of prime minister.[9] His policies were supported by the City of London's finance houses, its bankers, merchants and trading companies. Preferring the profits of industry to the spoils of war, Walpole generated expanding trade and revenue, and gave Britain an era of prosperity – a strong financial base from which to take on France in the struggle ahead.[10]

Like his father, George II spent much of his time in Hanover and in promoting its affairs in Europe. According to Horace Walpole, Sir Robert's son, George's passions in life were Herrenhausen, the army, and sophisticated women – though not necessarily in that order! As a result, George left the very able Caroline as guardian of the realm, and the equally able Walpole to govern the country in his absence. Unlike France, with its divine right and absolute monarchy, Britain had a constitutional king, with powers limited by law and parliament, especially over taxation. As the last verse of the National Anthem (1740) states: 'May he defend our laws, And ever give us cause, With heart and voice to sing, God save the King.' While the king had the right to appoint any minister he pleased, a minister could only hold office, if he were acceptable to the majority of the House of Commons.[11]

The office of prime minister, leader of the House of Commons and speaker for the cabinet, developed under Walpole and Caroline, aided this constitutional process. Walpole reported cabinet discussions to the King, and George would issue his instructions through Walpole. To the end of his parliamentary life, Walpole enjoyed the confidence of the King and his wife, until her death in 1737.

In 1736, aged 52, George went to Hanover to acquire a new mistress. He spent eight months there courting Amelia Sophia, the attractive young wife of Count von Wallmoden, 21 years George's junior. On Queen Caroline's death the following year, after a long and painful illness, he installed her as his mistress in the apartments in St James's which he had given to Henrietta Howard, who had served him faithfully for 20 years. Now, having elevated her husband to the post of gentleman of the bedchamber, as a reward for his wife's amorous exertions with her royal lover, George ordered her to resume her conjugal duties. But Henrietta had the last laugh. Her husband died and she married a man 12 years younger than herself.

Amelia Sophia Marianna (1704–65), the daughter of a general in the Hanoverian service, was related to three of the mistresses of George II's father, the von Platens.[12] An author can reasonably claim she was bred of a good pedigree for her royal duties! But one uncharitable wit posted a notice on the gates of Kensington Palace:

> Here lies a man of fifty-four,
> Who lost his wife and found a whore.

This was to prove an understatement, for he 'found' a good many more. On her deathbed, Caroline begged her husband to remarry. 'Never! Never!' he sobbed, 'I shall only have mistresses.' And for the rest of his life he kept his promise, choosing them for their physical rather than mental qualities.[13]

George made Amelia his official mistress, and created her Duchess of Yarmouth, after she divorced her husband in 1739. Walpole hoped 'her influence might be politically serviceable', but she proved entirely unfit for the role of a Pompadour. She took over from Walpole as the principal channel between the king and his ministers, and 'made an honest living selling peerages, on the sound principle that the less worthy the applicant, the more it would cost'.[14] Royal patronage was required not only in the great offices of State but also for those seeking preferment in the Church, the Law, and for sons seeking commissions in the armed forces. Friends and relatives, too, required government contracts or public office.[15] Amelia returned to Hanover after the death of the king, whose affection she never lost.

English society in the 18th century was founded on landed property,[16] and the ownership of land was the symbol of social distinction. Landowners fell into three categories of peers, gentry and freeholders – a social pyramid of status, wealth, power and influence, narrow at the top and broad at the bottom. While France was essentially a country of small farms, English estates and farms were large and prosperous – and during the century grew larger and even more prosperous, with enclosures and improved agricultural methods. Together, the nobility and gentry owned three-quarters of the land, employed about two-thirds of the population, and earned two-thirds of the national income. The entire constitutional machinery was controlled and directed by them. 'They controlled all government institutions, whether central or local, military or civil, spiritual or temporal, executive, legislative or judicial'.[17] Great Britain's destiny was in their hands.

The 'broad acres' of some 400 aristocrats, like the Dukes of Bedford, Devonshire, Newcastle and Richmond, gave them the right to govern, confirmed by birth and education. The great Whig families controlled the House of Lords, in which sat the peers and bishops, whose membership was determined by inheritance or crown appointment. They had a near monopoly of cabinet posts and the ownership of 'pocket' and 'rotten' boroughs. The gentry, who corresponded to the lesser nobility of France, were not legally part of the aristocracy at all. Their 750 knights and baronets, 4,000 squires and far more numerous gentlemen largely made up the House of Commons as elected members of parliament. The established Anglican Church, the universities and most of the higher schools were dominated by the squirearchy and enjoyed their patronage. As in France, the high offices of State, at court, and in the armed services were normally filled by the nobility. In England, this nobility divided their time between their clubs, hunting and racing, cards, cock-fighting, wine and women, 'till time and the gout sent them to the spa waters of the fashionable Bath and Tunbridge Wells'.[18] There, according to Defoe, men sometimes found a mistress but very rarely looked for a wife.

But the real government of the country was local, not parliamentary. The Tory squire, secure in his manor house, upheld the laws and liberties of country and church. He sat on the county bench as a justice of the peace, tried the poacher and punished rogues, vagabonds and 'sturdy beggars' under the Poor Law Acts. He appointed the parson, supervised the gaols, markets and police, and nominated men for militia service. He hunted his foxes, drank his port, and like Fielding's Squire Western, 'kept a good wench'. He entertained widely, supported by a plentiful supply of cheap domestic labour.[19]

The broad base of the landowners' social pyramid, 11 times as numerous as the gentry, was filled by large and small freeholders – yeomen who farmed or rented out to tenant farmers the land they owned.[20] The tenant farmers, in particular, prospered under the Georges, and are often called 'the pride of English agriculture'. This group had the vote and filled the unpaid but essential parish roles of church warden and overseers of the king's highway. They levied the 'poor rate' on the parish, and applied the proceeds to the relief of the poor, sick and aged. They apprenticed boys under 24 and girls under 21, and provided work for the able-bodied paupers.[21] As constables, they ensured the militia quotas of 10,000 parishes were met.[22]

At the bottom of the social hierarchy were the 'lower orders' – wage-earning craftsmen and artisans, petty tradesmen, farmhands and hired labourers, the unemployed and the unemployable. This, the largest occupational group, had no vote and no participation in politics or government. Their only remedy for grievances, especially during poor harvests, was to riot.

The early years of the 18th century would see the rise of a middle class in France and England. Trade and commerce boomed, and the trading classes – merchants, bankers, industrialists and small businessmen – began to make money, to invest in the Bank of England (founded in 1694) or the East India Company. The big landowners, too, were deeply engaged in trade and invested capital in mines, docks and real estate. Whilst France remained overwhelmingly agricultural, trade and commerce would make England the wealthiest country in Europe and provide the 'sinews of war' for her struggle against France. 'Tis not the longest sword but the longest purse that conquers,' wrote Defoe.[23]

In England, only the eldest son inherited his father's title and estate (primogeniture); in France, women could not pass on nobility but the family shared the title and inheritance. So younger sons, as English commoners with no special privileges, had to enter the professions (church, law or armed services), go into industry or commerce, or marry the richly endowed daughters or widows of the wealthy middle class; unlike France, there was no chasm between the classes. Compared with the French aristocracy, whose ancestry went back into the mists of time, English nobles were Tudor or Stuart upstarts. In England there was more social mobility and it was no social slur, as in France, to enter trade or commerce.[24] Many an English gentleman's wealth came from 'pieces of paper' (stocks and shares), not land. Defoe wrote:

> Tradesmen in England fill the lists of our nobility and gentry. Their daughters are adorned with ducal coronets and ride in the coaches of the best of the nobility. Gentlemen of the best families marry tradesmen's daughters and put their younger sons apprentices to tradesmen. Their children, or at least their grandchildren, become as good Statesmen, Judges, Bishops and Noblemen as those of the highest birth and most ancient families.[25]

English peerages were not for sale, as in 18th century France, where to be well endowed was becoming as important as to be well-born.

Elsewhere,[26] Defoe wrote:

> Wealth, howsoever got, in England makes
> Lords of Mechanicks, Gentlemen of Rakes.
> Antiquity and Birth are needless here:
> Tis Impudence and Money makes a Peer.

The Industrial Revolution had not yet begun to create in northern England a new population of bitter factory outcasts, and the English accepted the social order as a fact of life –

> God bless the squire and his relations,
> And keep us in our proper stations.[27]

England was still largely a rustic nation of scattered farms and hamlets, open fields and common land, clustered round its parish church, with a great variety of agricultural methods, land tenure and social groupings.[28] Three-quarters of her six million inhabitants in 1750 lived in the countryside.[29] Most, including the women and children, were employed on the land or in associated cottage industries. Although communications improved during the century, the stagecoach was still the most common method of travel, rumbling over the wretched country roads, slow, infrequent and uncomfortable. Passengers carried pistols or stout cudgels against footpads and highwaymen. Goods were transported mostly by sea or river barge.[30]

Winter brought unemployment; the seasons were a cycle of want and plenty, toil and drudgery, with a life expectancy of 35. The recurring round of birth, marriage and early death bore heavily on the poorer classes but most heavily on the women, tens of thousands of whom died in childbirth.[31] But life was healthier in the country than in the towns, crime less prevalent, and the seasonal calendar was enlivened by markets, fairs, feast-days and rural festivities.

London, with 700,000 inhabitants (1750), was the largest city in Europe and growing rapidly. With roughly ten times the population of the next largest English city, it towered over Manchester, Liverpool, Birmingham and Bristol. It was 'an irresistible honeypot for the young, offering work, money and excitement, or anonymity and escape'.[32] It was the centre of the court, of politics, law, fashion and the arts, and the capital of finance. It had theatres, concert and assembly rooms, clubs and literary circles, taverns and alehouses, and some 500 coffee houses, the second homes of many Londoners, where they could talk, read their newspapers and smoke their pipes.[33] There, too, wealthy Virginian and Jamaican plantation owners could keep abreast of colonial news, and merchants and travellers discuss trade and empire. London had something for everyone. When a man is tired of London, said Dr Johnson, he is tired of life!

To London came Horace Walpole's[34] powdered, patched and berouged lords and ladies, vacating their solid Georgian mansions for the four-month London season, with its round of theatres, balls and receptions. There they could dance, flirt, meet their friends, exchange scandal, play cards and sell off their daughters in the capital's marriage market. In the fashionable pleasure haunts of Vauxhall and Ranelagh Gardens, the extravagant ostrich plumes of ladies of quality could mingle with the peacock feathers of courtesans.[35] While the ladies shopped for the latest fashions, jewellery and furniture in Pall Mall or St Paul's, 'infinitely superior to those in the fashionable Rue St Honoré in Paris', their husbands saw their bankers and lawyers, attended parliament or gave orders to their tailor or coach-builder. The leisured class of London was creating a consumer society, supported by the products of a widening empire.[36]

The sons of the nobility, in velvet suits and embroidered ruffs, gambled away their patrimony at Whites, Boodles or Almack's in St James's Street before visiting the Bear Garden, 'where Cocks and Bulls and half-naked Irish women fight'.[37] Some would resort to the Bethlehem Royal Hospital (Bedlam)[38] to mingle with Hogarth's aristocratic ladies mocking the lunatic inmates, or sample the ladies of pleasure in the Rose Tavern in Covent Garden.[39] Other young sparks would invade the stage at the Theatre Royal, Drury Lane, to admire the stage's first duchess, Lavinia Fenton,[40] as 'pretty Polly Peachum', or cheer London's most popular actor, David Garrick, son of a captain in the Dragoon Guards. They would boo the players who displeased them, pick quarrels, chatter to their friends, ogle the masked ladies and make their assignations.

London was not only the national capital but the heart of a colonial empire. Its merchants exported manufactured goods in exchange for colonial luxuries and necessities. What the country did not consume, it re-exported to Europe. Through its busy port, with its wharves, ship-building yards, docks and arsenals passed two-thirds of England's foreign and colonial trade – the foundation of the nation's prosperity and strength in peace and war.

The Thames was a major thoroughfare, carrying goods and people, with London Bridge, now five-and-a-half centuries old, the only bridge spanning it until the opening of Westminster Bridge in 1750. A building boom, starting in 1713, moved the rich and aristocratic society of the court, government and the professions westward from the once fashionable Soho and Covent Garden. The villages of Chelsea, Marylebone, Hammersmith and Paddington were swallowed up, and Hanover, Berkeley and Grosvenor Squares built 'for persons of distinction'. To Queen Caroline we owe the Serpentine in Hyde Park, itself a popular resort for fashion, beauty and highwaymen. George II built the Horse Guards on the site of Henry VIII's Tiltyard, today a tourist attraction for the Household Cavalry to mount guard and for the annual Trooping of the Colour. After fire had destroyed Westminster Palace in 1698, the royal family took up its official residence in St James's, or lived in Kensington Palace, where George II died.

To the east of the City (still with its medieval walls and gates, its finance houses and Inns of Court), in Wapping and the hamlets around the Tower, lay a growing area of huts, shanties and workshops, the homes of migrant poor and riverside industry. Here, wrote the traveller Archenholtz,[41] 'the houses are old, the streets narrow, dark and ill-paved, inhabited by sailors and shipyard workers.' Here was to be found the darker side of the metropolis, where lived London's 'underworld' or criminal classes, the world chronicled by Defoe, Smollett and Fielding, and painted by Hogarth. The tangled lanes, dark alleys and sprawling suburbs were ideal breeding grounds for crime and criminals. For poverty led to crime, 'men rob for bread: women whore for bread: necessity is the parent of crime,' wrote Defoe.[42] Defoe wrote from experience, having suffered bankruptcy, the pillory and imprisonment in Newgate. Poverty led to the brutalisation of men, women and children, to violence, punitive laws and savage punishments in order to protect citizens, fearful of their safety and ill-served by an inadequate police force of beadle, Bow Street Runner or parish constable.

The death penalty could be awarded for 160 felonies, or they were punished with the pillory, whipping at the cart's tail, branding or transportation, usually to Maryland or Virginia.[43] Once every six weeks the procession of carts and hearses carried the condemned along Tyburn Road (modern Oxford Street) to be 'topped' at Tyburn Tree (Marble Arch). 'Hanging day' became a popular holiday, with scenes of excitement only matched at a Bridewell house of correction, where teenage prostitutes were daily flogged 'to feast the eyes of the spectators and arouse the appetites of the lascivious, rather than to correct vice or reform manners'.[44] The dirty, overcrowded and fever-ridden prisons still awaited the reformer, John Howard. The evils of drink, so graphically portrayed in Hogarth's Gin Lane (1751) were a national scandal, as the mortality rate soared and taverns proudly proclaimed 'Drunk for a penny, dead drunk for twopence: clean straw for nothing.'

Poverty was also the root cause of prostitution, which increased dramatically in 18th century London.[45] Vice always came in at the door of necessity, not at the door of inclination, said Moll Flanders. Young girls from the countryside and Ireland flocked to London to find work, independence and better social and marriage prospects. Many came as domestic servants, the 18th century growth sector, only to end up on the streets around Holborn and Co(n)vent Garden. Hogarth's Harlot's Progress (1732) shows the stagecoach bringing young hopefuls to London to be met by a procuress, 'on the watch for any fresh goods.'[46]

Domestic servants had low wages, long hours of drudgery, and no holidays: they were subject to brutal treatment on the one hand and lechery on the other by master, sons or male servants. Many working girls in London became common strumpets to supplement their wages or kept women for an easier life, especially as there was a large surplus of marriageable women in the metropolis. 'The market is against our sex just now,' said Defoe's worldly-wise heroine, Moll Flanders. 'If she have not money, she's nobody.' Defoe's Roxana (1724), an impoverished widow, opted to become a high-class kept woman rather than face starvation – 'Tis better to whore than to starve,' she reasoned.

J W von Archenholtz, an authority on the life and morals of contemporary England, estimated there were 50,000 prostitutes in London in 1760, ranging from fashionable courtesans to common street-walkers.[47]

The lot of Hanoverian women, who made up over half the nation's population, whether rich or poor, was in general one of sexual exploitation and legal and physical submission to a male – father, master or husband. In law, wives had no rights over their person, property or children, and every husband could legally beat his wife, provided 'he used a stick no thicker than his thumb,' ruled Judge Butler in 1782 – 'an ancient privilege still claimed and exerted by the lower rank of people'.[48] Custom, too, favoured obedience, and confined the role of women in society to that of wife, mother, housekeeper, domestic servant, maiden aunt, concubine or mistress. In a male-dominated society which held women in low esteem, male promiscuity and female exploitation and prostitution were natural consequences.

Marriage, for the propertied classes, was a duty, usually arranged, undertaken for the procreation of children, and always associated with money, marriage settlements and jointures. 'Who marrieth for love without money hath good nights and sorry days'; 'Poor beauty finds more lovers than husbands' were contemporary proverbs. The French had a similar proverb – '*la beauté ne sale pas la marmite*' (beauty doesn't salt the cooking pot). Property required 'a lady's chastity before marriage, and reputation afterwards, since a husband would not contemplate a cuckoo in the nest, nor would he wish to bequeath his property to a son, unless he was sure of paternity'.[49] Property begets affection. Lust and desire should be left to whores and courtesans. And royalty set the pace in both mistresses and children. George II had nine children; George III had 15!

Throughout the first half of the 18th century, church marriage was the exception rather than the rule: for the poor, 'the habit of disregarding marriage, had become common', largely for economic reasons. Large numbers lived in 'customary concubinage' – illegal according to the laws of Church and State, but recognised by the neighbours. Marriage was often clandestine, requiring neither licence, banns in church nor parental consent. Furthermore, it was considerably cheaper, saving the cost of the ceremony and lavish entertainment. A sworn statement that there was no legal impediment sufficed. Others went through a regular church wedding but were marrying bigamously. Consummation and conception normally preceded – indeed precipitated – marriage, as shown by the fact that a third of all brides were pregnant on their wedding day, and over half of all first births were conceived out of wedlock.[50]

In 1753, Lord Hardwicke's Marriage Act ('for the better preventing of clandestine marriages') forbade and invalidated anyone marrying under 21 without parental or guardian consent, and required the calling of banns and residence in the parish. It subjected clergymen convicted of performing clandestine marriages to transportation to America for 14 years. The Act attacked the national scandal of Fleet marriages, performed in almost every tavern and brandy shop around the Fleet Prison (but also elsewhere in London and in the country generally), by unscrupulous parsons in the prison's pay. For a small fee the parson would marry any couple brought before him – young heiresses abducted from boarding schools were married under duress to scoundrelly adventurers; young men were plied with liquor and paired off with Drury Lane trollops. Such marriages encouraged seduction for money, bigamy, and the dumping of a pauper and her children on another parish. These marriages were popular with soldiers and sailors, attracted by the cheapness, speed, legal informalities and anonymity.[51]

Since divorce was difficult to obtain and beyond the means of the poor, wife sales in some public place, such as market or tavern, were frequent during the century, though not recognised by Church or State. How else were the poor to obtain freedom from a marriage that had not worked?

> Thinking that his wife is his goods and chattels, the man puts a halter about her neck and leads her (often willingly!) to the marketplace, where he auctions her, as though she was a brood-mare or a milch-cow, to the highest bidder.[52]

The alternatives were bigamy or living in sin.

The family was the economic unit for the working class, on farm, in trade, craft or shop, the labour and wages of each member supporting the whole. Whether married or single, women and children ('children are the riches of the poor' according to a contemporary proverb) were expected to support themselves. 'None but a fool will take a wife, whose bread must be earned solely by his labour,' a master advised his serving-maid.[53] For girls the legal age of consent was 12, for boys 14, but the majority married after 21. Working-class women tended to leave home earlier and marry later. Wives living on farms, working in shops and in the cottage industries ran a home, bore children, earned their keep and supported their parents in old age. Tired women, it would seem, were likely to be more virtuous!

Invariably, the British soldier and his 'woman' (the term used in army regulations) came from the lower social orders. The soldier was considered 'the scum of the earth', whom only the lash could keep in order. In America, as in England, only six per 100 men were allowed to be married 'on the strength' of the regiment. The women would be of the same class as the soldier, picked up wherever he was stationed, and expected to earn their keep by washing, nursing and performing simple chores. Many, of course, would be unmarried; some relationships would be temporary, others of a more permanent duration.

The officers, on the other hand, came almost without exception from the upper and professional classes, and married within the same social strata. It was pardonable for a young officer to fall in love with a young 'beauty' of a lower station, but not to marry her. Wolfe would 'fall upon an officer delinquent without mercy. By this method I broke many an amorous alliance and dissolved many ties of eternal love and affection.' In any case, an officer had to postpone marriage in the interests of his military profession, and then to a girl or widow, preferably with money to pay for his commission and subsequent promotions.[54]

For William Pitt and General Wolfe, as we shall see later (Chapter 17), and their upper class contemporaries, there was the possibility of the 'grand tour' of France and Italy to complete their education, broaden their cultural and social horizons, and teach them another language. This was usually French, which had replaced Latin as the universal language. Paris was the goal for most tourists of both sexes, the cultural centre of Europe and the centre of gaiety and pleasure.[55] For the young, healthy and wealthy Englishman, freed from parental control, Paris offered opportunities for sexual adventures.

Its *filles de joie* ranged from the aristocratic courtesan (*femme entretenue*), to the shopgirls (*grisettes*) and the common street-walkers (*les putains*).[56] Pitt, for instance, pursuing the easy life of a cornet in a fashionable cavalry regiment (1st Dragoon Guards), toured France and Switzerland in 1738. He became infatuated with a French lady, 'though her lack of social station precluded any thought of marriage'. Contemporaries and anxious parents warned of the dangers of young men spending their time and money on gambling, drinking and whoring, especially with 'French actresses and Parisian opera girls'. English ladies were advised never to travel unescorted and to beware of ending up with a 'French dancing master's son for an heir'.[57] Better to concentrate on the glories of Versailles and the treasures of the Louvre!

But whatever the attractions of France and its women, Defoe and Protestant England hated the French as:

A nation of onion-nibbling peasants, oppressed by lecherous Papist priests, a tyrannous king and mincing courtiers.[58]

The British navy held similar opinions (see illustration 4).

Hark ye Monsieur! Was that your Map of North America? What a vast tract of land you had. Pity the Right owner should take it from you!

'Before the English learn there is a God to be worshipped,' said Count Fourgeret de Montbon, 'they learn there are Frenchmen to be detested.'[59] Treating the French and all foreigners with contempt was a national characteristic. We shall find the English military leaders applying the same contempt to the French in Canada and to the American colonials – often with disastrous results!

5

THE WAR CLOUDS GATHER

'War is the trade of kings' Dryden

In 1738 Captain Robert Jenkins, master of a Glasgow brig, stood up in the House of Commons to complain that Spanish coastguards had stopped his ship on the high seas, bound him to the mast, and torn off an ear. Mockingly, they told him to present it to King George. He now produced it, carefully packed in wool, for parliament's inspection. 'I committed my soul to God, and my cause to my country,' he claimed. Uproar broke out. Pitt declared that the nation's trade and honour were at stake. The House promptly passed a resolution that 'It was the undoubted right of British subjects to sail their ships in any part of the seas of America'. Spain, on the contrary, resented the expansion of British commerce 'in her Caribbean waters'. The Spanish looked upon traders like Jenkins as smugglers. Their ships should be seized, and the culprits handed over to the tender mercies of the Spanish Inquisition.[1]

Walpole, the British Prime Minister, was reluctant to go to war over a question which, he believed, could be settled by diplomacy. But such was the popular outcry among the British traders, the City of London, and the populace at large that Walpole was forced to declare the War of Jenkins' Ear on Spain in October 1739. 'They are ringing their bells now: soon they will be ringing their hands,' he warned the nation.

Within a year the struggle with Spain became merged into a wider struggle with France, England's traditional enemy, and with Prussia against Austria. The War of the Austrian Succession (1740–8), called in America 'King George's War', since it involved the king personally as Elector of Hanover, was followed by the Seven Years' War (1756–63). Both sprang from a common source – the emergence of Prussia. Once kindled, war spread rapidly, embroiling most of Europe, with many sharp vicissitudes of fortune.[2] For the wars of the 18th century were largely dynastic, with peoples condemned to bear the cost of wars which they had no part in promoting.

For Britain, the War of the Austrian Succession was no more than a continuation of the worldwide conflict with France for military and naval supremacy, and trade and empire, especially in India and North America. By 1740 the French empire had grown rich and strong. The French Caribbean islands were competing increasingly successfully with the English 'sugar' islands in trade with Europe and the North American colonies. The French Naval

Minister, the Comte de Maurepas, had built up a formidable French navy and had done much to modernise it; despite this, Madame de Pompadour had him dismissed, for reasons unconnected with his abilities. (He had ridiculed her.) By abstaining from expensive adventures abroad, and providing competent government at home, Cardinal Fleury had improved France's economy. Her position now, said Fleury, was comparable to France 'at the most brilliant epoch of Louis XIV's reign.' France was now outwardly ready to challenge Britain, 'to put to flight this usurping race', and to curtail its commerce, which had already made France's 'ancient enemies almost the masters of the fate of Europe'. With only a limited number of career posts open to them, the court nobility were seeking opportunities to practise their military profession, and Madame de Châteauroux, the current *mistresse en titre*, 'transformed from a royal plaything to an institution of State,' encouraged Louis XV to take military action. So the armed struggle would merge into the war known in America as the French and Indian War, and in Europe as the Seven Years' War.

In October 1740 the Holy Roman Emperor Charles VI lay dying, without a son to inherit the Austrian Habsburg empire. Salic law excluded females from dynastic succession, so Charles tried to ensure the peaceful accession of his daughter, Maria Theresa, to an undivided inheritance by persuading every important court in Europe to sign the Pragmatic Sanction.[3] Maria was a young, attractive woman of 23, with little experience of political affairs. Her mediocre husband had no military talents; her ministers were mostly old, timid, and incompetent. Her treasury was empty and her army weak. Furthermore, she could not count on the loyalty of her Magyar nobility.

Suddenly, in December 1740, to her complete surprise and that of Europe, Frederick II of Prussia, driven by a desire for personal glory and to consolidate his kingdom, seized Austria's richest province of Silesia. His action launched a series of wars in 1740–2, 1744–5, and 1756–63 against Austria, in order to retain it. The Queen of Hungary decided to take vigorous action, and became involved in a desperate struggle to save her inheritance from a greedy collection of the principal signatories to the Pragmatic Sanction. From every quarter 'the vultures' descended on her territory. France laid claim to the Austrian Netherlands; Spain demanded Hungary and Bohemia; Sardinia wanted Lombardy; Bavaria and Saxony required their share of the spoils in Bohemia. After the share-out, Maria Theresa would be lucky to retain Hungary and the eastern provinces of Austria.

Then came a remarkable change of fortune. The principles of honour, chivalry and good faith had not been banished completely from international relations. In 1741, at the Diet of Pressburg, the beautiful, distraught Maria Theresa, dressed in black and with babe in arms, made a dramatic and courageous appeal for help to the chivalry of her wild Hungarian nobles. Clashing their swords on their shields in an enthusiastic display of loyalty, the

Magyars shouted with one voice: 'Let us die for our King, Maria Theresa.'[4] Laying aside their separatist traditions, they supported her by raising a force of 20,000 men, mostly cavalry, and paying for her coronation. Fisher wrote:

> There are few errors in French history more calamitous than France's decision to join Frederick of Prussia in his attack on Maria Theresa. It was not only a blunder, involving her in an exhausting continental war, calling for so many risks and sacrifices, but a crime, for France had signed the Pragmatic Sanction.

As a result Canada and India would pass into British hands. George II also answered Maria's call, not from any romantic idea of chivalry, but to protect his Electorate of Hanover from the predatory armies of France and Prussia. He feared, too, that France would join Spain against England. Six years earlier, France had signed a secret treaty, the Family Compact, with Spain to recover Gibraltar for her and curtail England's commercial privileges with Spanish America. So, at the age of 61, George II was once again on the battlefield, leading a joint army of Britons, Austrians, Dutch and Hanoverians to victory over the French at Dettingen (1743).[5]

It is during the War of the Austrian Succession that we first hear of William Pitt, later Earl of Chatham. Pitt would be largely responsible for wresting Canada and India from France, by his policy of subordinating military operations in Europe to naval and colonial aims. As a young man of limited means, Pitt had obtained in 1731 a cornetcy in the fashionable 1st Dragoon Guards, thanks to his brother's marriage into the family of the wealthy Viscount Cobham, who owned the regiment. Four years later he entered parliament through the family borough of Old Sarum, making a name for himself by his wonderful oratory, and his attacks on king and government. 'We must muzzle this terrible young cornet of horse,' exclaimed Walpole.

After offensive remarks made about the King on the occasion of the marriage of the Prince of Wales, Pitt was dismissed from the army. In 1742 he attacked the practice of paying Hanoverian troops with English money, 'making Great Britain a mere province to a despicable Electorate'. Such remarks were hardly calculated to make him popular with the King but were highly popular in the country – and with the eccentric Duchess of Marlborough, who had never forgiven the Hanoverians for slighting her husband. The richest woman in England, the duchess died in 1744 and left Pitt a legacy of £10,000 for 'defending the laws of England and preventing the ruin of his country'.[6]

In 1746 Pitt hoped to obtain the post of Secretary at War, but the King strongly objected. 'His Majesty was determined not to have him at the War Office,' wrote Newcastle. Instead, he was given the lucrative post of Paymaster General of the Forces. Pitt's rival, Henry Fox, reluctantly accepted the post of Secretary at War from the King, which demanded hard work for less money than Pitt would receive. 'Greatly to his honour', chronicles the *Dictionary of National Biography*, 'and, unlike his predecessors, Pitt declined to accept a farthing from his new office, beyond the legal salary.' He refused to take the interest on the huge balances of army pay he handled, or to accept the one-half per cent commission which foreign powers paid on receipt of their military subsidies. The job was recognised as a legitimate means of making a fortune, and such perquisites had made Walpole and Fox very rich men. Fox, for instance, believed statesmen should live off the State, and that 'to buy support was the only way to carry on a government'. When Walpole accepted the post in 1714 gossips commented: 'He was very lean and needed to get some fat on his bones'.[7]

George II gave the direction of the Austrian War to Henry Fox, Pitt's contemporary at Eton, whose political career under Walpole had been supported by influence and money. His father, Sir Stephen Fox, had started life as a nobleman's footman before entering the household of Charles II. He accompanied the king 'on his travels', and was rewarded with the post of Paymaster General after the Restoration. He became a rich man but, losing his son and heir, he decided at the age of 77 to remarry. His son, Henry, squandered his patrimony in gambling and dissipation before 'falling light into the opulent bed of a Mrs Strangways-Horner. She kept him handsomely, went on a continental tour with him, and clandestinely married her 13-year-old daughter to Fox's brother, Stephen.' Henry entered parliament via 'a rotten borough', while Stephen secured a peerage as Lord Ilchester. Fox became Pitt's rival in parliament, but cared more for money than power and was content later to hold the post of Paymaster General for many years, amassing a fortune during the Seven Years' War.

In 1744 France launched an invasion fleet from Brest against England, under Marshal the Count de Saxe, a bastard brother of the Elector of Saxony, in the employ of Louis XV. Fortunately, a storm dispersed the fleet in the English Channel. Fox, then Secretary at War, created a storm of another kind by eloping with the teenage Caroline Lennox, the great-granddaughter of Charles II and his mistress Louise de Kéroualle. Despite the scandal surrounding their own marriage, (Caroline's mother, Sarah, daughter of the Earl of Cadogan, had been given as a 13-year-old bride to the 18-year-old son of the Duke of Richmond in settlement of a gambling debt), Caroline's parents and the Prime Minister, Newcastle, were outraged. The scandal soon blew over, and the couple settled down at Holland House, with its 64-acre park bordering Kensington Palace. But the marriage gained entry for Fox into the ducal houses, eventually raising him to the peerage and blessing him with four sons.[8]

The following year, while King and Parliament debated subsidies to Maria Theresa and sent money to support 18,000 Hanoverian soldiers in Flanders, the Young Pretender landed in Scotland in an attempt to dethrone George II.

The attempt was unsuccessful, and Prince Charles was defeated at Culloden, where the young James Wolfe served as brigade major in the Duke of Cumberland's army. The French, based at Louisbourg, took the opportunity to attack Annapolis, capital of Nova Scotia. New England was alarmed. Governor William Shirley of Massachusetts, an English barrister and son of a wealthy London merchant, decided on a bold counterstroke – the capture of France's impregnable fortress of Louisbourg, which menaced the New Englanders' fisheries and the expanding frontier settlements of Maine and New Hampshire. It also spoiled the colonists' lucrative sport of seizing ships laden with sugar, gold and silver bullion off the coast of Nova Scotia.

Shirley organised and equipped a force of some 4,000 New England volunteers,[9] and placed them under the command of William Pepperell, a colonel of militia. Pepperell was a prosperous Boston merchant whose father had emigrated as a poor man from Devon to make his fortune. New York sent a few guns, clothing and bedding; Pennsylvania sent provisions. Newcastle and the Royal Navy supported the expedition with a blockading squadron from the West Indies station under Admiral Sir Peter Warren, who happened to be cruising in the area. (Warren had a special interest in the venture. He had married Miss de Lancey of Boston, sister of the governor of New York, who owned large tracts of land in the Mohawk valley, and hoped to be made governor himself.) The expedition was highly successful. In barely six weeks, 'with the help of 500 Marines from the fleet and extraordinary good fortune', Pepperell and his amateur army succeeded in capturing Louisbourg and its garrison of professional soldiers (17 June 1745), mostly *troupes de la marine*. Had the capture been confirmed at the 1748 Peace of Aix la Chapelle, the position of the French in America would have become untenable.[10]

The colonists were immensely proud of their exploit, and rightly so! The New Englanders were raw militia, ill-disciplined and with no military experience beyond frontier skirmishes. A contemporary described the expedition 'as having a lawyer (Shirley) for contriver; a merchant (Pepperell) for general; and farmers, fishermen and mechanics for soldiers'. But speed, secrecy, daring, and a slice of good fortune won the day.[11] This was the first great military success in North America against France, and aroused intense enthusiasm in London, for Louisbourg was a growing threat to British interests.

The fortress was a home for a French fleet, and for pirates and privateers preying on British commerce. By 1745 the civil population of the town numbered 4,000; its garrison 2,000. Most of the French officers sent there lived in private houses and remained as permanent settlers, their sons succeeding them, for a commission was a family asset. The men lived in a barrack building on army rations, supplemented by hunting and fishing in the neighbourhood. Their barrack room or *chambrée,* sparsely furnished, was a favourite spot for lounging, talk and drinking when off-duty or free from obligatory work on the fortifications. Because of the isolation and climate, desertions were few and settlement limited. Soldiers were allowed to marry, and since few women came from France, officers and men found Canadian or Acadian wives. Married soldiers had the right to keep a tavern; officers sold extra food, tobacco, wine and brandy imported from France. The captain, having a monopoly on sales to the men of his company, could charge exorbitant prices and was able to maintain a substantial house.[12]

So parliament paid the expenses of the siege. Shirley and Pepperell were awarded baronetcies, and the colonial troops who survived the assault were formed into two regiments on English pay, and taken on the regular establishment as the 65 and 66 (later 50 and 51) Foot. Shirley and Pepperell became their respective colonels. The Royal Navy obtained nearly a million pounds prize money, shared out among those participating according to rank. Sir William Warren would himself receive £125,000 prize money during the war.

Shirley, his appetite whetted by success, wanted to complete the conquest of Canada the following year. Moreover, war gave him increased opportunities for wealth and patronage through military commissions, supply and clothing contracts. He was prepared to raise 10,000 American volunteers. Britain promised five regular battalions and a fleet. Three British regiments, the 29, 30 and 45 Foot,[13] arrived in April 1746 to occupy and garrison Louisbourg. The promised British provincial forces would march against Montreal via Lake Champlain.

The colonies voted a force of 4,300 men. The French frantically prepared their defences, but the promised British forces never arrived. Instead, they were directed by the Duke of Newcastle to attack the coast of France. A report that a huge French expedition was on its way to retake Louisbourg and Acadia, and burn Boston, frightened the New Englanders. A French fleet did reach the coast of Nova Scotia but was shattered by a terrible storm. The French admiral, Danville, died of apoplexy (or suicide): his successor, outvoted in a council of war, threw himself on his sword in despair. The remnants of the fleet struggled back to France in a state of starvation, having lost more than 2,500 men.[14] A second French fleet, attempting to regain Louisbourg, was caught by Admirals Anson and Warren off La Rochelle and utterly defeated. But the European combatants, tired of their aimless and expensive war on the continent, signed the Treaty of Aix-la-Chapelle in 1748. Under its terms, Britain, France and Spain reverted to the *status quo ante bellum* in Europe and overseas. The American colonists were dismayed to learn that their prize, Louisbourg, had been bartered in the treaty for an insignificant factory called Madras, soon to become the heart of the British empire in India. France gave up her conquests in the Austrian Low Countries, the fortifications at Dunkirk were to be demolished, and Prussia kept Silesia. The original cause of Britain going to war – the Spanish right of search – was not even mentioned!

One problem left unresolved by the treaty was the future of Nova Scotia (Acadia). It had been conquered by General Nicholson in 1710, who named it after his native Scotland, and was formerly transferred to Britain by France at Utrecht in 1713. The terms of the treaty expressly provided that:

> Such of the French inhabitants as are willing to remain and be subject to the
> Kingdom of Great Britain are to enjoy the exercise of their religion, according
> to the usages of the Church of Rome, as far as the laws of Great Britain do
> allow the same.[15]

Those who wanted to leave with their belongings would be permitted to do so within a year. Few, in fact, chose to leave. Britain, anxious to obtain their loyalty, treated them very leniently, refrained from taxing them, and made little effort to remove them. The population increased threefold and, until 1749, remained entirely French.[16]

But the French in Canada had no intention of giving up Acadia and its people, nor its lucrative fur and fishing trade. Led by the fanatical Joseph Le Loutre, vicar-general of Acadia, for whom religion and patriotism combined to make the expulsion of the English a holy crusade, the Jesuit priests threatened the inhabitants with eternal damnation, if they swore allegiance to a heretic king. Furthermore, Le Loutre threatened to abandon them, deprive them of their priests, and have their wives and children carried off and their property laid waste by his Micmac Indian allies. Faced with such menaces, the illiterate and superstitious peasants proved hostile to the British during the War of the Austrian Succession (King George's War). At best they were sullenly neutral to the small English military garrison (40 Foot) at the capital of Nova Scotia, Fort Annapolis Royal (named in honour of Queen Anne).

In 1749 the new governor, Colonel Edward Cornwallis, arrived with 2,300 settlers, mostly veteran soldiers and their families, to found a new colony. He chose the splendid harbour of Halifax, six miles long and over a mile wide, to counter the threat of Louisbourg. It would become a powerful naval base, with the advantage of being ice-free all year round. It was named after the Earl of Halifax (George Montagu), a wealthy clothier, who added Dunk to his name as a condition of marriage to Anne, daughter of Sir Thomas Dunk. This brought him an enormous fortune. He did so much to expand the commerce of America that he was often called 'the Father of the Colonies' (DNB).

In an advertisement in the London Gazette of 1749, the Earl of Halifax, President of the Board of Trade and Plantations, offered settlers 50 acres of freehold land, an additional ten acres for every women and child, a paid passage, and tax immunity for ten years. The offer 'for the better peopling and settling the Province, and giving encouragement to such officers and private men lately dismissed His Majesty's land and sea service', gave junior officers 80 acres, with an extra 15 acres for each member of their family (officers above the rank of captain were offered 600 acres and 30 extra acres respectively). The offer was also open to 'carpenters, shipwrights, smiths, masons, joiners, bricklayers, and all other artificers necessary in building and husbandry'. Clergymen were offered 200 acres, schoolmasters 100, 'to encourage the practice and teaching of the Protestant religion'?[17]

To the Board of Trade's offices in the Cockpit, Whitehall (the forerunner of the Colonial Office), there arrived a motley collection of:

> Physicians, surgeons, clerics and schoolmasters seeking appointments, and others wanting to furnish clothing, medicines, ploughs and other commodities for the settlers.[18]

Succeeding years brought fresh emigrants, until in 1752 the settlement of Halifax numbered over 4,000.

The French retaliated by building Fort Beauséjour on the Chignecto Isthmus, the narrow strip of land which today joins the provinces of New Brunswick and Nova Scotia. They also sent 'religious and political agents to stir up discontent among the French Acadians, already offended by the intrusion of the new settlers'.[19] The French commander, La Corne, and Father Le Loutre, for example, continued to induce the Acadians to transfer to 'French territory' and colonise the area around Fort Beauséjour. Three thousand did so, promising to take the oath of allegiance to the King of France.

But a new generation of Acadians, born under English rule and protected by British regular garrisons, was reluctant to move, especially as they had been offered fair and just terms to persuade them to remain. Le Loutre once more resorted to the tomahawks and burning torches of his terrible Micmac Indians to transplant the others forcibly. The fortifications of Louisbourg were rebuilt and its garrison increased. Versailles instructed the governor to use the Indians to harass the new settlement at Halifax 'but secretly, so as not to compromise the peace'. By 1755 the once peaceful life of Nova Scotia was ended, as the raids on frontier farms, the abductions of men, women and children, and the massacres became daily occurrences.[20] Clearly the British could not tolerate such a situation, and Governor Shirley and the New Englanders supported the elimination of France in Nova Scotia.

The new governor was Colonel Charles Lawrence, who had first arrived with his regiment, 47 Foot, in 1747 to garrison captured Louisbourg. Born into a military family, he was at 46 a veteran of 28 years' army campaigning. Lawrence decided to deport all Acadians who would not swear a binding oath of allegiance to the British crown.[21] After 40 years since the Treaty of Utrecht, it was time, he reasoned that the Acadians either became British subjects or were removed. In this strategic area, vital to both sides in the coming conflict, he considered the Acadians a security risk and a potential 'fifth column'. Neither lenient nor harsh policies would succeed in making them contented citizens.

The Board of Trade and Plantations was also in favour of firm action, despite war not having been declared between France and England. It recommended to George II that English settlement in the area would be impossible unless and until the French forts of Beauséjour and Baie Verte (Gaspereau) on the St John River had been destroyed and the hostile Indians subdued. Though the land belonged to the British crown, no peace was possible in Nova Scotia without such measures.

Lawrence gave command of the operation to Robert Monckton, son of Viscount Galway and his wife, a daughter of the Duke of Rutland. On 26 May 1755, Colonel Monckton sailed out of Boston Bay with 2,000 New Englanders and 300 regulars of 40 Foot (Hopson's) and 45 Foot (Warburton's), later the Sherwood Foresters, to invest the forts. On 1 June he anchored in front of Fort Beauséjour, which crowned the hill opposite Fort Lawrence and was commanded by Captain Vergor, who owed his position to his friend François Bigot, the powerful intendant of New France. After a feeble two weeks' defence both forts surrendered, but not before Vergor and his drunken French officers had looted much of their king's stores. Among the defenders were 300 Acadians, supposedly subjects of Great Britain, who claimed they were fighting under French threats. Le Loutre was among them, too!

The fate of Acadia was sealed. On 9 July Admiral Edward Boscawen sailed into Halifax with a British fleet. En route, Boscawen had defeated a French fleet off Newfoundland, capturing 1,200 French prisoners and a rich booty of wine and currency. Boscawen and Lawrence agreed to take the opportunity to rid the province once and for all of Acadians who refused to take the oath. The Acadians almost without exception refused. Accordingly, thousands were rounded up; during the summer and autumn of 1755 men, women and children were put on transports and scattered among the English mainland colonies.[22] Some escaped by land and sea to French Canada, or hid in the forests where, dispersed and bitter, they harassed the English settlers, 'more barbarous than the Indians'.[23] Some settled in Louisiana, and their descendants today form a large part of the French population there. A few returned to France. Le Loutre escaped to Quebec, but was eventually captured at sea. Under an assumed name, he was kept a prisoner for eight years in Jersey Castle.

Lawrence's 1755 operation achieved only partial success. Nominally in possession of Nova Scotia, the British in fact occupied only a few garrison strongholds. Lawrence's plan to colonise the province during 1755–62 was thwarted by the reluctance of New England farmers to settle in a land where they might be scalped at any moment by an implacable foe.[24] British regulars had to be sent to 'cleanse' the province completely, and stamp out French resistance on the St John River. While Lawrence directed operations from Halifax, Monckton was in command of military activities around Fort Beauséjour (which he renamed Fort Cumberland after the commander in chief). Colonel John Winslow, a colonial aristocrat in command of the New England forces, was sent to clear the settlements on Minas Basin.

The cancellation of the first Louisbourg expedition in September 1757 freed the 27, 43 and 46 Foot regiments for service in the garrisons of Annapolis Royal, Fort Cumberland and Fort Edward (Nova Scotia). Fort Edward, built by the British in 1750 on a hill overlooking the Avon and Windsor Rivers, became during the years 1755–62 the centre for the deportation of Acadians. The blockhouse still remains intact among the ruins of the old fort.

Visitors to the Grand Pré National Historic Park can see relics of the deportations, which Canadians regard as a national tragedy. In the park is a bronze statue of Evangeline, the heroine celebrated in Longfellow's famous narrative poem (1847). Her bridegroom was deported from Grand Pré on their wedding day. On the front steps of the reconstructed St Charles's Church, on 5 September 1755, Colonel John Winslow, the British commander, read the ultimatum for the expulsions, which continued for the next seven or eight years. Some 6,000–10,000 were deported from Nova Scotia after the fall of Beauséjour, although the numbers are uncertain. Today, 200,000 Canadians of Acadian descent mourn the expulsion of their ancestors.[25]

> So with songs on their lips the Acadian peasants descended,
> Down from the church to the shore, amid their wives and daughters.
> Wives were torn from their husbands, and mothers, too late, saw their children,
> Left on the land, extending their arms with wildest entreaties.
> While in despair on the shore Evangeline stood with her father,
> And the blaze of the burning village illumined the landscape.
> On the falling tide the freighted vessels departed,
> Bearing a nation, with all its household gods, into exile.

The Historical Records of the 43 Foot (the Monmouthshire Light Infantry)[26] provide a picture of contemporary regimental life in these isolated garrisons. The 43 Foot arrived at Halifax in June 1757, dressed in their three-cornered hats, wide-skirted red coats, long waistcoats, scarlet breeches, and long white spatterdash gaiters reaching to mid-thigh. They had survived a voyage in hired transport, packed so tightly they could hardly move, battened below deck in foul weather, miserably sea-sick, and frightened out of their lives. Devoured by vermin and often soaked to the skin, they had been fed on salt pork, usually mouldy and ill-cooked, eked out with biscuit full of weevils. 'A man in jail had more room, better food and commonly better company,' said Johnson.[27]

The regiment was posted to Fort Cumberland, a pentagon, beautifully situated on a hill and appropriately named Beauséjour (Fair Abode) by the French, who built it after the peace of Aix-la-Chapelle in 1748. The men strengthened it, and built good barracks, workshops and storehouses, receiving extra pay for the heavy work involved. On 13 October six companies sailed for the garrison at Annapolis Royal, and four companies went to Fort Edward.[28] The garrison at Annapolis was in very poor condition: the soldiers were shabby, their uniforms and discipline neglected. As was customary, the men of the old garrison were absorbed into the ranks of the new regiment. They were content to end their days in their new country, bound by ties of drink and women, rather than face the alternative of discharge and unemployment back home.

In this, the loneliest of garrisons, the soldiers were often employed by civilians, the officers socialising with the surrounding families to the neglect of their military duties. The men in the evenings would resort to the local tavern, drinking, blaspheming and singing their bawdy songs, which caused the New Englanders, with their Puritan upbringing, to accuse the redcoats of lewdness, profanity and of failure to observe the Sabbath.

> A lass is good, and a glass is good,
> And a pipe to smoke in the cold weather:
> The world is good, and the people good,
> And we are all good fellows together.

Lieutenant Colonel James, the 43rd's regimental commander, quickly restored good order and discipline. Patrols were sent out against prowling Acadians, and the guards instructed to report immediately sightings of enemy vessels, to stop piracy and attacks on coastal shipping. The sale of liquor in camp was forbidden. The extreme cold was the garrison's biggest problem. Although firewood was plentiful in the area, fuel had to be imported from Boston and other New England ports because of the activities of Acadian and Indian scalping parties. If parties of soldiers ventured out to cut wood, casualties resulted. In December, for instance, the corpse of a grenadier was found outside the camp, scalped and stripped of everything but his breeches. A roll-call revealed four Rangers and seven of the 43 Foot were absent, having been out cutting wood in defiance of repeated orders to the contrary. An armed patrol brought back their bodies 'stark-naked, barbarously murdered and scalped'. The following day the regiment was paraded to bury them, but they had to be laid out in the snow because the ground was too frozen to be broken by pick-axes.[29]

A grenadier who had deserted during an enemy attack relieved the boredom by returning to camp to surrender. He was tried by court martial for cowardice, and pleaded guilty. He was sentenced to ride the wooden horse half-an-hour every day for six days, dressed in a petticoat, with a broom in his hand and a placard on his back – 'Such is the reward of my merit'. With few distractions to while away the hours of boredom except the occasional visit of a hungry bear, the punishment was carried out 'to the inexpressible mirth of the whole garrison – and of its women, in particular'.[30] On subsequent occasions this man proved himself to be a remarkably gallant soldier.

The Irish officers of the garrison celebrated St Patrick's Day (17 March 1759) in the traditional way by entertaining 'their brethren in arms' to dinner, and bestowing half a dollar on each Irish soldier. An armed party of 50 men, including the chaplain, volunteered to raid the carefully planted French orchards. They returned with hampers, sacks and baskets filled with apples, 'no small luxury to the poor fellows so long rationed on salt provisions, sea biscuits soaked in water, and no vegetables'. Subsequent raids proved equally successful. A month later, 'to loud and protracted cheers', the regiment was ordered to hold itself in readiness for Wolfe's expedition to Quebec.[31]

6

WASHINGTON STARTS
THE WAR
IN NORTH AMERICA

'In order to plan a campaign, one should know one's enemies, their alliances, resources and the nature of their country.' Frederick the Great, 1747.

The Peace of Aix-la-Chapelle (1748) settled little. For France and England it proved merely a truce before both countries were plunged into the Seven Years' War (1756–63). France was willing to surrender all her conquests in the Low Countries in exchange for Louisbourg, while England gave up Louisbourg to regain Madras, a vital trading base in India which had been captured by the French.[1] But the trade and colonial struggle between the two powers immediately broke out again, even before war was actually declared.

Britain saw her rival gaining in the cod fisheries off Newfoundland, in the production of sugar, molasses, indigo and ginger in the West Indies, and in the fur trade in North America. The American colonies supplied Britain with the products of farm, forest and fishery – tobacco, cotton, timber, naval stores, furs and rice. Britain produced manufactured goods and African slaves, the West Indies sugar, rum and molasses in a 'triangular trade' designed to profit the home country and regulated by a series of Navigation Acts to eliminate foreign competition. The Caribbean, however, swarmed with illegal traders and a colonial contraband trade flourished, especially in exports and imports with France, Holland and Spain. Britain considered this illegal activity a loss to her balance of trade, on which her national strength and prosperity depended – and ultimately her ability to wage war.

Meanwhile, France continued to build forts to create a wide fortified corridor between Canada and Louisiana and stop the American colonists from pushing westward, seeking land and settlement beyond the Allegheny Mountains. It was this direct physical confrontation between the colonists, not trade, which would ultimately drag their unwilling home governments into war.[2]

Both Britain and France claimed the rich lands of the Ohio Valley. The Iroquois, too, claimed sovereignty. In 1747 the cream of Virginian aristocracy, including the Washington family, formed the Ohio Company to develop 200,000 acres of crown land in the Upper Ohio region. The company promised to settle 200 families there in the first seven years, to erect a fort, and to maintain a permanent garrison. In 1753 the new French governor, the Marquis Ange de Duquesne, decided to take offensive action. He told the Iroquois he intended to prevent the English occupying it, and would permit no interference. He sent a militia force of 1,500 men to occupy the sources of the Ohio and reclaim the territory for the king of France. Forts were constructed at Le Boeuf and Presqu'ile (modern Erie), some 20 miles further north. Garrisons were left at both forts, and at the captured British trading post of Venango (modern Meadville) on Lake Ontario, midway between the French ports of Niagara and Frontenac. The remainder of the force withdrew to Montreal. The following April the Marquis built Fort Duquesne (on the site of modern Pittsburgh) at the forks of the Ohio – thus securing the French lines of communication between the Ohio and the St Lawrence River.[3] Such actions in peacetime were tantamount to acts of war!

When the governor of Virginia, Robert Dinwiddie, a protégé of the Earl of Halifax and a shareholder in the Ohio Company, learned of the French actions, he sent 21-year-old Major George Washington to challenge this invasion of King George's territory. Washington, a land surveyor and adjutant of the Virginia militia, took with him a guide, an interpreter, five men, and the governor's request for the French to withdraw. 'The fort stands on land, notoriously known to be the property of Great Britain,' he wrote. 'It is my duty to require your peaceable departure.'[4] Washington, descended from a Northamptonshire squire, set off on the 500-mile journey to Fort Le Boeuf. At the captured Fort Venango he was hospitably received by French officers, who told him courteously but bluntly, over wine after supper, that their orders were to take possession of the Ohio and 'by God, they would do it'. They allowed him to continue to Le Boeuf, where Washington handed over Dinwiddie's letter, addressed to the Governor of Canada. The party returned home to Williamsburg with assurances that the letter would be forwarded to Montreal.

The newly-constructed fort at Duquesne clearly menaced the growth of the English colonies westwards. Dinwiddie, having received permission from the Duke of Newcastle to oppose force with force and to construct forts on the Ohio (though at colonial expense), selected Washington, now a colonel, with 300 men from his militia to attack Fort Duquesne; even though France and England were still officially at peace. In May 1754 Washington crossed the Alleghenies and ambushed a small French scouting party at the Great Meadows, on a tributary of the Monongahela River. The French commander was killed with nine of his men, and 21 prisoners taken. 'It was this volley, fired by a young Virginian in the backwoods of America, which set the world on fire,' said Walpole when news of the engagement reached England.[5]

Washington, anticipating a swift French revenge attack, hastily constructed a rough stockade, aptly called Fort Necessity. When the attack came from Fort Duquesne, Washington's smaller force of regulars and provincials, encumbered with 30 women and children from an independent company stationed at New York, were forced to surrender. Under the capitulation terms, Washington was permitted to return home with his company to Virginia, leaving the French the undisputed masters of the Ohio Valley.[6] A certain Captain Robert Stobo from Glasgow was left behind as hostage for the safe return of the French prisoners captured earlier. It has been claimed that it was Stobo, interned at Quebec, who revealed vital topographical details to Wolfe which helped him to scale the Heights of Abraham.

The capture of Fort Necessity (4 July 1754) was only a minor skirmish, but it alarmed the colonies and stung the home government, headed by the Duke of Newcastle, into action. Thomas Pelham-Holles, the first Duke of Newcastle, married to the granddaughter of the famous Duke of Marlborough and heir to a fortune based on the broad acres obtained from Henry VIII's dissolution of the monastic estates, had succeeded Robert Walpole as prime minister in 1741. He gained power in parliament, and kept it for 45 years by his rank, wealth, family connections and skill in political management and corruption. Fortescue[7] wrote of him, 'he was only less of a curse to England than Madame de Pompadour was to France'. Throughout his career, Newcastle's exaggerated vanity and excessive love of place and power made him jealous and suspicious of his colleagues. Hitherto he had been anxious to avoid an open breach with France, until he could negotiate with Prussia to protect Hanover. In America, his policy had been to encourage the colonies to form a defensive union against France, but not to resort to open warfare.

Now Newcastle, supported by Fox as Secretary of State for the Colonies, accused France of violating the Treaties of Utrecht and Aix-la-Chapelle by invading the territory of George II at Forts Necessity and Duquesne. Newcastle claimed the French were interfering with English trade with the Indians, and dividing the continent by constructing a chain of frontier posts from Canada to the ocean along the Mississippi.[8]

Cumberland, the King's son, who enjoyed the confidence of his father, and as commander-in-chief the admiration of the army, was invited to plan a military response:

> The colonies must not be abandoned, our rights must be maintained and the French made to stop their hostilities. Without military action, the Trade Commissioners warned the King, any further attempts to make settlements in the interior of America will be effectively prevented.

But neither England nor France wanted a formal declaration of war.[9]

If the American conflict was to have any hope of success, it was necessary to have the co-operation of all the colonies and the support of the native Americans. Dinwiddie appealed to the colonial assemblies for volunteers and money to form a common fund. Only the New England colonies seemed alive to the danger, led by Governor Shirley of Massachusetts, who, despite being married to a young French woman whom he had met on a visit to Paris, had lost none of his hatred for France.[10] The remaining colonies were, as usual, concerned more with their own provincial interests and disputes. New York and Pennsylvania, for example, were busy profiting from supplying Canada, including French warships, with provisions such as beef, pork and flour. To them a French threat of invasion was no more than a remote possibility. For Britain, such trading was illegal and little short of treason.

This attitude was typical of the colonial response to the war effort. Massachusetts, Connecticut and Virginia would do the most. Pennsylvania and the Carolinas would do little more than defend their own borders. New York and New Jersey were mostly content to leave their defence to the British regulars, who were responsible for most of the offensive action against the French in Canada; more, in fact, than all the colonies put together.[11]

In June 1754, 23 representatives of seven colonies – Pennsylvania, New York, Maryland and the four New England colonies – were persuaded by the Governor of New York, James de Lancey, on the instructions of Lord Halifax of the Board of Trade, to meet at Albany to negotiate an agreement with the Six Indian nations (the Iroquois) and seek a common defence and taxation policy. With 150 Iroquois chiefs in attendance, Franklin argued:

> Our enemies have the great advantage of being under one direction, with one Council and one Purse. With Britain so far away, the French can, with impunity, violate the most solemn treaties, kill, seize and imprison our traders, confiscate their property, murder and scalp our farmers with their wives and children, and take an easy possession of such parts of the British territories, as they find most convenient for them: which, if they are permitted to do, must end in the destruction of the British interest, trade and plantations in America.[12]

But Franklin's plan for unity against France failed. Every colonial assembly rejected it, because it gave too much power to the king's representative. They feared, too, that union would lead to new tax burdens. The British government rejected it for the power it gave to the proposed American House of Representatives.[13] The French jibe that the English would not unite their two million people against 100,000 French was well founded!

The Indians, who had once 'looked upon the great King George as the Sun and our Father and upon ourselves as his Children', now accused the

English of deserting them. 'You are all like women, bare and open, without fortifications, while our enemies are swarming all over our territories,' they grumbled.[14] Their numerous wars had taken a great toll of their tribes, and many had been 'christianised' by the French and supported France. Fortunately, Colonel William Johnson, the agent for Indian affairs, had gained their respect. This remarkable man lived among the native Americans like a feudal lord, with an Indian squaw, ruling a vast trading empire. In the war he was able to effect a reconciliation; for the Earl of Halifax the Indians were more useful to Britain than purchasing allies in Europe at the expense of large annual subsidies.

On 14 November 1754, George II announced in parliament his determination to protect his American plantations, in what he hoped would be no more than a local war, restore the *status quo*, and capture the new French forts. At first the King had been reluctant to send regular troops to America, although the French had been steadily reinforcing their own army in Canada with regular battalions.[15] Now parliament voted him £1 million to strengthen his forces, followed a fortnight later with a further £50,000 to raise two regular battalions, each of 500 men – the 44 Foot (Sir Peter Halket's)[16] and the 48 Foot (Thomas Dunbar's).[17] The complements were to be raised to 700 each by local enlistment. The 50 Foot (Shirley's) and 51 Foot (Pepperell's), broken up in 1748, were re-raised on the Irish establishment, also to be recruited to full strength in the colonies, the cost being borne by the king. The British troops embarked at Cork in January 1755 for the New World. On 27 April, Admiral Boscawen sailed to blockade the French Canadian ports and intercept French transports, which left Brest laden with troops a week later. But bad weather prevented Boscawen from intercepting more than a few French ships.

In command of the troops was General Edward Braddock, a Coldstream Guardsman with 45 years' service and a friend and nominee of the Duke of Cumberland.[18] A strict disciplinarian with a genuine concern for his men's welfare, he had fought bravely at Dettingen but his European experience would avail him little against Indian tactics and forest warfare – and, said Franklin, 'he had too mean an opinion of Americans and Indians'.[19] Braddock was aware of the dangers, however, and tried to give his scratch force some training in forest fighting. But time was against him. He was certainly not the stupid, hidebound figure that historical legend has painted him!

Braddock's warrant required him 'to vindicate our just rights and possessions'. Before leaving, he made a will in favour of his reputed wife, better known as Mistress George Anne Bellamy, 'whose beauty, highly publicised love affairs, and the patronage of an aristocratic society, caused to rise rapidly in her profession as an actress'. Miss Bellamy , the natural daughter of a brother officer, had been enticed from a boarding school when she was a young girl and 'protected' from her earliest years by Braddock, whom 'she called her second father, being many years younger'.[20] She played at Covent

Garden opposite David Garrick, and died in the Fleet debtor's prison. At his base camp at Fort Cumberland in America, Braddock soon found a couple of ladies, Mesdames Wardrope and Spearman, 'to help to dispel his loneliness in such a barbarous land'.

The 44 and 48 Foot had been formed in January 1741, two of the seven regiments raised as a result of the War of the Austrian Succession (1740–8). The 48 Foot was typical of these regiments. George II had authorised Colonel the Honourable James Cholmondley, an officer of the Life Guards, by beat of drum or otherwise,

> to raise Volunteers in any county or part of our Kingdom of Great Britain for a Regiment of Foot under your command, which is to consist of ten companies of 3 Sergeants, 3 Corporals, 3 Drummers and 70 effective private men in each Company, besides Commissioned Officers. And all the Magistrates, Justices of the Peace, Constables and other Civil Officers whom it may concern are hereby required to be assisting unto you in providing Quarters, impressing carriages, and otherwise as there shall be occasion. Given at Our Court at St. James's this third day of January 1741, in the 14th Year of Our Reign. George R.

According to the Regiment's records,[21] ensigns were expected to be well educated, and to have a good figure. Their commissions could be purchased for £400 (captains £1,500, lieutenant-colonel £3,500), though these fixed prices were usually exceeded.

> From 16 to 19 is the best age for entering the military profession, lads being then strong enough to bear any sort of fatigue and may be by that time supposed to have acquired some branches of polite and useful knowledge, particularly French, Drawing and Fortification.

Officers would normally be the younger sons of noble or wealthy families, who purchased their commissions and promotions through influence and patronage.

A victim of the system was Colonel Edmund Fielding, whose career was described by his son, Henry, in his famous novel *Tom Jones*. Edmund Fielding was promoted lieutenant on the battlefield for his valour by the Duke of Marlborough. But he had to remain in the same rank for 40 years, while others were promoted over his head. The reason: his wife, a beautiful and wealthy lady, would not 'purchase his preferment' by prostituting herself to a senior officer.[22]

Britain's soldiers were chiefly volunteers, recruited almost without exception from the lower social orders. Poverty and hunger largely filled the ranks,

64

preference being given to sturdy farmhands, with a large number of men from Scotland and Ireland. Each year regimental recruiting parties toured the towns and villages, assembled the crowds by 'beat of drum', and harangued them on the advantages of a military life. Some would enlist for the bounty, tempted by the ready cash; others craved excitement, adventure, loot and rape. George Farquhar's play *The Recruiting Officer,* written in 1706 but still performed, showed the wily Sergeant Kite at work in the market-place at Shrewsbury:

> If any gentlemen, soldiers or others, have a mind to serve their country and pull down the French King; if any 'prentices have severe masters, or any children undutiful parents; if any servants have little wages, or any husband too much wife, let them repair to the noble Sergeant Kite, at the sign of the *Raven,* in the good town of Shrewsbury, and they shall receive present relief and entertainment.[23]

Farquhar certainly knew the tricks of the trade, since he had been a second lieutenant in the 4 Foot, a recruiting officer for his regiment, and a playwright and actor. Born in Londonderry, the son of a poor clergyman, he married an officer's widow believing her to be a rich heiress. Disappointed, he was forced to sell his commission to pay his debts, and turn to the stage to make a living.

Such attempts to cajole, bribe or intoxicate recruits, however, did not fill the army's quotas, especially in times of war or national emergency. In 1704, for instance, when the army's annual requirement for the Marlborough wars rose dramatically, there were not enough guardsmen to perform the ceremonial duties at Kensington Palace and the Tower of London. Parliament authorised the use of the press-gang to enlist 'any sturdy beggar, any fortune-teller, any idle, unknown or suspected fellow in a parish that cannot give an account of himself'. The same Act released capital offenders for the forces, and offered insolvent debtors release from prison, if they would enlist or find a substitute. France was faced with similar problems and took similar remedies. In 1707 even the musicians of the Marseilles opera house had to join up, because 'they were dying of hunger'.[24]

For the unprecedented large numbers required for the Seven Years' War, the term of service was fixed at three or five years, and the minimum height of a recruit lowered to five feet four inches (1.6m). He had to be 'able-bodied, free from rupture and any other distemper, not a Papist, nor under 17 or above 45 years of age'.[25] Sailors and colliers never make good soldiers, noted the Regimental records, 'being accustomed to a more debauched and drunken way of life than what a private Sentinel's pay can possibly admit of.'

Parliament voted a private soldier the annual sum of £12.3s.4d for his pay, a quarter being retained in England for his clothing, the maintenance of Chelsea Hospital for 'olde, lame or decay'd soldiers in ye service of the Crown',[26] and the perquisites of the Paymaster-General, the Secretary at War, and the regimental agent. The remainder was sent to the commander-in-chief in America for the regimental paymasters to meet the subsistence of the men on the regimental rolls. After further deductions for the surgeon, spruce-beer (brewed locally for scurvy), and camp necessaries, the soldier was lucky if he received one shilling and eight pence a week (three shillings, New York currency). The colonel provided his men with the bare necessities, such as a coat, breeches, shoes and stockings. He owned the regiment, and expected to make a profit on his investment. He could defraud his men in a variety of ways, and was as open to corruption as any other government servant of the day.

Army life was tough, pay uncertain, and discipline and punishments severe. Desertion and fraudulent enlistment abounded. Week after week deserters were brought out into Hyde Park, tied to a tree or the halberds, and flogged with hundreds of lashes of rod, strap or birch. Such savage punishments deterred others, and reinforced respect for the law among civilians. The sentence of death was pronounced in America by courts martial, often carried out by fellow deserters, and the condemned man required to carry his own coffin or dig his own grave.

The soldiers were unruly and insolent, the officers conceited and overbearing, complained parliament; and in the absence of barracks, there was the burden of free quarters. Billeting troops on innkeepers was cheaper and they could be removed from towns and villages during fairs, horse races and elections to avoid rioting, drunken fights and damage to property. During a fracas in November 1756, for instance, the Light Dragoons blew up an inn at Cobham. Soldiers debauched the manners of all the people – their wives, daughters and servants. Where soldiers were quartered, the men would not go to church for fear of leaving their womenfolk unattended. The most honest man in England, wrote Fortescue,[27] had but to don a redcoat to be dubbed a lewd, profligate wretch. Such was the country's low regard for the military profession!

7

BRADDOCK, THE NAVY, AND THE ARMY WOMEN

'Marriage Is Good For Nothing In The Military Profession' – Napoleon

General Edward Braddock arrived with his two regiments at Alexandria, Virginia, on 20 February 1755. He had under his command five other British regiments, seven independent companies, and detachments of Royal Artillery. Three of these British regular battalions formed the permanent garrison of Nova Scotia. The 40 Foot (Hopson's) had been in the province for nearly 40 years: the 45 Foot (Warburton's) was one of the two regiments sent to Louisbourg in 1746. The 47 Foot (Lascelles's) had arrived from Ireland in 1750 with 290 private soldiers, 130 women and 50 children to form part of the settlement of Halifax. The seven in-dependent companies were the permanent garrisons of New York and South Carolina.[1]

The French reacted quickly to the news of the British plans, secretly obtained by bribery by the French *chargé d'affaires* in London, and instantly communicated to Paris before Braddock's departure.[2] The French fleet from Brest, which Boscawen failed to intercept, carried 3,000 regulars (the six French regular battalions were La Reine, Bourgogne, Languedoc, Guienne, Artois and Béarn) under Baron Dieskau, a German veteran who had served under the famous Marshal Saxe. Also sailing in the convoy to the St Lawrence and Montreal was the new governor, the Marquis de Vaudreuil, appointed by Louis XV to succeed the ailing Duquesne. Both governments professed peace, but both gave secret orders for offensive action. Neither France nor Britain declared open war until the following year.[3]

It required great feats of seamanship in the 18th century to keep a naval fleet of wooden ships at sea in bad weather. Fog and contrary winds hampered Admiral Edward Boscawen and his attempts to blockade the Canadian coast. At sea, convoys came home in autumn and battle fleets were recalled to winter quarters, to be refitted and remanned for the next operational season. Unlike the French, who sent out squadrons to the colonies for short periods as they were needed, the British kept small squadrons permanently based in West Indies dockyards at Jamaica and Antigua, victualled and supplied with naval stores from North America. Useful for blockading ports or interrupting illegal trade, these squadrons were too weak to engage a powerful enemy fleet.[4]

The navy was the key to British strategy, governed by the geographical truths that only a 25-mile Channel separated her from an often hostile continent, and that she needed to safeguard her overseas possessions. Only a Pitt, however, would put those possessions in India, North America and the Mediterranean before the strategy of maintaining the balance of power in Europe. Parliament supported the navy financially, and the people preferred it to a standing army, which they always associated with absolute rule and a threat to civil liberties.

So the army was kept to a minimum, at the expense of the more popular and cheaper militia. The militia was poorly trained and officered, inadequate for national defence, and could not be mobilised for service overseas. When Pitt introduced his Militia Act in 1757, abolishing the system whereby property owners supplied men, equipment and horses, the militia also proved ineffective as a fighting force. Thereafter the county provided its quota of men by compulsory ballot, paid for out of its rates. But those chosen by lot could purchase substitutes, only 28 days' drill per year was required, and the new militia proved extremely unpopular. From 1749 to 1754, parliament had reduced the army and navy to 19,000 and 10,000 respectively. The administration of both was chaotic, with different departments responsible for different duties in both services – state of readiness, movement, personnel and pay – and there was very little communication between them.

Both French and British relied on their merchant fleet in time of war to supplement their navies with ships and men. Some merchant vessels could easily be converted into warships, but in Britain ships continued to be built according to the size of available slipways, and not according to specification and need. The French built the better ships, and the more heavily armed. But with the British carrying half the world's sea trade, their navy had the advantages of numbers and quality of both officers and seamen.

The majority of British naval officers came from the ranks of the aristocracy or gentry, but neither birth nor wealth was essential for midshipmen. Most started as captains' servants between the ages of 13 and 16. Anson, Hawke and Boscawen, for instance, began their naval careers in this way at the age of 15. After six years and a qualifying examination they could be commissioned as midshipmen, but competition was fierce. French naval officers were just as aristocratic and feudal as their army compatriots but even more exclusive, looking down on the bourgeois officers of the merchant fleet drafted into war service. They lacked, however, the sea experience of British officers.[5]

Ships in the Royal Navy were manned by volunteers, in theory, attracted by prize money. But in times of emergency and rapid expansion, press-gangs were used to impress the dregs of society – vagabonds, sturdy beggars, rogues and debtors, many of them landsmen who had never seen the sea, let alone sailed aboard a ship. The result was that large numbers deserted during the Seven Years' War, in which 135,000 sailors were lost by disease or desertion and only 1,500 killed in action. An Act of 1755 permitted foreigners who had served for two years aboard a British merchant ship to be called British seamen, and foreigners were extensively recruited to make up numbers. Pay was 19–24 shillings a month, subject to deductions, and payable in arrears. Food was often of poor quality, inadequate, and supplemented by over-generous allowances of rum. Quarters were cramped and insanitary; scurvy was rife, and fevers in tropical climates deadly. Brutal floggings were necessary to maintain discipline.[6]

Tobias Smollett served as a surgeon's mate on board a king's ship before marrying a wealthy widow, running through her money, and then settling down to write his famous novels. In the *Adventures of Roderick Random* (1745) he described his experiences aboard a troopship which sailed from Cartagena on 5 May 1741 to Jamaica, on the failed expedition to Cuba under Admiral Lord Cathcart. The object was to destroy the Spanish port of Portobello, from which the treasure fleets left for Spain. The men were pent up between decks in small vessels, unable to sit upright. They wallowed in filth: myriads of maggots were hatched in the putrefaction of their sores, with no dressings and only their allowance of brandy to wash them. Nothing was heard but groans, lamentations, and the language of despair, invoking death to deliver them from their miseries. 'The dead, from dysentery and yellow fewer, were thrown overboard into the harbour, where, after a few hours, they rose to the surface among the transports, whilst sharks and birds of prey fought for a meal.' Of every ten men who left England only one returned – and Cathcart himself fell victim to disease.

Braddock's two newly-arrived regiments settled down at their camp at Alexandria (Washington), where the ladies of the staunchly loyal colonies of Virginia and Maryland 'appreciated the British regiments more than the gentlemen of the colony, who were not overpleased at the supercilious bearing of the British officers'.[7] George Washington, whose estate at Mount Vernon was only a few miles from the camp, was a frequent visitor. He, too, bitterly resented a British order which placed all the king's British officers over all provincial officers, irrespective of rank or service. To save Washington from this indignity, Braddock gave him a position on his personal staff.

Braddock assembled 1,500 regulars and some 1,200 colonial militiamen at Wills Creek, an old trading station on the Potomac transformed into a military post and renamed Fort Cumberland. Braddock had little faith in the provincials, whom he considered 'unfit for military service' – an opinion he would later regret. He ignored their different backgrounds and terms of service. Provincial officers and men enlisted for a campaign, which they understood would last from March to November. By law they could not be compelled to serve for more than 12 months. So each provincial regiment had to be raised annually, leaving little time for training and the inculcation of military habits of discipline, dress and sanitation, in camp or on the line of march.[8]

With Braddock also were 50 Indian warriors, with as many squaws and dusky maidens. Their appearance astonished the British soldiers. Their faces were painted red, yellow and black, their ears slit and hung with pendants. Their heads were close-shaved, except for the feathered scalp-lock at the crown. They spent their lives hunting, fishing and making war. Braddock welcomed them, but their chief remarked: 'He looked upon us as dogs and ignored anything we said to him'. Indian squaws carried out all the domestic duties of the village. They tended crops, reared children, cooked meals, and handled captives, including torture and execution at the stake. Divorce was easy, and casual liaisons between the unmarried were permitted. Polygamy was forbidden, but women were sometimes provided as sleeping partners for visiting dignitaries. If widowed, they cut their hair as a sign of mourning: when their hair grew again, they could remarry. War prisoners were often adopted by families which had lost sons of their own.[9]

Braddock established a field hospital at his Wills Creek headquarters under Master-Surgeon James Napier, with a Mrs Charlotte Brown as matron in charge of the women orderlies – selected army wives, paid sixpence (the equivalent of today's 2.5p) a day and their rations. An order of 7 April 1755 read:

> A greater number of women having been brought over than those allowed by the Government sufficient for washing, with a view that the Hospital might be served: and complaint being made, an agreement was entered into, not to serve without exorbitant wages, so a Return will be called for of those, who shall refuse to serve for sixpence per day and their Provisions, that they may be turned out of camp, and others got in their places.[10]

Besides the wives and mistresses of the soldiers would be the usual camp followers, 'who were apt to make trouble and change their partners'.

The army frowned upon marriage, and its officers were expressly required 'to discourage matrimony amongst the men as much as possible', wrote Wolfe in 1751. 'The Service suffers by the multitude of Women already in the Regiment' – especially as some of them 'are not as industrious, nor so useful to their husbands, as a Soldier's wife ought to be … A bad soldier's wife must be got rid of as soon as possible.'[11] Marriage was considered incompatible with military efficiency: women and children hindered the regiment's mobility and cluttered up the baggage train.

The army preferred the single soldier, and offered him an escape from 'too much wife and squalling children'.[12] A soldier could not legally be prevented from marrying, but he could be prevented from enlisting. If a soldier made a false attestation he was treated as single, and a wife had no redress. Furthermore, the army could insist on an enlisted soldier obtaining the prior permission of his company commander to marry – 'rash or improper marriages tended to encumber soldiers for life, to break their spirit, and damp every hope of promotion'.[13] The army had the same marriage policy in North America as it had adopted at home. Marriage was to be discouraged: a soldier had to seek official permission to marry; the woman's character had to be investigated and only the industrious encouraged. But many women followed the army, despite such regulations.

On 18 May 1755, three weeks before his departure, General Braddock authorised six women per company of 100 men in his two regular British battalions (44 and 48 Foot) to accompany his force. This was the normal allocation for service overseas. A ballot, often held on the quayside to maintain hope to the last possible moment, decided who should embark. Braddock also allowed four to each company of the Virginia and Maryland Rangers, five in the artillery detachments and 'five in the detachment of seamen' (In 1755, permanent corps of marines were established under Admiralty control; every ship, except the smallest, carried a detachment of marines under their own officers). Free rations would be provided only for authorised women; half of the soldier's ration for each woman, and a quarter for each child 'born in wedlock'. The women of each regiment were to march under the orders of the provost in the baggage train and 'none under any account are to appear with the men under arms'.[14] Many would find official employment; others found jobs locally.

On 9 June, the day before Braddock set out for Fort Cumberland in western Maryland on his march to Fort Duquesne, he wrote to the governor of Pennsylvania asking him to provide subsistence for 28 named women, sent under escort with the letter, of whom he wished to be rid. Two days later he further reduced the number of women allowed on the march to two per company – for operational reasons! Lists of those authorised to remain with the troops in camp were to be sent by regimental commanders to the brigade major. Those unauthorised who remained in camp would be severely punished and, if caught a second time, would suffer death – so severe was the food shortage! The fate of the children is never mentioned.

The Duke of Newcastle, Secretary of State at the time, strongly supported the army's policy on marriage in general and the regulations allowing some to serve overseas:

> The soldiers would be disgruntled, if the women did not accompany them to do the cooking, washing, sewing, and to serve other purposes for which women naturally go with the Army.[15]

The women, as camp followers, were subject to military law overseas. General Braddock ordered the Articles of War to be read out regularly on morning parade, 'at which time, the servants, women and followers of the Army, are to attend with their respective regiments and companies that they belong to'.[16] Again, this was standard British practice, since the women were mostly illiterate and orders would need to be explained to them.

Punishments were severe:

> Any sutler or woman stealing, purloining or wasting provisions – Death.
> Any sutler caught giving liquor to the Indians will be severely lashed (250 lashes).
> Any soldier or woman caught outside the boundaries of the Camp without a regimental pass will be tied up and given 50 lashes.
> A Sergeant, who had been keeping company with and debauching a soldier's wife, while the husband was on guard duty, was sentenced to death (sentence commuted), while the wife was drum'd out of the Fort at the Cart's Tail, ducked, and sent to Boston for trial by the civil magistrates.[17]

The flogging of women was permitted in England until 1817, and of soldiers until 1881.

Although some army officers considered the embarkation of the wives helped recruitment, or at least prevented desertions, others believed that army women debauched the troops or spread venereal diseases, despite regular medical checks. General Braddock, for example, ordered his soldiers' wives to be examined three times within one month to ensure they were 'clean', and added that the women who were not so, or who tried to avoid inspection, were to be barred from marching with them.[18]

From provincial diaries, occasional glimpses can be seen of army 'women' – usually enlivening camp life (and the soldiers' existence) by creating a disturbance. One such entry in 1760 noted: a mighty discord amongst the regulars this night, disputing who had the best right to a woman, and who should have first go at her. Another recorded (1758) a fire in camp, 'where was a number of women's huts: which made great disturbance.'[19]

Whatever the regulations, there were always more women with the regiments than officially authorised. The chaplain of the 20 Foot said the regiment had 150 in their camp in 1756; other regiments had at least 200, some 300, not all 'lawfully married'. The redcoat's reputation for arrogance, drinking, debauchery and insubordination was notorious.[20] Despite this, 'women adore a martial man,' wrote the dramatist William Wycherley; '*Ah! Que j'aime les militaires,*' sang the French![21] Literature and military history provide many examples of women following their husbands or lovers overseas, to join the ranks of the 'unrecognised women'. Without army rations or support, they had to survive on the scraps their men could provide, or earn their own keep in dubious ways.

Phoebe Hessel, who had five husbands, donned her husband's uniform and served for many years in the 5 Foot. She was wounded by a bayonet at the Battle of Fontenoy, and fought bravely at the Battle of Bunker Hill (1775) in America. Her sex was eventually discovered when she was stripped to the waist to be whipped for a misdemeanour. She died aged 108. The exploits of 'Mother' Ross, who enlisted as Christian Welch in the Scots Greys, are legendary. Like many another, on the death of her husband she 'remarried' her protector, Captain Ross, to become, as many an army widow, a sutler, selling provisions and drink to soldiers in exchange for cash and loot. She is buried in Chelsea Hospital's graveyard (1739).[22]

However harsh such punishments may seem, they must be judged in the context of the violence, disorders and brutal conditions prevalent in 18th century Britain, and against the low status of working-class women. As late as 1805, for example, a drummer in the 4 Foot went to the market-place in Hythe and for sixpence bought the wife of an Irish labourer building the Shorncliffe canal. 'She was not more than 20 years, and of a likely figure', records the regimental history. Coming from such backgrounds, the army women who marched with their men at home and abroad were tough, resourceful, loyal to their partners, and ever ready to share their dangers and deprivations.[23]

As for the hopes and fears of the military wives and girlfriends who waited at home for their loved ones to return, let Frances, the wife of Admiral Boscawen, speak for all of them:

Portsmouth, 30 August 1755.
Here is the sea, and here are ships: and men of war come in daily, but not the ship, which my eyes have ached in looking for everyday upon Southsea Common, spying for sails around St Helen's Point.[24]

Married in 1742, she bore Boscawen five children. When he died of fever in 1761 she erected a handsome memorial to him in the parish church of St Michael Penkivel in Cornwall, inscribed by 'his once happy wife, as an unequal testimony of his worth and her affection'.[25]

The long periods of separation bore heavily on the womenfolk, but also on senior officers like Boscawen. Spending many months at sea, they often deferred marriage until later in life. Instead, some senior officers kept mistresses, like Admiral Lord Colvill, who commanded the North American station in 1765, and Rear Admiral Augustus Keppel. The exigencies of the naval service allowed them freedom 'to hunt in pastures new', with many commanders carrying 'lewd women to sea'.[26] For sailors, many of whom joined the service in the hope of prize money:

When storms and tempests all are o'er,
And Jack receives his prize on shore,
Then for his doxies all he'll send,
What's dearly earned, he'll freely spend![27]

8

BRADDOCK'S DEFEAT
ON THE MONONGAHELA

The plan of campaign for the year 1755 was finally decided at a full council of colonial governors, which included Shirley, Dinwiddie, and British officers assembled at Alexandria. The French were to be attacked at four points simultaneously: the two main thrusts would aim to clear the French and their Indian allies from the forks of the Ohio River.[1] The two regular battalions from England, the 44 Foot (Colonel Sir Peter Halket) and 48 Foot (Colonel Thomas Dunbar), were to advance on Fort Duquesne under the command of General Braddock himself; 50 Foot (Shirley's) and 51 Foot (Pepperell's), recently raised in the provinces and taken into the king's pay, would reduce Fort Niagara (at the Falls) under the command of Colonel Shirley, governor of Massachusetts.

Subsidiary attacks would be on Crown Point by a force of provincial volunteers from New England, New York and New Jersey, and some Indians, under Colonel William Johnson, appointed because of his influence over the Indian tribes. Crown Point on Lake Champlain was the key to the chain of lakes, leading due north from Albany to Montreal. As we saw in Chapter 5, another force of New Englanders under Colonel Robert Monckton, deputy to the governor of Nova Scotia, was ordered to capture the French fort of Beauséjour at the head of the Bay of Fundy, and subdue Acadia completely.

It was an ambitious plan, but it contravened one of the recognised principles of war. Instead of concentrating the British forces, it dispersed them piecemeal. Furthermore, the commander would have saved time and money, if he had started from Pennsylvania in the north, instead of taking the more difficult route from Wills Creek in Virginia to the Ohio.[2]

The British excused this fourfold assault in peacetime on the grounds that all the positions to be attacked were on British soil and had been seized by the French. This was an act of self-defence, with limited objectives, to drive the French back to their 1714 position. The French argued they had held Crown Point for 24 years and Niagara for 75, without any attempt to dislodge them.

In preparing for the expedition, Braddock found it difficult to obtain the horses, wagons and forage he needed. He grew impatient with the provincial assemblies for their unwillingness to vote the money, their delays in providing the food and supplies, and their poor quality and exorbitant prices.[3] The other colonies were half-hearted in their efforts to support Virginia in the drive to the Ohio. Their frontiers were not threatened; the Carolinas with a small white population had no troops to spare in their fears of a Negro insurrection; New York feared the conflict would arouse their Indian neighbours. 'Pennsylvania and Maryland refuse to contribute in any Shape towards the Support of the Campaign against Fort Duquesne,' reported the *London Chronicle*, May 17–19 1756. These internal rivalries and inadequate colonial support would be important factors in Braddock's eventual failure. So, too, was their contempt for a British general 'fighting on the banks of the Potomac, as he would have fought on the banks of the Rhine'.[4]

European warfare in the 18th century, wrote Winston Churchill,[5] involved masses of men marching up to each other shoulder to shoulder, three or four ranks deep, and mechanically firing volley after volley into each other at duelling distance, until the weaker wavered or broke. All the gaps, which at every discharge opened in the ranks, would be promptly filled. Keeping an exact, rigid formation, platoon by platoon or rank by rank would carry out the numerous unhurried motions of loading and unloading. In a space no larger than the London parks put together, regiments would stand for hours, knee-deep among the bodies of comrades, writhing or forever still. In their ears rang the hideous chorus of screams and groans of pain, which no anaesthetic would ever soothe. In the forests of North America such tactics proved of little value. On a smaller scale but on the same principles, Braddock planned to fight his battle.

On 10 June 1755, Braddock's expedition finally got under way from Fort Cumberland, where he had assembled some 1200 regulars and some 800 provincial soldiers. The tragedy which followed is one of the most well known in military history. Braddock's army faced a 110-mile journey through dense forests, uninhabited wilderness and over steep rocky mountains. Behind the scouts and advance guard, 300 axemen hacked a path through the undergrowth. Over stumps of trees, roots and stones on the narrow forest track, the long train of pack-horses, wagons and cannon toiled, with the regular soldiers and militiamen marching alongside. Progress was painfully slow, just three miles a day, and the forest damp caused fever among the men.[6]

It took the force eight days of hacking, drilling and blasting to reach Little Meadows, less than 30 miles from Fort Cumberland; there a camp was formed. 'Instead of pressing on with vigour,' wrote Washington to his brother, 'they halted to level each mole-hill, to erect bridges over every brook, which means we were four days in travelling 12 miles.' Walpole commented sarcastically that 'General Braddock seemed in no great hurry to get scalped'. It took, all told, 32 days to cover the 110 miles to Fort Duquesne.[7]

On 7 July the force was still about a dozen miles from its destination. Fort

Duquesne's French commander was well informed about Braddock's advance by his Shawnee and Delaware Indians. He also knew that his troops were too few to withstand a long siege, especially against artillery, and decided to contest Braddock's crossing of the Monongahela River. He arrived too late to establish an ambush. For his part, Braddock had been sent a detailed plan of Fort Duquesne's defences, smuggled out by the British prisoner Captain Robert Stobo (see Chapter 6), for which he would have faced a firing squad had the two countries been at war.

Learning that 500 French were on their way to reinforce Fort Duquesne, Braddock decided, on Washington's advice, to leave a third of his force, with the heavy baggage and most of the womenfolk, under Colonel Dunbar to follow on at their best speed. He would push on with some 1,200 of his fittest troops to capture the fort before the arrival of these reinforcements.[8] To avoid a narrow defile and possible ambush, the British force twice forded the Monongahela River, keeping to their parade-like formations. The scarlet-coated regulars and blue-uniformed Virginians marched in columns of four, the officers on horseback. The light cavalry, horse-drawn artillery, and dozens of pack-horses followed.[9]

On the afternoon of 9 July the British force, with colours flying and drums beating, moved into more open country, barely six miles from the fort. Suddenly the advance guard of 300 regulars and a grenadier company, commanded by Lieutenant-Colonel Thomas Gage (later to command the troops at Lexington, Concord and Bunker Hill) of the 44 Foot, was halted by a wild war-whoop from a hillock ahead and a burst of musketry from unseen marksmen concealed in the long grass and tangled undergrowth to the flank. They had been surprised by a concealed force of 250 French regulars and militia and 600 Indian allies. Without hesitation, and in accordance with their European training, the leading redcoats – raw East Anglian farm boys – formed to face their enemy with a crashing volley. But European tactics were useless against an unseen foe, skilful bushmen and Indian marksmen, expert in forest lore. The advance party was thrown into wild disorder.

The main body, a quarter of a mile back and just clearing the river, was marching in column formation on either side of the convoy of baggage, supplies and cattle, the whole protected by flank guards. As soon as the general heard the sounds of firing ahead, the main body 'hastened to succour them but found the remains of the Advance Guard retreating'.[10] Formations and men became intermingled: control was lost. The confusion spread, and what was once a disciplined body became a huddled, bewildered mass as the men were picked off by the deadly fire.

Only the Virginians, accustomed to such warfare, fought like the Indians from behind cover. The general maxim of the Indians, wrote Henry Bouquet of the Royal Americans, 'is to surround their enemy. They fight in extended order, never in a compact body. When attacked, they never stand their ground but immediately give way, to return to the charge, when the attack ceases.'[11]

An eyewitness wrote:

> The Enemy kept behind Trees, and cut down our Troops, as fast as they could advance. The soldiers then insisted much to be allowed to take to the Trees, which the General denied and stormed much, calling them Cowards.[12]

Braddock, furious at what he considered such cowardly and ill-disciplined behaviour, strove bravely to re-form his panic-stricken men. 'We would fight, if we could see anybody to fight,' they replied.[13]

The slaughter was terrible. The ground became strewn with dead and wounded animals and men. After the fighting had continued for a couple of hours, Braddock ordered the retreat, which became a race for life. Regulars and provincials splashed in panic over the ford, which they had crossed in such pomp only a few hours earlier. Everything was abandoned – arms, accoutrements and supplies flung away in the utter rout. Left behind were the guns and mortars so laboriously manhandled over the mountains and Braddock's military chest with his plans and orders. These included the plan of fort Duquesne, bearing Robert Stobo's incriminating signature.[14]

Fortunately, the Indians were too busy looting, scalping and torturing the wounded and prisoners to pursue the fleeing troops. As it was, the British lost nearly 500 British and Americans dead, 500 horses and all their artillery and stores.[15] Sir Peter Halket was shot dead, and his son, a lieutenant in the same regiment (48 Foot), stooping to raise his father, was killed beside him. Thomas Gage was wounded. Eight of the women who had accompanied the expedition were slain and scalped, and three or more were made prisoners.[16] The French commander at Venango kept one for himself, and two were sent to Canada to be sold. The enemy suffered barely 50 casualties – the engagement was more of a massacre than a battle!

Washington, one of the few officers to escape, led the remnants, barely 600, back to Fort Cumberland, where a crowd of invalids, with most of the soldiers' women, had been left behind. The Fort was turned into a hospital for the shattered remains of the once-proud army, whose abiding memories were the wild war-whoops of the savages and the death throes of animals and men. Dunbar had hurriedly retreated to Philadelphia, leaving Fort Cumberland to be defended by this spent force – he was shortly afterwards permanently removed from military command. Thus, says Parkman,[17] was the frontier left unguarded, soon to face a storm of blood and fire as the Indians attacked from Maine to Virginia – homesteads burnt and women and children massacred by a foe, whose confidence and prestige had grown enormously as a result of the conflict.

Braddock, after having had four horses shot under him, was finally mortally wounded by a bullet in the chest while riding the fifth.[18] He was carried from the battlefield to a stopping place called Great Meadows, some miles away, and died at sundown on 13 July 1755. 'We shall know better how to deal with them next time,' he murmured as he died. He was buried before dawn in the middle of the track, the retreating vehicles driven over his grave to prevent desecration by the relentless pursuers.

Years afterwards, in 1823, the grave was discovered by labourers employed on the construction of a road nearby. Some of the bones in the area, still distinguished by military buttons and badges, were carried off. Others were reburied at the foot of a broad spreading oak, which marked the spot, about a mile to the west of Fort Necessity. In 1913 a proper monument was erected near Farmington, Pennsylvania.

Whether Braddock's final words were reported to Britain's commander-in-chief, His Royal Highness the Duke of Cumberland, in 1755 is not known. What is certain is that Cumberland grasped the full significance of Braddock's defeat. Strongly supported by the Duke, Parliament decided on 4 March 1756 to raise a regiment of four battalions, each of 1,000 men, in America, known as the Royal Americans, the 60 Foot. The men would be largely provincials under a British colonel in chief, with a fair sprinkling of foreign Protestant officers. Henri Bouquet and Frederick Haldimand, Swiss officers of distinction serving in the bodyguard of the Prince of Orange, who was married to the Duke of Cumberland's sister, were appointed lieutenant-colonels of the 1st and 2nd battalions respectively.[19]

The object of raising the Royal Americans, later the King's Royal Rifle Corps (the Green Jackets), was:

To form a body of regular troops capable of contending with the Red Indian in his native forest, by combining the qualities of the scout, with the discipline of the trained soldier.[20]

The woodcraft of the hunter (*Chasseur, Jäger*) and the physical hardihood of the backwoodsman would be allied to practical skills of the scout (or rifleman). These military attributes would be learned not in the English camp training areas, but in practice, among the hills, valleys and forests of America, using the native American as the finest model of a scout the world has ever known. In forest warfare the full-dress army uniform was quickly discarded in favour of more suitable and less conspicuous tones.[21] The camouflaged battledress of modern times is the direct descendant!

The Regiment recruited most of its early volunteers from the western settlements of the American plantations, far from civilisation and luxury. There lived a large colony of backwoodsmen, partly English, partly Swiss, Tyrolese and German. They were strong and hardy people, accustomed to the country and inured to the climate, whose conditions and habits were well adapted to oppose the enemy, whether French or Indian, and conduct frontier warfare in New France along its rivers, lakes and fortresses. Their officers, too – Stanwix, Jacques Prevost, Haviland, Bouquet, Haldimand and John St Claire – would leave their mark on North American history. So did Lord Howe, Lawrence, Monckton and Bradstreet, who carried their training methods and traditions into the British army. Some were native-born Frenchmen; others spoke French fluently.[22]

Braddock's bravery, fidelity and honour as a soldier have never been questioned. But he was traditional, methodical, inflexible – a product of the Prussian military system.[23] On the day, his formations and battle tactics were faulty, his officers lost control, and the soldiers panicked. Some blame the panic on the rawness of the British troops, on Irish drafts or American recruits. Others praise the steadiness of the French regulars and the superb fighting qualities of the 650 Indians, who formed the bulk of his troops.[24] But war on the Hudson was very different from Dettingen or Fontenoy. Braddock's defeat on the Monongahela, unprecedented in British military history, brought cynical recriminations in England:

> They knew that those who run away,
> Might live to fight another day,
> But all must die that stood.[25]

British shame and humiliation was matched by unbounded joy in France. Read's *Weekly Journal* recorded:

> If the British Parliament doth not interpose to force Virginia, Pennsylvania and Maryland to unite their forces, it requires no great skill in politics to foretell, that these colonies will be lost to Britain. Yet people this way are no more alarmed than if they were in China, because the enemy have not yet surrounded their habitations.[26]

The American colonists' faith in the invincibility of British soldiers was permanently shattered. But the lesson was not lost on their successors:

> Over the bones of Braddock and his redcoats, the British soldier, in different garb, and with different fighting methods, advanced again to the conquest of Canada.[27]

9

JOHNSON AT
CROWN POINT

In contrast to Braddock's failure on the Monongahela, Colonel William Johnson's advance on Crown Point (Fort St Fédéric), with his 3,000 provincials and 400 Indians, enjoyed a partial success.

Johnson was a native of Ireland. When his parents refused to let him marry, he emigrated to America in 1738[1] and took over the management of the estate of his uncle, Admiral Sir Peter Warren, whose American wife's dowry included an immense track of wild forest land in the Mohawk Valley. He married his mistress, a German girl:

> One of those unfortunate immigrants, driven by need to America, and indentured to the captain of the ship, by which she came for her passage money – a human chattel for a term of years.[2]

Ships' captains would sell the immigrants on arrival to an employer, usually for four or five years, depending on the amount to be redeemed. A comely or clever woman might escape from the bonds of servitude by becoming a wife or mistress.

In this, Johnson's mistress resembled the 'casket girls' who were sent to New Orleans to supply the market for wives in Louisiana, carrying in their caskets a dowry from the French government. She made him an excellent wife and gave him three children. After her early death he consoled himself with a number of mistresses, including a niece of King Hendrick of the Mohawks, 'famous for her beauty', who also provided him with three children.[3] After her death in 1743 he took as his housekeeper Mary 'Molly' Brant, a young Mohawk squaw, sister of the chief, who bore him eight children.

Johnson learned to speak the Mohawk language fluently, 'liked their men and loved their women',[4] and was adopted as a Mohawk chief. He gained an extraordinary ascendancy over the warlike Six Nation Indians. Once the scourge of English and French alike, these tribes were now the passive allies of the English, carrying on a clandestine trade between Albany and Montreal, some 225 miles away. To retain their friendship, Johnson entertained them lavishly and could drink, whoop, paint his face, dress and dance, if need be, the war-dance of the wildest of the Mohawk warriors.

The Indians, in turn, looked to Johnson and the English to protect their tribal land claims and support their profitable fur trade, as well as provide them with gifts. After all, the council which Braddock had called to Alexandria in April 1755 had appointed him 'sole superintendent of the affairs of the Six united Indian Nations, their allies and dependants', with the rank of colonel.

For the Crown Point expedition, in early July Johnson collected 1,000 Iroquois men, women and children at his manor, where he lived in the style of an English gentleman. On this occasion he feasted his guests on oxen, roasted whole, and then harangued them for three days after the Indian fashion before flinging down in their midst the wampum belt, inviting them to war. Only one-third took up his challenge to join his expedition, bringing with them their squaws and children. The remainder refused to take active measures against the French, pleading they had relatives among them. In fact, the Mohawks did not love indiscriminate carnage for its own sake. Craftily, they argued that if they were expected to do the devil's work, they should receive the devil's wages: and there were times when such wages were more likely to be paid by the French than the English.[5]

Johnson assembled his force at Albany, where he arrived with Shirley in July to compete for men, materials and supplies for their respective expeditions. Boats had to be built and supplies gathered, so there was little time to train the recruits in the co-ordinated loading and firing demanded by European battle tactics. Two days after his arrival, Johnson sent Colonel (later General) Lyman with a first contingent of 1,400 Massachusetts and Connecticut militia to cut a wagon road up the Hudson to the Great Carrying Place. The road was to be 30 feet (nine metres) wide and well cleared, to provide a fit surface for the army's ammunition and supply train to follow. At the Great Carrying Place, near the ruins of Fort Nicholson, Lyman would build Fort Edward that autumn, which at first bore his name.[6] Five hundred men were kept there to complete and guard the stockaded storehouse, as Lyman's provincials slowly advanced along the 14-mile portage to Lake George.

Meanwhile Albany, the little Dutch settlement on the Hudson River, where the Dutch had established a trading post even before the arrival of the 'Mayflower' in 1620, had never seen such a gathering of armed men. They camped in their thousands in tents around the town, strolled down from the fort on the hill to the river, and gossiped in front of the two rows of substantial Dutch-style houses which made up the town. One of these men was Robert Rogers, soon to gain fame as a scout and ranger.

Rogers volunteered for service under John Winslow in February 1755, answering Governor Shirley's call for recruits to drive the French from the Bay of Fundy. Two months later he was appointed captain in the New Hampshire regiment. Now he joined the off-duty soldiers and eyed the red-cheeked, buxom Dutch girls in their clean, rustling skirts and trim white caps, and wrote in his diary: 'I went to bed. Dreamed about Playing with a Dutch garl.'[7]

Johnson ordered Rogers to reconnoitre Crown Point, which dominated the American border areas from its site at the narrowest part of Lake Champlain. The thick, black, limestone walls, bomb-proof four-storey inner tower and 40 mounted cannon of Fort St Frédéric stood out in stark contrast to the burned remnants of wooden palisades that the English had constructed at Forts Saratoga, Nicholson and Anne.[8] The French had sent out dozens of raiding parties from Crown Point to terrorise the New England frontiers – a fort so strong would need cannon to be transported there to demolish it. Rogers with four men in his bateau covered routes no white man had trod without Indian guides since the campaign began. He penetrated to the heart of French territory, and returned with intelligence about the enemy's position and strength.

In July Johnson ordered a second contingent of 1,100 men to take the field artillery to Colonel Lyman. He ordered that frequent stops should be made *en route*, to keep the column together – a lesson learned from Braddock's defeat, the news of which had just arrived at Albany. On 8 August 1755 Johnson set off with the third and last contingent, while the second was still on the road to Fort Edward and the first was busy cutting the 12 mile supply road from Fort Edward to Wood Creek.

When Johnson reached Lyman's camp at Fort Edward, he realised that a surprise attack on Crown Point was impossible. The French were well informed of his movements and were concentrating at Fort Ticonderoga (Carillon), whose strong natural position made it possible to resist forces considerably superior to their own. So Johnson abandoned the Wood Creek road, and pushed on with 2,000 of his men to the shores of the lake, which he renamed Lake George (Lac St Sacrement). There he established a camp on what was to be the site of Fort William Henry, named, like Fort Edward, after one of the King's grandsons. This route would allow him to move his cannon more easily for an attack on Crown Point.[9]

The New England regiments, settling into the camp at Fort Edward, did not have any women with them and difficulties soon arose, since the New York and Rhode Island units had laundresses, nurses, wives and prostitutes in their camps.[10] Johnson, whose own womanising was notorious, replied to complaints from his second-in-command, Colonel Lyman:

As to bad Women following or being harboured in our Camp, I shall discountenance it to the utmost of my Power. As to Men's Wives, while they behave Decently they are suffered in all Camps and thought necessary to wash and mend. Immorality of all kinds I will use my utmost power to suppress and chastise. I hope we shall not soil the Justice of our Cause with

a Conduct rebellious against that Almighty Power upon whose Favour depends
the Success of all human Enterprises.[11]

But within a month of Johnson's arrival at Fort Edward, Lyman succeeded in
sending all women back to Albany.

The French, from Braddock's captured correspondence, were fully aware
of Johnson's intentions against Crown Point, and made their plans accordingly.[12]
Originally they had intended to strike at the biggest thorn in their flesh – Fort
Oswego, the British outpost on Lake Ontario, which stood on the vital French
line of communication through the Great Lakes. Only the width of Lake Ontario
separated it from the French Fort Frontenac on the other side.[13] Oswego was
constructed in 1727 by William Burnet, the provincial governor of New York,
as a fortified trading base to protect the flourishing trade in deer and beaver
skins between Oswego and Albany. It was of great strategic importance for
British military operations against Forts Frontenac and Niagara, and for naval
operations on Lake Ontario or its connecting waters.[14]

The task of capturing Oswego was given to Baron Ludwig Dieskau, with
18 companies of regular French troops of the recently-arrived Guienne, Béarn,
La Reine and Languedoc regiments, supported by 1,600 Canadian militia and
600 Indians. Now, the new governor general of New France, the Marquis de
Vaudreuil, changed the direction of Dieskau's operation. He ordered him to
push down the Richelieu River with all speed to attack Johnson's base camp at
Fort George, named by Johnson after George II 'in order to make known the
King's undoubted dominion here'.[15] This would open up for the French the
way to Albany, and down the Hudson River to New York.

Leaving some troops to reinforce the garrison of Crown Point, Dieskau
made for Ticonderoga, 15 miles further down Lake Champlain. Here he left
the bulk of his army to build and man the new fort while he continued his
march south with 900 regulars and Canadians and the 600 Indians. From his
scouts he learned that Johnson had reached Fort Edward. Dieskau decided to
attack the fort, cut Johnson's supply lines, destroy his boats, stores and
ammunition, and take advantage of the fact that Fort Edward was still unfinished.

When Johnson learned of Dieskau's advance, he sent out a small force to
attack him. But the force was ambushed and had to withdraw. The confident
Dieskau, advancing, like Braddock, with his white-coated regulars marching
in perfect formation, was met by a stout defence, which decimated his regulars
and disheartened his Canadian and Indian allies. The French were put to
flight; Dieskau was wounded and taken prisoner. The British made no attempt
to pursue the enemy.

The Mohawk Indians, true to their ethics of warfare, howled for Dieskau's
torture and death. They wanted revenge for the loss of their chief, Hendrick,
killed in the earlier ambush along with many of his braves and white followers.

'They want to burn and eat you, and to smoke you in their pipes,' Johnson told Dieskau.[16] 'But never fear. They will have to kill me first, before they take one of my prisoners.' He sent Dieskau to be looked after by his own sister in Albany, despite her husband having been killed during Dieskau's offensive. Later the baron publicly thanked Johnson and his officers for their kindness to him and his men. He also praised the fighting qualities of Johnson's provincial troops. 'In the morning they fought like good boys: about noon like men, and in the afternoon like devils.'[17] The comparatively raw American colonials had fought and won a battle against French regulars – no mean feat!

Johnson made no effort to follow up his victory, and allowed the French to make their way back to Ticonderoga. A council of war decided to strengthen the camp against any further attack. Work was started on constructing a stronghold on the southern end of the lake, which Johnson named Fort William Henry. The dead were buried, many unidentifiable, since they had been stripped and scalped. Some had been killed while bound as prisoners, which added to the hatred against the French for allowing these murders.

The Mohawks returned home, disappointed with their loot. Robert Rogers returned from a reconnaissance to Crown Point and Ticonderoga, reporting that the latter fort was being strengthened rapidly. By the end of November, beset by sickness, poor rations and worn-out clothing, his men mutinous and deserting in the bitter early winter weather, Johnson allowed Lyman to preside over a council. The decision was taken to withdraw to the Hudson. Captain William Eyre, Johnson's experienced military engineer, was left to finish the construction of a solid fort to hold a garrison of 500 men – Fort William Henry was born! With the French in Ticonderoga and both sides building defensive fortifications, Lake George had become a military waterway, with the opposing cannons only a few days' march apart.[18]

Victory did not end the bickering of the colonies, but in London Johnson's limited success was hailed as a great victory by a country desperately looking for military laurels after the humiliations of Braddock's defeat. Parliament voted Johnson £5,000, and the king gave him a baronetcy.

Meanwhile, Shirley's expedition against Niagara was planned to round off the summer campaigns. The starting point for his trek to Oswego was Albany, destined to become for the next five years the principal base of military operations against the French. Regiment after regiment, with drums beating, banners waving and all the trappings of war, transformed its peaceful streets into a garrison of army red and provincial blue.

Shirley realised that extensive preparations were necessary if his plan was to be successful. Early in the spring he sent four companies of troops to strengthen Oswego's defences.[19] Three hundred ships' carpenters were employed to build a schooner, the first representative of the English navy on Lake Ontario, and to construct boats and bateaux. During the summer Shirley made his way up the Mohawk river to Oswego, with 500 men of the New Jersey Regiment (the Jersey Blues), the 50 Foot (Shirley's) and 51 Foot (Pepperell's). These two latter regiments, paid by the king, counted as regulars, though in effect they were raw provincials, recently recruited.

At Oswego, Shirley learned of Braddock's defeat and the death of his eldest son, killed at Braddock's side. His other son, Captain John Shirley, died of fever at Oswego as he waited for supplies.[20] Sickness broke out, and the autumnal storms were so severe that small craft could not venture on the lake. The French, forewarned of his plans, strengthened their garrisons at Niagara and Frontenac. Shirley, realising the task set him was beyond his capabilities, reluctantly abandoned the enterprise in October. The soldiers exchanged muskets for spades, saws and axes to work on the defences. On 24 October Shirley set out for Albany, leaving 700 of his men to strengthen the garrison under Colonel Mercer in readiness for a new thrust in the spring.

With Braddock's death, Shirley became temporary commander-in-chief of the British forces in America, 'until the King's pleasure be known'.[21] Despite the loss of his sons, his enthusiasm for action against the French remained undiminished. In December 1755 he held a council of war at New York, and a comprehensive plan of operations for 1756 was decided. But Shirley upset a number of powerful New York politicians, including the governor, James de Lancey, and Sir William Johnson, all of whom had powerful friends in England. They resented his demands for men and supplies, and contrived to have him removed from his military command – but not before he had advised the British government that Fort Frontenac was the key to the west, and that it would be easier and less costly to take than attacking Fort Niagara. Three years later events would prove him right.

So, after 16 years as the royal governor of Massachusetts (1741-57), Shirley was recalled. If he had begun his career as a place-seeker, he ended it as a true patriot. He saw more clearly than other colonial statesman of his day that the struggle in America between France and Britain allowed no compromise. After a spell as governor of the Bahamas, he returned in 1769 to Boston for the last two years of his life.

Except for the capture of Beauséjour in Acadia (see Chapter 5),[22] the 1755 campaign had been a disaster for the British. They had been routed on the Monongahela, failed at Niagara, and had had a barren victory on Lake George. The Indians were now free for the next two years to swarm out of Fort Duquesne into the defenceless frontiers of Virginia, Maryland and Pennsylvania to pillage and massacre with fire and tomahawk. 'They kill all they meet,' wrote a French priest,[23] and after abusing the women and maidens, they slaughter and burn them.' Men returning home after a day's work found their homes smouldering, their families dead or carried into captivity. Washington with his 1,500 provincial militia, assisted by the British regular Independent Companies, had over 350 miles of homesteads and farms to protect, and could do little to stop the marauding Indians. Settlers piled their belongings on to wagons and fled beyond the reach of the scalping parties.

Month after month during the winter of 1755–6, the great continent lay wrapped in snow. While the provincial governments continued their squabbles, Forts Oswego, Edward, and William Henry shivered in the grip of winter. Bands of New England rangers, muffled against the piercing cold, scoured the forests from the forts, seeking out prowling Indian war parties, or spied out the secrets of Ticonderoga. So the guerrilla war went on – and, like hibernating bears, both sides awaited the coming of spring.[24]

10

WAR DECLARED
– MONTCALM ARRIVES

O n 18 May 1756, after a year of open hostilities, England declared war
on France. The French and Indian War in North America now became
a part of Europe's Seven Years' War, which would be waged in four
continents and prove to be the most terrible conflict of the 18th century.[1] Each
of the Great Powers fought for its own interests, seeking allies in Europe to
secure those concerns. For Britain the war provided an opportunity to defeat
France in India and North America, a colonial war based on trade and sea
power.

Great Britain was allied to Holland and Austria. George II, King of England
and Elector of Hanover, feared Prussia and France would attack his vulnerable
Electorate, and on 16 January 1756 concluded an alliance with Frederick II
(the Convention of Westminster) 'to unite their forces against any foreign Power
that might introduce troops into Germany'. The Duke of Newcastle, seeking
further security for Hanover and knowing that Russia was a danger to east
Prussia, arranged to subsidise Russia to keep 55,000 troops on the border
against a 'common enemy', unspecified. When Frederick invaded Saxony,
Britain had to decide whether to support Prussia against the two Catholic
powers, Austria and France, or protect Hanover with subsidies to the German
states in order to keep France occupied in Europe, and commit her major
military and financial resources at sea and in the colonies. Pitt called the latter
strategy 'conquering America in Germany'.

In an age when the affairs of a nation were governed by the personal
whims of the sovereign, the destinies of France, Austria and Russia were largely
controlled by three women – two empresses and a concubine.[2] All three hated
Frederick the Great of Prussia, a misogynist, who found in the three dominant
women of his day 'a perpetual invitation to scurrilous and well-advertised
wit'.[3] Maria Theresa, the devout, unforgiving empress of Austria (Frederick's
'Apostolic Hag'), hated him for stealing Silesia, 'the fairest jewel of her crown',
in 1740.

Elizabeth, the sensuous and vain Tsarina of Russia (1741–61), was insulted
by his coarse jests about her liking for vodka and her notorious weakness for
handsome grenadiers.[4] Frederick openly compared her lustful appetites with

those of the Roman empress Messalina. More interested in clothes (on her death, she left a wardrobe of 15,000 dresses) than in politics, she was content to leave state affairs to her chancellor, Bestuzhev, and her lover Alexis Razumovsky, a Cossack who had first attracted her by his singing in her chapel choir. She appointed him chamberlain and a field marshal. This last surviving daughter of Peter the Great had seized power with the help of the palace guard and was a strong supporter of Austria. Her death on the last day of 1761 helped to save Frederick when, after military defeats, he seemed to be on his knees. Elizabeth's heir, Peter III, a fervent admirer of Frederick, reversed her anti-Prussian policies and ordered his army out of Prussia. His short reign ended when he was murdered with the connivance of his wife and successor, Catherine II, 'The Great', who withdrew completely from the war.

Madame de Pompadour would not forgive him for insulting her as the fish-wife, Mlle Poisson. He named one of his bitches after her, and told his court that she slept beside him in his bed and was considerably less expensive to maintain than his brother's Pompadour at Versailles. Frederick, a man of depraved morals himself, ridiculed Louis for the millions he squandered on his mistresses, and hurled insults at the French army, while he drove his own soldiers into battle like cattle, with terrible brutality. Henry Martin, the French historian, claims Louis XV believed that an alliance between Catholic France and Austria against Protestant England and Prussia would redeem his personal sins. 'He dreamed of a Holy War from the recesses of the Parc aux Cerfs'.[5] Louise XV certainly admired the Austrian empress and disliked the treacherous Frederick, whom he wished to punish for concluding with Britain the Westminster Convention against him.

Maria Theresa, secretly allied to Russia, in 1756 concluded 'a diplomatic revolution' by allying herself with France, her traditional enemy. The mastermind behind this diplomatic achievement was Prince von Kaunitz, since 1753 her State chancellor and one of the most notable figures in Austrian history. A Bohemian noble and landed proprietor, he devoted his service and considerable diplomatic talents to his Queen and country. Clear-sighted and cunning, he 'taught the pious empress queen that in international affairs a bit of mendacity was a tragic necessity'. Maria Theresa came to rely completely on his political experience and judgement. He believed that Prussia had replaced France as the hereditary enemy of the Habsburgs, and knowing that the French cabinet, with the exception of Machault, was pro-Prussian, he approached Louis through Madame Pompadour to further his diplomatic aims. Pompadour's success in influencing the French king was rewarded with a jewelled portrait of the Austrian queen as a token of her appreciation.

At first Louis XV had tried to avoid war with George II, fearing England's naval power. But in an act of the utmost folly, Louis allied himself with Maria Theresa by the first Treaty of Versailles (May 1756), angered by the ingratitude and lack of faith of his *protégé*, the king of Prussia, in making a defensive alliance with England. When Frederick suddenly invaded Saxony (August 1756), France was drawn into the conflict by 'the Alliance of Petticoats', as Frederick derisively called this diplomatic treaty, which did not serve France's interests. By the second Treaty of Versailles (May 1757), Louis XV placed the resources of France at the disposal of Austria.[6] Since France could now hardly invade the territories of her new ally, Britain's traditional fears for the Low Countries, now the Austrian Netherlands, were removed.

France, already struggling with her ancient enemy in the backwoods of America and on the plains of India, would have been better advised to have concentrated her efforts on the defence of her overseas possessions rather than fighting a continental war against the might of Prussia. But King, court and Pompadour were continentalists and anti-colonial. Canada, except for her Newfoundland fisheries, was of less commercial value than the West Indian islands of Martinique, Guadeloupe and St. Dominique (today's Haiti). France was fighting for a few areas of snow, wrote Voltaire, and draining her treasury for more than Canada was worth.

Henceforth, France would be committed to a European struggle: her army would have preference over her navy – and France would lose an empire. But the Austrian alliance was hated by the French people, and many outside court circles. 'It was more criticised in Paris than in London,' wrote Pompadour's foreign minister friend, Cardinal de Bernis,[7] who presided over both treaties. 'France has neither generals nor ministers, and no directing will. Everything is going to pieces ...No sooner does one succeed in propping the building at one corner than it crumbles at another,' he wrote. It would be left to his successor, Choiseul, eventually to attempt to clear up the mess in August 1761, by signing a second Family Compact with Spain in the hope of gaining better terms for France in a war settlement. 'Whoever attacked one crown, attacked the other,' stated the Compact, which drew Spain into the conflict.

The people and their generals blamed Pompadour, while Britain was left free to pursue her colonial interests and concentrate on her sea power. British trade increased during the war, while the French flag almost disappeared from the trade routes of the world. The French population, at home and in her dominions overseas, suffered beneath the crushing blows of the Royal Navy. For Britain and Pitt, Europe was of secondary importance – only George II and Newcastle thought differently.[8]

Early in the New Year, Newcastle and the Duke of Cumberland met to decide who should command the British 1756 spring offensive in North America. Their choice was John Campbell, fourth Earl of Loudoun and one of 16 Scottish peers, who had been proposed in 1752 for the governorship of New York. Commissioned into the Royal Scots Greys in 1727, Loudoun had been a captain in the 7th Dragoons, a lieutenant-colonel in the 3rd Foot Guards and colonel of the 30 Foot. After the battle of Dettingen (1743), he had served in Flanders as ADC to the King. To help defeat the Jacobite rebellion, he raised a regiment of Highlanders, which was almost completely wiped out at the Battle of Preston (1745). It was considered that his rank and wealth would ensure that he could support the style and dignity of high command in the colonies. Apart from his military duties, Loudoun, as commander-in-chief, had to persuade the colonial assemblies to work together against the common enemy and provide the men and money for their own defence.[9] Like Amherst and Forbes after him, he would find he could only plead and cajole for their help, never order or requisition men and supplies.

While Loudoun was preparing to leave and the British government was assembling the regiments, transports and supplies for the expeditionary force, the French seized the initiative. They appointed their own commander-in-chief and sent troops to New France. Thanks to a centralised system of selection and administration, they arrived some months earlier than the British. They also concentrated along the Channel coast 60,000 French troops to invade England, in a daring attempt to halt the flow of British soldiers to North America. So successful was the threat that Newcastle decided not to reinforce America, and parliament requested the King to summon 12 battalions of his Hanoverian army to England as a deterrent. The move was successful. Belle-Isle, the French War Minister, realised the invasion of Britain would be too dangerous, and cancelled the plans.

The French nobility always expected the king to provide suitable opportunities for them to serve in the army, 'the most aristocratic and top-heavy army in Europe'. But none of the French court favourites relished a military command in the backwoods of America.[10] Compared to a command in Europe, it meant banishment and financial sacrifice, and Louis XV's choice of commander-in-chief, Louis-Joseph, Marquis de Montcalm-Gozon, was not a wealthy man.[11] He was a French aristocrat of splendid lineage on both sides, brave, honest and scholarly, and already a resolute and experienced general.

Montcalm's father had bought his son a captaincy at the age of 17. Marriage to another aristocrat added influence, property and ten children to his modest inheritance. He was a good husband and father, and devoted to his family home at Candiac, near Nîmes. He was proud, courageous, incorruptibly patriotic, and ambitious for a marshal's baton and a seat in the French Academy as a scholar. He went to Paris to thank the king personally for his appointment, and was delighted when Louis XV gave his young son the rank and pay of a colonel – one of the few abuses of court favour in his career, for he took no part in the corrupting pleasures of Versailles! He arrived in Canada with a poor opinion of Canadian officers and officials, which increased when he got to know them better. He believed colonial methods of fighting were outdated, and would be replaced in the future by European-style campaigns, regular troops and professional artillery.

Among the goodly number of young, lighthearted and debonair officers he took with him was his chief aide-de-camp, Colonel Louis Antoine de Bougainville. Though only 27, Bougainville was already famous in the world of science, had served in the French embassy in London, and would become an admiral of the French Navy and a peer of France. He would survive the French Revolution, and die on the eve of the fall of Napoleon. It is from his pen that we learn much of the inner story of the last days of New France.

Montcalm's deputy was Brigadier François de Lévis, a member of a great French family, marquis, later duke and marshal of France. He was a capable soldier and skilled in the art of managing men. Third in the chain of army command was Colonel François-Charles de Bourlamaque, quiet and reserved, with few social gifts but highly dependable. While Louis XV and Pompadour could send 100,000 men to fight the battles of Austria, they could only spare two regiments, La Sarre and Royal Roussillon, of 1,200 men to reinforce the French regulars of some 2,500 already in New France.[12]

As usual French ships were earlier in the field than the British: Montcalm embarked at Brest on 3 April 1756, with a brilliant staff and two splendid regiments, and reached Montreal safely on 11 May. (Loudoun's arrival in New York was delayed until 23 July.) He found Quebec equal to the best of French cities, the peasants living more like the lesser gentry of France, and the hospitality excellent. 'The Canadian ladies were witty, lively, devout and gamblers for high stakes: those in Montreal were adept at conversation and dancing,' he reported to the Canadian Pierre de Rigaud, Marquis de Vaudreuil, appointed governor-general of New France and Louisiana in 1755. His father had held the same position from 1703 to 1725. His mother, though Canadian born, had considerable influence at Versailles, where she had been governess to the children of the Duc de Berry, Louis XIV's grandson.

Vaudreuil, born at Montreal in 1704, belonged to one of the most ancient families of France, and was related to de Lévis. His wife, 15 years older and a widow, when he married her in Paris in 1743, was adept at seeking places for the children of her first marriage and her many relatives. She helped to sharpen her husband's antagonism to those of his own rank and caste who came from France. Vaudreuil loved his Canadian people and distrusted Old France and all that came out of it. Living in the governor's chateau of St Louis in Quebec, he ruled Canada on behalf of Louis XV, the supreme civil power but also the executive chief in all military matters, both at headquarters and in the field. 'Whenever operations are in question, the Governor shall have the right to determine them alone,' were his orders.[13]

Vaudreuil was well-meaning but vain, weak and timid. He was very conscious of his own importance in the court at Quebec, and easily susceptible to the flattery of the corrupt circle which surrounded him. He served the King and the colony, said Parkman,[14] in some respects with ability, always with an unflagging zeal; and he loved the land of his birth with a devotion that goes far towards redeeming his miserable defects. 'The best excuse that can be made for him,' wrote the Canadian historian William Wood,[15] is that he was 'almost as great a fool as a knave.'

Montcalm, subordinate to the governor, was responsible for operations and commanded the regular army (*troupes de terre*). Vaudreuil was in charge of the overall strategy of the war and controlled the 1,500 colonial regulars (*troupes de la Marine*, in which he had served as a captain), mostly recruited in Canada, and the Indians (*les sauvages*).[16] He alone could call up the enlisted militia. Both Vaudreuil and Montcalm, outwardly courteous, were jealous of each other and criticised the other's actions and conduct of the war. Worse, however, was Vaudreuil's insistence on exercising his final authority over military matters, about which he had little knowledge and less experience. Since the court of Versailles encouraged even subordinate officers to communicate their opinions, Vaudreuil, Montcalm and others corresponded at length about Canadian affairs, criticising each other's conduct and apportioning blame. Their bitter feud represented the two parties which would soon divide Canada, those of New and Old France, and split army loyalties. The regulars supported Montcalm, the administration and colonial troops Vaudreuil.[17]

Worse than the jealousy was the corruption in Canada. The leading figure in this was Vaudreuil's intendant, François Bigot, an able but corrupt rogue, who knew how to manage the governor and impose his will on the weaker man. Like all his class (*noblesse de la robe*), he was a lawyer and a professional government administrator. Related to a marshal of France, he had powerful French connections, including Madame Pompadour and Maurepas, the Minister of Marine, whose favour at court had gained Bigot the post of intendant in Canada in 1748. He was responsible for finance, police and administration, including government contracts, public works and the regulation of prices. As an additional duty he controlled supplies to the forces, like a modern quartermaster-general.[18] There was no accounting system, and honesty was unknown.

Corruption was traditional in the colonial service, and officials expected to make their fortunes – but never were a king and his subjects more flagrantly cheated. Bigot developed the system, using his position as an opportunity for fraud and corruption to line his pockets on a gigantic scale, afterwards covering up the evidence. From time to time he visited France, bought an estate, and equipped his house with a wealth of pictures, plate and *objets d'art* to prepare for the day of his return. In 1754 he wrote to Captain Vergor, in command at Fort Beauséjour: 'Profit by your place: all power is in your hands: do it quickly, join me in France, and buy an estate near mine.'[19]

Bigot surrounded himself with a swarm of lesser swindlers, like the contractor Joseph Cadet, the Canadian son of a Quebec butcher. Cadet supplied munitions and, under a nine-year contract awarded him by Bigot, all the food and refreshments needed for the king's service in the cities and garrisons of Canada – a monopoly which netted him a fortune. Mercier, who had arrived from France 20 years earlier as a private soldier in the colonial regulars, was now commandant of artillery making a fortune manufacturing and transporting guns and ammunition at enhanced prices. The command of a fort (like Vergor's) or a detachment provided opportunities for fraud and embezzlement.[20] The king's stores were purchased and resold for private gain; the troops were defrauded of their provisions, stores and equipment. So widespread was the corruption that the court of Versailles questioned the wisdom of pouring the resources of France into that bottomless pit called Canada.[21] The war only increased the opportunities for peculation, and multiplied the immense fortunes of this band of corrupt officials. After the defeat of France, Bigot, Cadet, Vaudreuil and some 20 others faced retribution in the Bastille, banishment from France, and heavy fines.

'Bigot,' wrote Parkman, 'was untiring, both in work and in pleasure.' Following the examples of his masters at Versailles, he kept a young, well-born and attractive mistress, Madame Angélique de Péan, whose complaisant husband, a Canadian major, was rewarded with huge army contracts.[22] Bigot, nearing 60, was besotted with his paramour, 20 years his junior, and refused her nothing. She 'played the Pompadour' with grace and favour, obtaining for relatives and favourites positions, perquisites and opportunities for wealth and extortions. Her balls and receptions were nightly occurrences at the Intendant's palace; her salon was the centre for fashionable society, where they could forget the misery outside and the enemy at the gates. Péan, meanwhile, found consolation in the bed of Madame Pénisseault, wife of his military partner, another of the couples seeking position and fortune at the expense of Versailles!

Montcalm visited Quebec in January 1757 and noted the corruption and reckless social round of dinners, dances, balls, masques and flirtations. He wrote in his *Journal*:

> Monsieur L'Intendant lives there in grandeur, and has given two fine balls, where I have seen over 80 very charming ladies, beautifully dressed. I think Quebec a town of very good style, and I don't believe we have in France more than a dozen cities, that could rank higher as regards society. Its population is not more than 12,000. The pace of life was determined by alcohol, sex and gambling, wrote another.[23]

Montcalm wrote a full report to Marshal Belle-Isle, Minister for War (12 April 1758) on the civil administration as he found it.

There is no confidence in Monsieur de Vaudreuil or M. Bigot. The government is good for nothing; money and provisions will fail. The farms are scarcely tilled at all. The people are dispirited. M. Bigot appears to be occupied only in amassing a fortune for himself, his adherents and sycophants. Cupidity has seized officers and store keepers; the commissaries are making astounding profits. Everybody appears to be in a hurry to make his fortune before the Colony is lost. Transport is given to favourites. Everything is done badly and at high prices. I have often spoken respectfully to Vaudreuil and Bigot on these matters; each throws the blame on his colleague.[24]

Female influence was freely employed, wrote Wood,[25] to further all sorts of nefarious undertakings. Anyone with a sufficiently attractive wife could make his fortune by exiling himself to some distant post, and taking his commission on the public stores there, whilst his wife remained in Quebec to brighten the social circle at the palace and act as a decoy for those who were worth fleecing at cards.

The third member of the powerful triumvirate ruling Canada was the Catholic archbishop. He guarded the interests of his Church, its landed possessions, and the souls of his Canadian faithful. The Church would play an important political part in support of the war, and use its French priests, like Father Le Loutre, to foment unrest among the Acadians in Nova Scotia.

Canadian colonial society itself came to be divided into two main groups. The establishment looked to France for the advance of their careers and those of their children. They regarded themselves primarily as citizens of France, resident overseas. The mass of Canadians, on the other hand, the provincials – habitants, artisans, town workers and shopkeepers – had few ties with France. Their economic and social life was firmly rooted in Canada, where the majority of them had been born.[26]

Montcalm's forces consisted of six regiments of regulars from France, some 4,000 men, including 1,100 regulars of the Louisbourg garrison. The regiments were named after the noblemen who owned them, or after the province from which they were recruited. The men were expected to remain in Canada for the duration of the war. Food and pay were bad, and at the end of their service they could only hope to enlist on the meagre half-pay of one of the 135 companies of *invalids*. Montcalm's regular troops were commanded by French officers, *noblesse* to a man, who would always fight bravely and die for their country when called upon.[27] The French historian Martin wrote:

Fine clothes and good living were their birthright. During the Seven Years' War in Europe, their baggage trains stretched for miles, while their armies were encumbered with crowds of chefs, hairdressers, musicians, lackeys, players and courtesans. They resembled the cohorts of Darius and Xerxes, rather than the armies of Condé and Turenne.[28]

Bougainville wrote[29] that French officers lived in war as they lived in peace, with every kind of luxury to be found in the French camps. The very subalterns had their mistresses with them, and officers often left their men on the march to accompany their ladies in their carriages, wrote another commentator.[30] If fight they must, said Parkman,[31] they preferred to die gloriously after a ball or a champagne supper, and with the kisses of their concubines still wet on their lips – but, added Fortescue,[32] in the trenches of a Flemish town, rather than in the trackless forests of North America!

Also included in Montcalm's forces were 2,000 paid colonial regulars *(troupes de la Marine),* recruited by the French admiralty for colonial service and descended from the three companies of *infanterie de marine* which had landed in Canada in 1684. They were used to police the colony or garrison the outlying forts. Most had been enlisted in France (the officers from the seigneurial families, promoted on merit in Canada), and were encouraged to settle as colonists when they retired.

In addition, he could call upon 15,000 citizen militia – in fact, all the effective male population of the Canadian provinces between the ages of 15 and 60 – who could be called into service by the governor. They were supplied with clothing, arms and rations, and equipped by France, but given no pay: their furloughs for harvesting were both necessary for the food chain and inevitable, whatever the state of the conflict. They rivalled the Indians in endurance and their skills of forest warfare, excelling as raiders and skirmishers.[33] But to regulars they appeared ill-disciplined, and given to boasting that every true Canadian was equal to three Englishmen![34] To the French they were 'criminals, who should have been broken on the wheel but who had been deported to Canada instead: scoundrels, who had inherited all the traits of their gallows-bird ancestors'.[35]

To the white fighting force of Canada must be added the native American Indians, who covered the vast areas of the interior from Lake Superior to the Ohio River, from the Allegheny Mountains to the Mississippi. Some 30 tribes had allied themselves to France, and considered they should be consulted in all military planning. There were 650 Indians at the defeat of General Braddock; 1,800 at Fort William Henry; but less than 1,000 at the siege of Quebec.[36] 'They make war with astounding cruelty,' wrote Montcalm to his wife, 'sparing neither men, women, nor children, and take off your scalp very neatly – an operation which generally kills you.'[37] Montcalm needed their services, but their bloodthirsty habits and lack of discipline disgusted him.

In the spring of 1756, Indian scouts reported that 10,000 English were preparing to renew the attacks of the previous year on Niagara and Fort

Frontenac, and massing for a campaign against Fort Carillon (Ticonderoga). Montcalm immediately sent his deputy Lévis with reinforcements to Ticonderoga, a massive square fort built on the crown of a promontory, with bomb-proof shelters, stone barracks, and ramparts constructed of tree-trunks and tightly-packed earth and gravel (this first fort was quite distinct from the modern reconstruction).

For his spring offensive, Shirley ordered General John Winslow to form three companies of Rangers out of the 2,000 New Englanders returning from the 1755 campaign in Nova Scotia.[38] Only those used to travelling and hunting were to be enlisted, and men of courage and loyalty. Each company would have 60 men; the officers to be paid as regulars, the men the same wages as the provincial troops. The king would arm, feed, and clothe them with a hunting coat, vest and breeches, Indian stockings and shoes. They took an oath of fidelity, and every ranger received five pounds sterling for every Indian scalp he brought in. Robert Rogers was given command of one of these independent companies of Rangers, which were subject to military discipline and the articles of war. More companies would be raised in subsequent years under Loudoun to work alongside Colonel Gage's Light Infantry.

While waiting for Lord Loudoun to arrive, Shirley sent troops to guard the dangerous route to Oswego, and stored provisions at the fortified posts *en route*. He also assembled at Albany 5,000 untrained levies, raised by the New England colonies for the planned expedition against Crown Point and Ticonderoga. General Winslow of Massachusetts was given command of these levies, who each volunteered to serve for a year. Each colony clothed, armed, paid, victualled and transported its own troops. This led to duplication and confusion, until Loudoun formed a commissary-general to co-ordinate these services, giving receipts for goods supplied. Each regiment had a complement of 500 men, the officers being chosen by the men themselves. Discipline was understandably poor.

Shirley arranged for stores and provisions to be assembled at Fort Edward before being ferried across country to Fort William Henry, 14 miles away. The attack on Ticonderoga would be made from there. In command at Fort William Henry was Colonel Jonathan Bagley, who kept gangs of men busily building several hundred boats as fast 'as rum and human flesh can move them'.[39] The fortifications of both forts were strengthened, the forests cleared, and the 'portage' road between the two forts improved.[40]

Meanwhile, the French reacted quickly. In May Vaudreuil sent 1,100 Canadian soldiers and Indians to harass Oswego and cut its communications with Albany:

> They swarmed about Oswego like hornets, and along the line of communications, irritating and annoying their enemies so seriously, as to

interfere with their plans. Fort Bull at the Wood Creek carrying place, with its large quantities of supplies for Oswego was captured and destroyed, and the garrison murdered. Ships-carpenters at Fort Oswego were killed and captured; Fort Ontario nearby was attacked and river convoys raided.[41]

Lieut-Colonel John Bradstreet, born in Lincolnshire but an American regular officer, commanded the provincial bateau service, a corps of rivermen ferrying supplies between the British forts around New York. He safely conducted a convoy of military stores and provisions to the beleaguered garrison. But news reached Shirley that Oswego was starving and several councils of war suggested the fort should be abandoned. During the winter half of Shirley's own regiment (50 Foot) had died from hunger and disease. 'The men were so weak,' reported a regimental officer, Captain John Vicars, 'that the sentries often fell down at their posts and lay there, till the relief came and lifted them up.'[42] But Shirley knew that Oswego had to be defended at all costs. It was the key to the expeditions against Forts Niagara, Frontenac, Ticonderoga and Crown Point (Frédéric). So throughout these early summer months he collected recruits, often of the poorest quality, and sent them to Oswego to reinforce the ranks of the two emaciated and depleted regiments.

On 17 June Captain Robert Rogers, whose exploits as a scout would make him a household name in the colonies, was lying hidden with his companions keeping watch on Fort Ticonderoga. On one of his earlier raids he had brought back to Fort William Henry a Frenchman, his wife and 14-year-old daughter.[43] His reconnaissance report, compiled from such sources, was eagerly awaited at Albany, where Shirley and Winslow were putting the final touches to their preparations before Loudoun's imminent arrival.

11

LOUDOUN AND
FORT OSWEGO

The eagerly awaited Earl of Loudoun arrived in New York on 17 July 1756. He had been appointed lieutenant-general 'with every power, civil and military, that can legally be given him'. As commander-in-chief he commanded all British naval and military forces in North America; he was also superior in rank to all the royal governors, and had responsibility for co-ordinating the efforts of each colonial government. He was accompanied by his aide-de-camp, and by his secretary and judge advocate, John Appy, responsible for the administration of military law in the colonies. As befitted Loudoun's rank and wealth, he arrived with his valet and footmen, servants, groom, postilion, coach and coachman – and his mistress, Jean Masson.[1]

Loudoun went straight to his army headquarters at Albany. What he found totally depressed him. In March Colonel Daniel Webb had been ordered by Newcastle to replace Shirley as commander-in-chief, but with instructions to hand over command to General James Abercromby until Loudoun's arrival. The well-meaning but gullible Shirley had left an over-optimistic report on the British position at Oswego and the dangers to which it was exposed, the poor state of Shirley's and Pepperell's regiments (50 and 51 Foot), and the lack of supplies, despite the efforts of Bradstreet.[2] What he did not yet know was that the Brest squadron had eluded the blockading British fleet and arrived safely in Quebec, carrying reinforcements.

Abercromby reported to Loudoun the arrival in New York of the 35 Foot and 42 Highlanders (the Black Watch) in June. But the levies expected from the colonies were, as usual, late in arriving and inadequately equipped; even worse, each contingent was jealously kept under the orders of its own provincial assembly.[3]

Loudoun settled down with his retinue and mistress in a house in Whitehall, New York, rented from the widow of Colonel John Moore, a distinguished merchant of considerable wealth. The mansion stood close to Fort George, within whose walls it was customary for governors to reside. There he entertained lavishly, while pondering the urgent military situation. He quickly decided to abandon any attempt to capture Forts Frontenac and Niagara, and to concentrate all his efforts on Fort Carillon (Ticonderoga). For Governor

Shirley he had nothing but contempt, blaming him for the empty military chest, the lack of supplies, and the true situation at Oswego, which Bradstreet at last revealed to him.

Meanwhile, General Winslow was at Lake George, with his provincials split between Fort Edward under Phineas Lyman (2,800) and 2,500 under his own command at Fort William Henry. But of this force 27 per cent were sick – 840 men at Fort Edward, and 600 at Fort William Henry. In his report of 5 August to Loudoun, Lieutenant-Colonel Ralph Burton wrote, 'The Fort at William Henry stinks, five to eight men, with officers in proportion, being buried daily'.[4] So disgraceful were the conditions that latrines, kitchens, graves, and the slaughterhouses for cattle were all intermixed throughout the encampment. Stores and artillery were in great confusion, and the men indolent and dirty, neglecting the most elementary rules of hygiene, and failing to wash regularly themselves or their clothes. For the officers had little experience of looking after their men's welfare and hygiene. Loudoun advised opening up the tents to dry the ground inside, burying all refuse, and constructing and re-siting a proper slaughterhouse. Fort Edward was reported cleaner, but conditions were not good enough to keep the soldiers healthy.[5]

Lord Loudoun had brought with him from England Doctor Richard Huck, a physician and friend. Huck had been the surgeon in Loudoun's Scottish regiment during the 1745 Jacobite rebellion, later transferring in 1750 to the 33 Foot. In America, Huck joined the staff of the army's chief surgeon and director of hospitals, James Napier, whose medical staff numbered four surgeons, three apothecaries, 12 surgeon's mates of warrant officer rank, and ten hospital mates. These personnel were distributed among the general army hospitals established by Napier at New York, Albany, which comfortably housed 300 patients, and Halifax, Nova Scotia.[6]

Forward of these base hospitals would be a 'marching' or 'flying' hospital, equipped to accommodate 200 sick or wounded soldiers. Further forward still would be the army's regimental hospitals, situated on or near the battlefield. Here the regimental surgeons and their mates would operate on the wounded, collected from the battlefield. Each flying hospital was equipped with its own tents and transport, and had its own medical and nursing personnel and drivers. When the army advanced again, these patients would be transferred to general hospitals, 12 to 40 miles behind the forward troops and situated in a suitable large town on the line of communications.[7]

Soldiers' wives were employed in the wards as nurses, to prepare food, wash linen, and keep patients clean and comfortable.[8] Provided in the ratio of six to a company of 100 men, or sometimes one to every 25 patients, these women were given army rations. They were forbidden to ride on wagons reserved for stores and the sick. No soldier patient was allowed to have his wife employed as one of the nurses, and if any of the nurses' husbands were taken ill, they were dismissed or suspended until their husbands recovered. But married men 'of good character, who live near the hospital and have careful wives' were allowed to remain in the hospital if taken ill, at the discretion of the surgeon.[9]

Napier appointed a hospital board of senior medical officers to lay down hospital regulations, dismiss unsatisfactory non-medical staff, and report to the commander-in-chief any negligent commissioned medical officers. Each regiment had a surgeon, provided with medicine chests and instruments, which were carried on batt horses. He would establish the tented regimental hospital or hire a suitable building, in which the sick and wounded slept two in a bed. One wagon was allocated to each regiment, to convey the wounded to hospital and return with the bread issue. The surgeon purchased the medicines, paid for by the stoppage of one penny a month from each private soldier and one and three-quarter pence from each NCO. The army paid for a nurse, a soldier's wife, who received sixpence a day. The soldiers acted as sick attendants, changed every 24 hours, to do the heavy work.

The hospital sergeant shopped in the local market for milk, eggs, vegetables, chickens and fish, and collected two shillings and sixpence per week from the patient to pay for his special diet. The basic ration of bread and meat was drawn by the soldier's company and sent to the regimental hospital. Sick parade was obligatory: any soldier found sick in his quarters was subsequently punished by his commanding officer. A sentry was posted at the hospital 'to prevent visitors, whether authorised or not, from bringing in strong liquor'. 'The Army is undone and ruined by the constant use of salt meat and rum', was Wolfe's experience.[10]

During winter a sickness rate of seven or eight per cent was common, with an average of some 40 to 50 men in each regimental hospital in North America. Fifteen to 20 men from each regiment were treated as being more seriously ill in the general hospital, according to the army's medical statistics. The army's annual losses by death, desertion and discharge were 15 per cent for troops in New York, and double that for Nova Scotia, where extreme cold and isolation took their toll. The commonest illnesses were fluxes, enteritis, venereal disease, fever, scurvy and smallpox. To prevent scurvy, spruce beer was brewed and issued on a regimental basis. At some garrisons half the meat ration was exchanged for fresh vegetables, where these could be obtained – many of the worst patients being sent to New Jersey, where fresh vegetables were more plentiful.[11]

Relationships were not improved for Winslow and his provincial officers by a royal order, given at the court at Kensington on 12 May 1756, which Loudoun had brought with him. This stated that all provincial commissioned officers were to rank only as senior captains, when serving alongside regular troops. In effect, this meant that the whole of the provincial army could be placed under a British major. Naturally, the order caused great discontent among the colonies and further hampered recruitment. But Winslow and his officers agreed to obey – the alternative was mutiny!

Concentrated on a 40-acre island site in the Hudson River at Fort Edward were Rogers and his independent company of rangers. They were courageous men, experienced in hunting, tracking and long marches. Shirley had given Rogers this command in May 1756 with orders 'To make Discoveries of the proper Routes for our own Troops, procure Intelligence of the Enemy's Strength and Motions, destroy their Out-Magazines and Settlements, pick up small parties of their Boats upon the Lakes and keep them under continual Alarm'.[12] Lyman had employed these rangers on frequent patrols, and attached British regular officers to them to gain experience.

On one of these expeditions, one of the Rogers's captains was captured and scalped. Another wounded officer was made to watch as the captain's head was put on a pole, and another ranger stripped and tied to a stake:

> The squaws cut pieces of pine, like skewers, and thrust them into his flesh and set them on fire, dancing around him and ordered me to do the same. Love of life obliged me to comply. They cut the poor man's cords and made him run backwards and forwards. I heard the poor man's cries to Heaven for mercy: and at length, through extreme anguish and pain, he pitched himself into the flames and expired.[13]

On 12 August Loudoun sent Webb with 44 Foot and some of Lieutenant-Colonel John Bradstreet's boatmen to reinforce Oswego. Webb had scarcely reached the Great Carrying Place when he learned that Oswego had already fallen. Montcalm had learned from reconnaissance reports that the English forts around Oswego were weak and could be easily captured. Oswego itself was held by barely 700 utterly demoralised men. During the winter they had lived on half rations (two ounces of pork and eight ounces of bread per day), and were so weak from starvation, scurvy and dysentery they could hardly stand on guard. Now, undernourished and without proper shelter and pay, they were mutinous. 'Sick men lay on the bare ground, and even those who were not formally on the sick list, were incapable of physical exertion.'[14]

Montcalm had over 3,000 French regulars and Canadian militia, plus 250 Indians 'naked, painted, plumed and greased, stamping, whooping, brandishing lances and tomahawks, and performing the war dance to the thumping of the Indian drums'.[15] Ferrying his force across Lake Ontario by night, on 10 August Montcalm landed his army, well supplied with artillery, within half a league of Fort Ontario, one of the three forts at Oswego. Surprise was complete.

Colonel James Mercer, commandant at Oswego, realised that Fort Ontario was too weakly held by the remnants of 51 Foot and withdrew them to the main fort, Pepperell, held by Shirley's 50 Foot and a number of sailors, boatmen and labourers. On a hill a quarter of a mile away stood the unfinished stockade called New Oswego, Fort George, defended by Colonel Schuyler and 150 volunteers from New Jersey. Mercer desperately needed reinforcements, and sent messengers to the New York contingents to hurry to his aid. But the scouts were captured by Indians, taken to Montcalm and forced to divulge their information. Mercer held a council of war with his officers, and decided to hold out until the arrival of Montcalm's artillery would render further resistance useless.

When Montcalm had mounted his cannon, the shells crashed through the fort's timber and rotten masonry. His Canadian militia and Indian allies forded the river at night and worked their way behind the forts to cut off any retreat. Colonel Mercer, the heart of the defensive effort, was killed. The garrison became disheartened, increased by the tears and entreaties of the 120 women and children, and fear of the Indians, whose blood-curling yells could be heard above the din of battle.[16] After three days of battering, the garrison raised the white flag. Over 1,400 surrendered to the enemy, who fell to plundering, drunkenness and scalping. 'The capitulation terms were disgracefully violated, and to Montcalm's disgrace as a soldier,' reported the Black Watch's *Records*.

> Montcalm handed over more than 20 of the unfortunate prisoners to the Indians, as sacrifices to the 'spirits' (*manes*) of men of their tribe, who had fallen in battle. He tried, in vain, to exonerate his conduct, by alleging that the British soldiers had given drink to the Indians.[17]

A French engineer tried to explain away the acts of cruelty shown to the prisoners, who had surrendered and been offered the honours of war under the surrender terms. 'It is dreadful to make war with such people as the Indians, especially when they are drunk. In that condition nothing can check their fury,' he wrote.[18]

Having levelled the forts to the ground, the victors returned in triumph to Montreal, loaded with prisoners and booty. The captured regimental flags were hung in the cathedral and Te Deums sung in honour of victory. The British victory at Louisbourg 11 years earlier had been avenged, for the two regiments captured, named after Pepperell and Shirley, were the same two which had shared in that triumph. These two decimated regiments were struck off the roll of the British army.[19]

Vaudreuil, who had long planned an attack on Oswego, claimed the credit for the concept: Montcalm was credited with having carried to a successful conclusion his first experience of forest warfare. Louis XV struck a medal to commemorate the achievement, which was received in France with great joy.

The loss of Oswego (August 1756) was a great blow to the British forces. Webb hastily withdrew down the Mohawk River, alarmed by a report that the French were advancing on New York. Instead, Montcalm withdrew his 5,000 men to defend Ticonderoga. Loudoun was furious with Webb for his panic-stricken retreat, and ordered Winslow not to take any offensive action against the reinforced Ticonderoga. In fact, neither of the opposing generals made any further offensive moves, both sides watching each other across Lake George. Thus, the 1756 campaigning season in America ended in a stalemate.

The regular troops on both sides now settled in quarters for the winter of 1756–7. The French retained a strong garrison at Ticonderoga; their Canadian militia returned home. At Fort William Henry, Loudoun left 400 regulars of the 44 Foot, later joined by the 35 Foot (the Royal Sussex), newly arrived in America. At Fort Edward four companies of rangers were garrisoned and 500 regulars of the 48 Foot (Northamptonshire Regiment). The remainder of the regular units and three other regiments wintered at Albany, and the 42nd Foot (Black Watch) at Schenectady.[20] The provincial militia, as was their custom, returned home.

Only the Indians remained active, emboldened by the early French-Canadian success. Throughout the long winter months, for the second year running, they ravaged the North American borders with fire and tomahawk. New York, New Jersey, Pennsylvania, Maryland and Virginia tried to protect their frontiers with wooden forts and a chain of blockhouses. Manned by ill-disciplined volunteers, they proved inadequate to protect the isolated settlers and their families from the savage marauders seeking information, loot, scalps and prisoners.[21]

In England, the news of the surrender of Oswego after such an early capitulation was received with consternation and dismay. Horace Walpole wrote: 'The nation is in a ferment. Oswego, ten times more important than Minorca, has been annihilated.'[22] British military power was at its lowest ebb. Oswego marked a new phase of the war. Less and less would the struggle in North America be a matter of border forays, of the burning of settlements and Indian scalping parties. Instead, more and more the conflict became warfare on a larger scale; both mother countries would play a larger part, with more soldiers, more artillery and stronger fortifications. Increasingly, the war became a struggle between the regular battalions of France and Britain, the Canadian militia and the American provincials playing a subordinate or supporting role.[23]

The disastrous events of 1756 made Pitt's accession to power an inevitable necessity.[24] Braddock's defeat at Fort Duquesne, the loss of Oswego, the capture of Calcutta and the horrors of the Black Hole in India, and finally the loss of Minorca, the main British base in the Mediterranean, demanded a scapegoat to satisfy public anger. Newcastle was accused of lack of leadership and strategic acumen, and blamed for his half-hearted support of the colonies. 'To the dock with Newcastle, and the yard-arm with Byng,' cried the ballad-singers.[25] Admiral Byng had been sent to relieve the besieged island of Minorca, but after a half-hearted attempt had withdrawn to Gibraltar. He was court-martialled and found guilty not of cowardice but of neglect: of avoiding action rather than taking it. The king refused to use the royal pardon, so 'Byng was shot on his own quarter-deck, because Newcastle deserved to be hanged,' wrote Fortescue.[26] Voltaire commented that Byng was shot *pour encourager les autres*. New leaders and new initiatives were required.

George II refused to call the popular favourite Pitt to form a government, because of Pitt's opposition to continental subsidies and the sacrifice of British to Hanoverian interests. Instead, he called on Fox to form an administration. Pitt refused to work with Fox and, unable to approach the King directly, sought the support of Lady Yarmouth for his own list of ministers. The King was furious 'because he liked to pretend that she had no interest in State matters'.[27] On 4 December 1756 the King gave way, and replaced Newcastle with the fourth Duke of Devonshire. Pitt was appointed Secretary of State for the Southern Department (the colonies). But this compromise was short-lived, suiting neither court nor Commons. Finally, in June 1757, Newcastle was appointed First Lord of the Treasury, and accepted Pitt's dominant position in cabinet and Commons as Colonial Secretary, virtually the prime minister. Fox, withdrawing from contention, accepted the post of Paymaster General of the Forces. For the rest of the war he held this lucrative office, and contented himself with amassing a large fortune. The King reluctantly accepted 'a disagreeable situation'.

The post of managing the army, Secretary at War, George II gave to William Wildman, Viscount Barrington, a nominee of Newcastle. After completing his education with a 'grand tour' and marrying a wealthy widow, Barrington settled down at the War Office in 1755, with an office in the newly-opened Horse Guards in Whitehall. Close by were his colleagues, the army's commander-in-chief, the forces' paymaster, the judge advocate general, and the Board of Ordnance in Palace Yard, Westminster. Barrington was responsible for day-to-day military administration. Policy was decided by the Secretary of State for the Southern Department and Colonies in nearby Cleveland Row, who had a seat in the cabinet.

In charge of the Admiralty, as First Lord, was Lord George Anson, best known to posterity for his voyage round the world. The booty obtained on this voyage made Anson rich for life. In 1748 he had married Lady Elizabeth Yorke, daughter of the Lord Chancellor, the first Earl of Hardwicke (author of the 1753 Marriage Act, which ended the scandal of clandestine marriages in England and Wales). The marriage was 'the happiest event of his life', and brought Anson added wealth and influence with one of the great Whig dynasties. Pitt came to rely on the professional advice and expertise of his Admiral of the

Fleet, and his many years on the quarterdeck and at the Admiralty made him popular with the Navy and invaluable to the civil departments, especially in wartime. To Anson, Pitt owed the many improvements in the navy, in shipbuilding, dockyard administration and in naval supplies. He also reconstituted the existing marine regiments into the Royal Marines (1755), which by the end of the war would rise from 5,000 to 20,000 men. Orders from the Admiralty to the fleet bearing Anson's signature were accepted by the officers without query.[28] Much of the navy's success during the Seven Years' War was due to him.

Traditionally, Britain relied on her navy to defend her shores and protect her trade. In the War of the Austrian Succession and during the early years of the Seven Years' War, Admiralty policy had been to deploy squadrons piecemeal, which had resulted in a number of indecisive engagements. Under Pitt and Anson, Britain developed a strategy of 'engagement and blockade' to gain the maritime supremacy on which her colonial empire and national existence depended.

One of Pitt's first orders on taking office in December 1756 was to arrange with Anson for the immediate formation of a naval squadron for service in the English Channel. Brest and other ports were to be blockaded and the French battlefleets confined to port, thus preventing any French reinforcements being sent to the colonies. The British learned to rotate these blockading squadrons to keep up the pressure. If a French fleet dared to venture out of port, as, for instance, to attempt an invasion of Britain, commanders like Boscawen at Lagos and Hawke at Quiberon Bay (1759) would seek them out and destroy them. Keeping a strong naval squadron in the Channel became the bedrock of British strategy. 'The defence of America was secured in the Channel and in the Strait of Gibraltar' became a maxim of Naval historians.[29]

12

PITT TAKES CHARGE

Every great war has produced at least one dominant personality, whose genius helped to decide the issue. The Second World War produced Winston Churchill; the French and Indian War produced William Pitt, Earl of Chatham. By the force of his own abilities, and his extraordinary popularity with the common people, he dominated the English political stage in the 18th century.[1]

William Pitt (1708–78) was a commoner who did not possess the social standing to hold the nation's supreme post. Trade was despised in the highest circles, and Pitt's grandfather had founded the family fortune by trade in India. So on 4 December 1756 the King appointed the Duke of Devonshire to form the government, with Pitt as Secretary for the Colonies and leader of the House of Commons. Newcastle was First Lord of the Treasury. 'I know that I can save the country, and that no one else can' was Pitt's ultimatum to parliament when it met at the end of the year. The nation listened to his passionate, if arrogant, oratory, and trusted him.

The King, in his address to the House, declared that 'the success and preservation of America' would be the main object of his attention and solicitude.[2] Pitt, promoted to the virtual command of the forces of the crown, the colonies, and foreign affairs, promised this policy of making America the main theatre of war would be carried out with 'a new resolution of vigour and dispatch' in 1757. The thousands of mercenary Hanoverian and Hessian troops, awkwardly strutting around the streets of London, would be sent home: instead, a national militia would be recruited to be responsible for home defence in the event of a French invasion: the regular army would be freed from such duties for service overseas. More regular troops would be recruited and sent to the colonies.

Before the end of December, Pitt wrote a private letter to Loudoun:

To assure you of the thorough satisfaction your conduct has given me, and I will not fail to support you to the utmost of my power through the many difficulties, you find in the executing of your orders. Nothing can be worse than our situation here at home, without any plan, or even a desire to have one: great numbers talked of to be sent you, but without any consideration of how, and from whence, without considering what they should carry with them.[3]

In January 1757, Pitt ordered seven regiments from Britain to be made ready to attack the French fortress of Louisbourg, which commanded the sea approaches to the St Lawrence and the heart of New France.[4] Six regiments would be drawn from Ireland, the seventh from England. In addition, Pitt arranged for an adequate siege train and supplies to be assembled at Plymouth.

Pitt's programme for raising the new regiments was put into immediate effect. Fifteen foot regiments each raised second battalions, which were later given regimental status and numbered 61 to 75 Foot respectively. A dozen years earlier the Jacobite rebellion had found support among the Highland clansmen of Scotland. Now Pitt enlisted two Highland regiments, 77 Foot, raised by Archibald Montgomery, later Earl of Eglinton, and 78 Foot by Simon Fraser, whose father had made him join the Jacobite army in 1746 at the head of his clan and afterwards was pardoned by the King. Thus commenced the 'glorious record in the British army of the men, who marched in kilts to the wild music of the bagpipes'. 'By putting arms into their hands, Pitt converted the mutinous subjects (which Culloden could not subdue) into loyal subjects'. During the Seven Years' War, those hardy and intrepid men would 'serve with fidelity as they fought with valour, and conquered for you in every part of the world,' boasted Pitt.[5]

With little more than 30,000 regulars and another 19,000 allocated to the colonies, it was necessary to increase the home militia ('mouths without hands, maintained at vast expense; in peace a charge, in war a weak defence,' according to Dryden[6]) to meet the needs of home defence and threats of a French invasion, and release more regulars for overseas service. The nation was stirred with a military ardour not felt since the Civil War, wrote Fortescue,[7] and there was a rush for commissions in the army (see the illustration of anti-French propaganda).

But Pitt's position was by no means secure. The king could make and unmake ministers. In April 1757 George II dismissed Pitt because his son, the Duke of Cumberland, the army's commander-in-chief and commanding the troops in Hanover, would not work with him. Though the King and the House of Commons were ready to keep Pitt out of office, the nation demanded his return. Stocks fell, and London voted him the freedom of the city. Finally, after a ministerial interregnum of 11 weeks, Newcastle came back as prime minister to manage the House of Commons 'by peddling civil and ecclesiastical patronage', and gave Pitt a free hand to carry on the prosecution of the war.[8] Thus in July 1757 was created the great ministry which for four years would lead the nation to victory.

While Britain was deciding its political leaders, France concluded the second Treaty of Versailles with Austria (1 May 1757). Louis XV promised to employ an army of 100,000 men in Germany, and to pay very large subsidies to Austria, Sweden and Saxony. There was to be no peace, until Maria Theresa had recovered Silesia, in return for which Austria would cede part of the Netherlands to France. Pitt's reply would be the unsuccessful expedition in September against Rochefort.

To decide his war strategy, Pitt studied meticulously the reports on the military situation in the American colonies. A major source of information on the New World was the Board of Trade and Plantations, with its collection of books, maps, reports, pamphlets and letters from merchants, proprietors, foreign settlers and colonial governors around the world. Here, too, came the Commissioners of Customs or of the Treasury, or the Lords of the Admiralty, to gather or leave information concerning their departments.[9] Pitt studied with minute care the scene of every operation, knew the roads and streams, with their rapids, which the troops must use, the ships and routes needed, and the stores and equipment required. This information, together with the advice of Field Marshal Ligonier, his army commander-in-chief (who succeeded the Duke of Cumberland), and Admiral George Anson, formed the substance of his detailed directions to commanders, both military and naval, and of the military contracts issued.

Pitt became even more convinced that France must be expelled from the North American continent, an objective which called for the unrestricted expenditure of British resources, both financial and military. The colonies needed regular regiments to do the fighting, and the British navy to dominate the Atlantic and the approaches to the St Lawrence. British money was needed to finance the campaigns; the American assemblies would have to provide the supplies. And the need was urgent![10]

Loudoun's plan of operations for 1757 involved an expedition to capture Quebec as the principal objective. Instead, Pitt wrote: 'Your Lordship is directed to begin with an Attack upon Louisburgh, and to proceed, in the next Place, to Quebec. The King judges the Taking of Louisburgh to be the more practical Enterprise.'[11] He reasoned that Louisbourg, 180 miles nearer to Quebec than Halifax, was the better harbour from which the British navy could operate against the Gulf of St Lawrence. Pitt ordered that as many regiments as possible should be sent to Nova Scotia, and announced that he would send there a powerful fleet and another 8,000 men. With 17,000 regular soldiers already in the colonies, he considered Loudoun would have a strong enough force to capture the fortress, before a main attack on Quebec later in the summer.

Accordingly, Loudoun assembled in New York an army of 5,500 regulars, whom he planned would join up with Pitt's reinforcements when they arrived in Halifax – chosen for the rendezvous for the attack on Louisbourg. With Governor Lawrence of Nova Scotia, Loudoun assembled at Halifax stores for 12,000 men for six months. He felt obliged to take with him General James Abercromby to command the expedition in the event of his death, but found, when he arrived, that Pitt had added Generals Peregrine Hopson and Lord

Charles Hay to his staff. General Webb, whose illness from palsy during the spring of 1757 rendered him timid and ineffective, Loudoun planned to leave behind at Albany. He would also leave behind Colonel George Monro of the 35 Foot, John Young of the 60th Royal Americans, and 5,000 troops to man the essential garrisons on the New York frontier and protect the areas of Lake George and the Hudson River.

During the winter of 1756–7, Vaudreuil too had been making his plans for the 1757 campaigning season. He decided his next objectives would be the capture of Fort William Henry at the end of Lake George, and Fort Edward on the Hudson. These two garrisons protected New York. He feared Loudoun would use these forts as bases for an attack on Carillon (Ticonderoga) and Fort Frédéric (Crown Point) on Lake Champlain – the covering defences of Montreal. In February, Vaudreuil sent his brother Rigaud with 1,500 men, well equipped for a winter expedition, to probe the Fort William Henry defences and spoil any English offensive preparations. Rigaud burned more than 300 boats on Lake George, stores, a hospital, and some outhouses, before withdrawing six days later.

When spring came, Loudoun was still at New York awaiting the arrival from England of Pitt's promised reinforcements. Pitt had asked for an early April start for the Louisbourg expedition, so the powerful British fleet under Admiral Francis Holbourne could block the St Lawrence to prevent French reinforcements, and deter Montcalm from striking a blow elsewhere. But Holbourne's fleet was delayed in assembling the regiments and supplies. On 20 June, unable to wait any longer, Loudoun sailed for New York, risking a French attack on his unescorted transports. Fortunately, he met up with Holbourne's fleet *en route*.

Meanwhile, Pitt was raising and assembling his new regiments. On 3 February 1757 the adjutant-general sent an order to the officer commanding 43 Foot stationed at Galway in Ireland:

> His Majesty has been pleased to direct the second battalion of his first and Royal Regiment of Foot (58 Foot), and also the 17, 27, 28, 43 and 46 regiments of Foot, to prepare for foreign service and march ... to Cork, where they are to embark on board such transport vessels as the Lords of the Admiralty shall send for that purpose. The said regiments shall recruit and raise, as far as time will permit, in and near their present quarters, and on the march to the said place of embarkation, and in and near Cork and Kingsale, as many able-bodied men as will be sufficient to complete their respective corps. The above six regiments are to carry with them their tents and camp equipage.[12]

The 55 Regiment, quartered at Galway, received similar orders.

One of those ordered to embark was Captain John Knox, whose marriage in 1751 to a wealthy woman in Cork had enabled him to purchase a commission as an ensign in the 43 Foot. In his famous journal of the four-year campaign in North America to the fall of Montreal, he wrote:

> The officials and population of Cork received the troops with great generosity. Instead of raising prices, they gave of their best at the lowest prices. Considerable sums of money were raised by voluntary subscriptions to enable those poor distressed women, not permitted to accompany their husbands overseas, to return to their respective countries: and such of the soldiers' children, as their mothers could be prevailed upon to part with (instead of accompanying them overseas), were happily provided for at the public expense.[13]

Elsewhere, Knox states that six women per company per regiment were officially recognised in America for rations 'in like manner and proportion as the men', from the day the regiments embarked in Ireland until the middle of December 1758, 'at which time they were struck off rations by order of General Hopson' (officer commanding the embarkation) for operational reasons. It was the custom for these six places 'to go overseas' to be decided by ballot, preference being given to those without children, or, at least, no more than one.[14]

The fleet, under Admiral Holbourne, sailed from Cork on 8 May 1757 bound for Halifax, capital of Nova Scotia. With dreadful storms and fog, the voyage lasted almost eight weeks. Knox wrote:

> Every Sunday the duty of Chaplain was performed by an Army Officer, on deck when the weather permitted, and was very decently attended by the greatest part of the men and women on board. The master of our ship, a very sober, moral man, always attended divine service with great devotion, but if the attention of the helmsman was diverted from his duty, and consequently the ship yawed in the wind, our son of Neptune interrupted our prayers with some of the ordinary profane language of the common sailors, which immediately following a response of the Litany, made us laugh.[15]

As fast as transports arrived at Halifax, the soldiers disembarked and established their camp. The men were employed on clearing and levelling the ground, and practising landings and attacks. A body of rangers under the command of Captain Robert Rogers marched out every day from Forts Edward and William Henry to scour the countryside. 'These light troops,' wrote Knox,[16] 'had no particular uniform at present: they only wore their clothes short, and are armed with a firelock, tomahawk and scalping knife, and carry a bullock's horn full of powder.' Their officers usually carried a small compass fixed in the bottom of their powder-horns to guide them in close country.

Loudoun took with him to Halifax two battalions of the 60th Foot, the Royal Americans. The 2nd Battalion was commanded by Frederick Haldiman, a Swiss who had begun his career under 'my old master', Frederick the Great. Haldiman would serve in North America for 20 years, becoming Governor of Canada, and honoured with a tablet in Henry VII's chapel in Westminster Abbey.[17] The specialist light infantry, the Royal Americans, were joined in Halifax by 22, 42 and 46 Foot. All together, Loudoun had an army of 11,000, nearly all regulars, ready to sail for Louisbourg. They would be divided into three brigades under Hopson, Abercromby and Lord Charles Hay, with the reserve under Charles Lawrence, and a detachment of 370 Royal Artillery under Lieutenant-Colonel George Williamson.

As the army waited impatiently to set sail, it was in great spirit. There were a few of the usual disciplinary cases. For example, on 19 July, a general court martial condemned two men to death for desertion; they were executed the next morning. 'Both died very penitent,' reported Knox, 'acknowledging the justice of their punishment.' Most of all, the British soldiers dreaded the tomahawks and scalping knives of the Indians, who frequently preyed on the camp disguised as wild animals. At the end of July four sailors, who had wandered out of the camp contrary to orders, were captured by an Indian raiding party. Two were scalped and two carried off as prisoners – probably for information, speculated Knox.[18]

Warfare to the Indians was not just a desire for revenge or loot, or to replace deceased persons in the tribe. They were trained from youth as warriors and hunters to inure themselves to hunger, pain and fatigue, and war was also a means of demonstrating courage, endurance and martial skills. These characteristics were recorded by the French as early as 1609, when Champlain joined an expedition of the Hurons against the Iroquois, their deadly enemies.[19] Warfare followed a ritual, from the raising of the war-party and frenzied dancing around the village campfire, to the insistent beating of drums, their faces painted and naked limbs glistening with sweat, to the rush to grapple with the foe, and to the ultimate torture and killing of prisoners:

> The Indians lit a fire, from which each took a brand and burned their prisoner without pity, and at intervals threw water on him to prolong the agony. Next, they tore out his nails and put live coals on his raw flesh and *membrum virile*. Then they scalped him, and poured drops of melted gum upon his head, which forced piteous cries from the poor wretch. Others made incisions in his arms near the wrists and forced out the sinews with sticks shoved underneath. In victory, other prisoners were reserved to satisfy the women, who add yet others to these horrible tortures, so pitiless and without mercy. In this way they pass several days with dances and songs.

Marc Lescarbot, a French lawyer and voyager who accompanied Poutrincourt from 1606–7, described these manners and customs of the Indians in the first *Histoire de la Nouvelle France* in 1609.

> In warfare, they kill all who can resist but pardon the women and children, cut off their hair as a sign of inferiority and contempt, make them slaves or purchase their liberty. The scalps, which they dry or tan, make trophies in their cabins or are hung about the necks of their women as a precious jewel. They have a custom, too, of fattening prisoners, giving them for bed companions to the fairest maidens, and then eating them.[20]

Loudoun applied the Mutiny Act to the British army in North America for disciplinary purposes. He issued warrants for the convening of general courts martial, which tried officer cases and the most serious military crimes, such as theft, mutiny, desertion and sleeping on guard duty, for which the death penalty was usually awarded. These courts also heard cases on appeal from the regimental courts martial, which dealt with lesser offences. Loudoun signed death warrants, and exercised the royal clemency where appropriate. The provost staff acted as arresting officers and executioners.[21]

Deserters were seldom shot or hanged for first offences: soldiers were too precious. Instead, cat-o'-nine-tails lashings were awarded. James Grayer of the 45 Foot, for example, received 500 of his 1,000 lashes on his bare back the day after his sentence for desertion had been awarded – 100 at the head of the paraded 22 Foot, 100 at the head of the 2nd Battalion, Royal Americans, and 100 lashes at each of the 48, 57 and 55 Foot regiments. The remainder of the sentence was to be carried out 'when the sergeant of the regiment thinks him able to bear it'. Loudoun often reduced a sentence, and sometimes remitted it altogether. An officer's sentence was usually dismissal from the service for conduct unbecoming an officer and a gentleman.[22]

The army women, as camp followers, were subject to the same military law, which was frequently read out to them on parade with the men so that all knew the regulations, especially as many, probably the majority, could not read.[23] Army women, both wives and female camp-followers, were placed under the responsibility of the provost staff in camp and on the line of march.

Compared with British military punishments, those meted out to provincial troops by their commanders, at least during the first three years of the war, were much more lenient. Usually, they took the form of admonishments. Corporal punishments were seldom inflicted: provincial soldiers were horrified at the savage whippings and executions exacted on British redcoats. But in 1757, when Loudoun established a fully combined command, the full provisions of the Mutiny Act were applied to regular and provincial soldier alike. Provincial officers, however, tended to award less severe sentences, seldom more than 200-300 lashes; most were less than 50.[24]

At the beginning of August 1757 all was set for the Louisbourg expedition to sail.

13

THE MASSACRE
AT FORT WILLIAM HENRY

L ined up in Halifax's splendid harbour, which today is acknowledged to be the world's second largest natural harbour, was a powerful fleet of 18 warships, a dozen frigates and 200 transports. Three weeks of persistent fog and unfavourable winds prevented the expedition from sailing. But on 4 August 1757, escorted by naval ships, the packed transports and freight-ships, heavily laden with siege equipment, finally weighed anchor.

Off the coast a French schooner was intercepted, bound from Cape Breton for France. The skipper pretended to throw a packet overboard, but a thorough search of the ship revealed a small bag hidden under a pile of dried fish. It contained letters addressed to the French Minister of Marine,[1] announcing the arrival in Canada of three squadrons of 18 warships, five frigates, and two regular battalions of French troops. The garrison of 3,000 men, supported by an army of 4,000 and a powerful fleet, was so superior to Admiral Francis Holbourne's resources that to pursue his attack on Louisbourg was futile. Furthermore, the season was now too far advanced for the assault to be certain of success, and a disastrous hurricane dispersed his fleet with heavy losses.

On 24 September the expedition was abandoned, and the ships and troops returned to New York. Pitt[2] unfairly blamed Loudoun – 'like St George on the inn signboards, Loudoun was always on horseback but never advancing' – when he signalled the recall of his commander-in-chief. 'Loudoun was so engrossed in schemes for improving the condition of his men, that he seemed to have no time for employing them against the enemy,' wrote Archibald Forbes of the Black Watch.[3] Delays had led to the failure of the Louisbourg expedition – delays which would also be responsible indirectly for Montcalm's success at Fort William Henry.

Taking advantage of Loudoun's inactivity at Halifax and the known British weakness in the area of Lake Champlain, Montcalm decided to strike. On 30 July he moved south from Fort Carillon (Ticonderoga), with 4,000 troops (half regulars, half Canadian militia) and 2,000 Indians drawn from a number of different tribes. They were lured by hopes of loot, scalps, drink, prisoners to be taken and sold, 'and the chance to teach their young men how to carve up a human being destined for the pot. I shiver at the frightful spectacle, which they are preparing for us,' wrote Bougainville in a letter to his brother.[4]

Montcalm's destination was Fort William Henry. Bradley[5] graphically described the scene. The surface of the lake was ruffled by the splash of thousands of oars and hundreds of Indian paddles: 250 boats carried 4,000 men, and swarms of savages in bark canoes glided in the van. The cream of French Canadian chivalry was there, and six famous regiments from Old France, with officers and men now hardened by American campaigning – the *troupes de terre* of Béarn, La Sarre, Guienne, Languedoc, La Reine and Royal Roussillon. Nearly all the available force for resisting them lay in the two forts, William Henry and Edward, situated at either end of the 14-mile carrying stage between Lake George and the Hudson River.

Fort William Henry, square in shape with corner bastions, was constructed of hewn logs, the intervals between the logs filled with packed earth, sand and gravel. It mounted 17 cannon.[6] Like many similar forts, it was impregnable to rifle fire but a poor defence against artillery. At best it could delay but not withstand a determined assault. The fort stood at the head of the lake, close to the water's edge. On the left were two stretches of marshland, separated by a low, flat, rocky hill on which stood an entrenched camp, some 600 yards (550 metres) away. Beside the camp ran the road to Fort Edward. Three sides were protected by V-shaped ditches and log fascines; the north by the lake and a steep bank. As there was not enough room for the whole garrison within the fort, the bulk of the provincial troops were stationed in the entrenched camp on the hill.

The 2,800-man garrison consisted of 600 regulars of the 35 Foot, 100 Royal Americans, 100 New York Independent Company, 800 provincials from Massachusetts, 750 militiamen from New York, New Hampshire and New Jersey, and 140 rangers, with some 250 provincial officers.[7] The British regulars were accompanied by their women and children, and there were some Mohawk scouts. In command of Fort William Henry was Lieutenant-Colonel George Monro of the 35 Foot.

When the attack began on 3 August it was clear that, unless it was speedily relieved before Montcalm could bring up his cannon, the fall of Fort William Henry was only a matter of time. General Daniel Webb, the military commander of the region and colonel of the 48 Foot, was at his headquarters in Fort Edward with 2,000 men, mostly newly-raised militia. Believing he was facing 11,000 French troops, he had requested urgent reinforcements from New York, and on 9 August, the day Monro surrendered, 3,300 militia arrived – too late to intervene.[8] But faced by Montcalm's superiority, he advised Monro to surrender if necessary on the best possible terms.[9] Unfortunately, this letter had been intercepted by Montcalm's scouts. Having read it, Montcalm sent it on its way. Monro replied that it was his duty to hold the fort for as long as he could – and, dying early in November, spent the last two months of his life cursing

Webb for having left Fort William Henry to its fate.[10]

By 8 August the position of the besieged was desperate. Sorties from the entrenched camp, and another from the fort, had been repulsed. More than 300 men had been killed or wounded. Smallpox was raging and the casemates were crowded with the sick. One hundred and fifty head of cattle belonging to the garrison had been captured by the Indians. Most of the fort's cannon had been smashed by the French bombardment at 200-yards range. Ammunition was running low, the walls were breached, and an assault was imminent. Two offers of surrender terms had been rejected, and the men, without rest for five nights, were exhausted and barely able to keep awake.

On the morning of 9 August, after a council of war had unanimously advised capitulation, a white flag was raised. An emissary went to Montcalm's tent to ask for honourable terms. Montcalm did not want prisoners: he could barely feed his own men. It was agreed that the troops would be allowed to march out with the honours of war (drums beating, colours flying, and all ranks retaining their arms and baggage),[11] and that they would be escorted to Fort Edward by a French regular detachment. The terms also specified that they should not bear arms against France for 18 months, and that 'all French officers, soldiers, Canadians, women and Indians' held by the British should be handed over at Ticonderoga within three months.[12] The sick and wounded English, who could not be transported to Fort Edward, would be in Montcalm's care, and all stores and artillery were to be left behind.

The Indians, summoned to the tent, had the terms explained to them by interpreters, and agreed the conditions, despite being earlier 'flattered with great hopes of plunder and scalps'. Were the French naive in believing the Indians understood and accepted terms which were alien to their culture, or were they unable to control them? Montcalm must have known what had happened at Oswego the year before, and should have taken adequate precautions to protect the defenceless garrison.

The soldiers evacuated the fort with the women and children, and marched to join their comrades in the entrenched camp, also included in the surrender terms. As soon as they left the fort a crowd of Indians clambered through the embrasures in search of rum and plunder. Soon cries arose from the sick, unable to leave their beds: all 87 were butchered. Unable to find much loot, the Indians rejoined their comrades around the entrenched camp, complaining bitterly the French had deceived and betrayed them. 'Only the bayonets of the 35 Foot stood between the Indians and the terrified women and children,' records the official history of the regiment.[13] Montcalm posted a guard of 200 French regulars inside the entrenched camp. As the Indians searched the tents, toying with the long hair of the frightened women and menacing anyone who tried to intervene, the situation turned nasty. Montcalm and his officers used threats and entreaties to hold them back, and announced the English would leave the camp at first light. After the Indians had been cleared from the camp, Montcalm left at about 9pm.[14]

After a troubled night, during which an attempt was made to march the garrison out of the camp, to the fury of the Indians, the real horror began, as the garrison apprehensively marched out at dawn. Despite the French escort of 450 regulars ordered to conduct the troops in safety to Fort Edward, and in full sight of the French army, the Indians 'fell upon the poor fellows with the most barbarous rage'. Baggage, especially that of the officers, was seized, rum demanded; anyone who resisted was stripped of clothing and equipment, and scalped.[15] Seventeen wounded men had been put in the charge of the French surgeon. They were taken out of their tents, killed and scalped, in front of the horrified surgeon and soldiers of the colonial regiments. The French pickets posted nearby did nothing to stop them.[16]

There were 2,500 men pledged not to fight Frenchmen or their allies, writes the historian Ian Steele,[17] and dozens of women, children, and other camp-followers, whose position had not been specified in the capitulation. It was one thing to trust French honour, quite another to assume that all the Indians were aware of the terms and would not take them literally. Even without Indian anger, desire for revenge or drunkenness, what could the English on parole expect from warriors who had spent weeks canoeing 1,000 miles to fight for martial trophies that were their only pay, symbols of esteem and for some the entry to manhood? Neither age nor sex was spared. Women and children, who were in the rear of the column and so most vulnerable, were murdered and scalped on the spot, or dragged off to the forest as prisoners.

Montcalm, Lévis and Bourlamaque were in their quarters. As soon as they heard the uproar, they rushed to the scene. 'Interpreters, officers, priests, Canadians, all made strenuous efforts to save them. But the savages, drunk with blood, rum and homicide, would listen to no one.'[18] Montcalm reminded them of their pledge, but it was too late. Hundreds of warriors, emerging from their camp (a chain of tribal camp-fires) astride the Fort Edward road, and seeing the scalps, plunder and prisoners taken in the entrenchment camp, went seeking their share.[19] All the French guards were prepared to do was urge the besieged to flee to the woods, back to the fort, or anywhere that promised an asylum. The Indians chased after them to capture prisoners, many of whom were later bought back by French officers. Bougainville, who did not witness the massacre, was in Montreal, when a party of Indians and 200 English captives reached the town. Many of the prisoners were ransomed by the Canadians, who also bought the plunder from the Indians with kegs of brandy.

The escorted garrison was expected at Fort Edward, and General Webb had arranged for a guard of 500 men to meet the supposedly protected column. Instead they met the first of the terrified soldiers, fleeing for their lives, 'mostly stript of their Shirts and Breeches'. Later a larger group, 'a part of the remains of the Army, arrived in the most distressing Situation,' recorded Colonel Webb.[20] They told horrific tales of the massacre of the men, women, children and wounded, and of the stampede for loot and prisoners. Some 600 men, but only ten of the 80 or more women, reached Fort Edward. A week later Montcalm arranged for 500 of the missing soldiers, wives, servants and sutlers to be heavily escorted to Fort Edward by 400 French grenadiers and Canadian volunteers.[21] In the following months, others returned to the colonies from Montreal or Indian villages, where they had been sold by the Indians or were redeemed by Montcalm and others, who returned them via Boston and Louisbourg. The final figures of killed and missing will never be known.[22]

Fort William Henry was demolished; then, with the corpses, it was set on fire. The mighty funeral pyre blazed all night. The noise and confusion of the 10,000 combatants, and all the rage, terror and agony, disappeared. No living thing remained, save wolves coming down from the mountains to feast on the remains.[23]

The memory of the massacre did not die, and would have its effect on the campaign. From that time onwards, recorded the regimental historian of the battalion most concerned, the 35 Foot would fling themselves upon their foes with a cry for vengeance – 'Remember Fort William Henry!'[24] Nine months after the massacre, all the paroled officers of the regiment petitioned General Abercromby to be allowed to join in the attack on Louisbourg.[25] Abercromby informed all the British units serving in America, and Governor Vaudreuil, that the capitulation terms were considered null and void because of the 'murdering, pillaging and captivating of many of His Majesty's good subjects'.[26] Amherst, the future commander-in-chief, was outraged, especially at the murder of women and children. He would cite the Indian massacre at Fort William Henry as a reason for denying French troops the honours of war at Louisbourg, and later when Montreal capitulated. Loudoun blamed the atrocities on the French court at Versailles, and on Montcalm and Vaudreuil, as part of a more general policy of 'barbarities', committed by their Indian allies and permitted by the French, to spread fear and terror along the colonial frontiers.

Montcalm, as commander, was blamed for his failure to take adequate steps to prevent such a crime, despite his valiant attempts to save the survivors. 'It is with great difficulty, that we can restrain the Indians of the far West, the most ferocious of all men and cannibals by trade,' wrote Bougainville before the siege.[27] The horror and indignation were felt in Britain and America as violations of accepted conventions by the French, but typical of Indian savages. Historians have tended to rationalise the massacre according to the national views of the British, American, Canadian, French and Indian participants. 'The massacre at Fort William Henry was too useful an atrocity, not to be exploited as a weapon of psychological warfare,' claims one historian.[28] It was certainly a blot on Montcalm's reputation.

After the capture and demolition of Fort William Henry, General Webb daily expected Montcalm to push forward and attack him at Fort Edward. Vaudreuil ordered Montcalm to do so. But Johnson with a band of Mohawk Indians rushed to Webb's assistance, while provincial militia levies poured into the fort. Montcalm knew his supply system was inadequate to venture further: his militiamen were anxious to return home, enjoy their booty, and bring in the harvest – desperately needed by the inhabitants and French troops, despite food supplies arriving from France. He may also have believed Quebec would be attacked in his absence. Whatever the reasons, Montcalm withdrew to Montreal.[29] Loudoun breathed a sigh of relief, for many British and colonials believed that, if Fort Edward had fallen, the way to Albany and New York would have been wide open.

At the end of the 1757 campaigning season, Lord Loudoun settled his troops in their winter quarters. Most were allocated to New York and the Albany areas.[30] The 28 and 43 Foot were garrisoned under Colonel Lawrence in the Bay of Fundy. The 2/1 Foot, 40, 45, 47 and 78 Foot (Fraser's Highlanders) camped under General Hopson at Halifax. Colonel John Stanwix was placed in command of the 4th Battalion Royal Americans and Montgomery's Highlanders (77 Foot), and provincials from Virginia, North Carolina and Pennsylvania, together with the independent companies. Their task was to guard the frontiers of Pennsylvania, Georgia and South Carolina. Before barracks could be built to house the influx of British regiments, many soldiers were quartered in private houses without the owners' consent. The British Mutiny Act was considered sufficient authority.[31]

Conditions for quartering in North America were very different from Britain, and Loudoun's measures caused much anger. Public houses were few; only single-roomed grog shops were available, and the cost of food was much higher than in Britain. In Pennsylvania, for instance, the men stricken with smallpox in Bouquet's battalion of the Royal Americans (60 Foot) 'had to lie on straw in rooms unwarmed by fire'.[32] There was no parliamentary or local assembly legislation to cover quartering in the colonies, so Loudoun made his own regulations, justified by the 'war emergency'. He ordered that officers and men should be quartered, either in public or private houses, at the expense of the colonial assemblies, who could construct barracks as an alternative. If they refused, he threatened he would use force, or increase their quotas.[33]

Loudoun's biggest quartering problem was in Albany, the centre of his military operations and administration, and the home of Dutch fur traders. In 1756 Albany's 330 families had been forced, much against their will, to provide shelter for some 150 officers and 1,450 men. In 1757, when Loudoun's much enlarged army went into winter quarters, eight regiments had to be accommodated in New York county, and three in Albany town itself.[34] Albany's newly-constructed barracks was impressive, with a main block, stone cellars, and windows of glass. The barrack rooms were furnished with double beds, each sleeping four men, head to toe, and provided with tables and chairs. But until they were completed in November 1757, Loudoun was compelled to quarter some 1,300 soldiers and their womenfolk on the town, pressing into use the Dutch church and the town gaol.

Loudoun moved his own quarters from his house in Whitehall to the security of the governor's house in Fort George, New York. On 30 November he joined the St Andrew's Society at the King's Arms for a Scottish ball, where 'there was scarcely ever before, so great a number of elegantly dressed fine Women seen together at one Place in North America'.[35] The fourth Earl Loudoun was one of the 16 representative peers of Scotland, and thus the principal guest of honour. Scottish officers almost outnumbered the English officers in America, and 'a great many of His Majesty's Officers, several of the highest rank, were invited, who had never before seen a public Company of Ladies in this Part of the World,' reported a local newspaper.

Present, too, was John Appy, Loudoun's secretary and judge advocate of the forces, whose family had been driven into exile from France by the revocation of the Edict of Nantes in 1698. Like many other French Huguenots, he had taken refuge in London, where Loudoun had recruited him to his staff. In London, Appy had spent much of his time with other young bloods among the taverns and bagnios of Charing Cross and Covent Garden, 'in pursuit of ladies euphemistically described as more fair than honest'; they would take the ladies by chair-hire to Ranelagh Gardens, and the playhouse at Drury Lane.[36] According to Appy's own account, he saw at Drury Lane the famous Irish actress Peg Woffington, who took the town by storm, masquerading as a boy 'in breeches parts'. She was said to have been 'the handsomest woman that ever appeared on the stage, courted, caressed, and sought after by all ranks'. He also saw there Mistress Bellamy, General Braddock's lady friend,[37] who was stabbed on the stage by Peg during a quarrel 'almost in sight of the audience'.

A week after the St Andrew's ball, on 7 December, Appy married at Trinity Church, New York, Elizabeth, stepdaughter of the deputy paymaster in North America, Abraham Mortier, like Appy of French Huguenot extraction. Leaving New York on his honeymoon, he narrowly escaped a fire at Fort George, which that evening destroyed most of the barracks and stores, due to the carelessness of tailors working in one of the rooms.

With winter upon them, the French would also have problems. Two successive harvests had been poor, provision ships from France had been intercepted, food was scarce and the people were hungry. Even the French troops were reduced to eating horse-flesh.[38] Only the skill and tact of Lévis averted a general mutiny. Their Indian allies were afflicted with smallpox, caught from digging up and scalping enemy bodies like that of the Ranger captain, Richard Rogers, who had died of the disease just before the siege of Fort William Henry. This was 'God's revenge for the killings', noted Jonathan Carver, a Massachusetts' soldier who had witnessed the massacre.[39] The French Canadian administration was proving corrupt, and war profiteering was widespread. 'What a country,' wrote Montcalm to his beloved wife, 'where knaves grow rich and honest men are ruined.'[40]

Nevertheless 1757 had been a successful year for the French, both at home and abroad. In Europe, Britain and Prussia stood alone against the mighty coalition of France, Austria, Russia and Sweden. The French had invaded Hanover, defeated the Duke of Cumberland at Hastenbeck, and forced him to surrender his Hanoverian and Hessian army, supported by British subsidies. To divert French resources from America and Hanover, Pitt had launched an amphibious attack on Rochefort. The port was too well garrisoned and the expedition failed. These forces might have enabled Loudoun to take Louisbourg or hold Fort William Henry.

In Quebec and Montreal the winter festivities of 1757–8 carried on as usual. Sleighing and skating were popular pastimes on the frozen St Lawrence and in the snow-covered forests. In Quebec 'there were always soldiers about and romantic fur traders coming in from the interior'. As it was the seat of government and the home of the king's representatives, the governor and the intendant, a smart and raffish society had grown up – a pale imitation of Paris. According to contemporary accounts,[41] Montcalm's officers enjoyed the social rounds, and were continually falling victims to the charms of Canadian ladies 'more adapted for husband-catching than for intellectual pursuits'. What chiefly upset Montcalm was that most of these young ladies 'were comparatively dowerless', poor prizes for French *noblesse!* Governor Vaudreuil, on the other hand, encouraged these liaisons with an eye to possible settlers and an increase in the married population of his native Canada.

Montreal was smaller and probably duller, more of a frontier community, and more commercial than Quebec. But neither had natural resources, except furs, which could be exploited and turned into transportable wealth. Both had the usual marks of Latin civilisation – 'churches, schools, convents, monasteries and officials'. And a road had been completed to link them by land as well as by water.[42]

By the end of the year, Loudoun's position as commander-in-chief of the British forces was untenable. Pitt wanted success with new blood, and Loudoun was recalled – to enjoy the lady friends he had left in London! He ended his days, unmarried, as governor of Edinburgh and Stirling castle and colonel of the Third Foot Guards. He was a victim of circumstances beyond his control. Surgeon Huck served throughout the French and Indian War, greatly to the medical benefit of the troops. He married in later life the niece and heiress of

Admiral Sir Charles Saunders, commanding the British navy at Quebec. From him Huck acquired a large fortune, and assumed the admiral's family name and armorial bearings as Richard Huck Saunders. His two daughters married into the peerage.[43]

14

LOUISBOURG ATTACKED
AGAIN – THE PREPARATIONS

The failure of the 1757 expedition to Louisbourg was largely caused by delay. Pitt, as Secretary of State responsible for campaign planning and troop movements, determined there would be no such mistakes in 1758. The plans to attack Louisbourg and Quebec had already been made, since it was customary to make strategic plans for the ensuing year during the late autumn. Campaigns were fought in the summer months, and dispatches took months to reach distant theatres of war. But new commanders and additional troops were required, and another fleet prepared to watch Toulon and Rochefort, to prevent the French navy from interfering in American operations.

Pitt wanted new and younger officers to command his 1758 campaign, with priority being given to the Louisbourg expedition. In Loudoun's place as temporary commander-in-chief, Pitt appointed General James Abercromby, a well-meaning 'copy-book' soldier of 52, who was specifically instructed to lead the attack on Ticonderoga in person. For the Louisbourg expedition, Pitt accepted the wise counsel of the heads of his two fighting services. Admiral George Anson, who by his victory over the French at Finisterre (1747) and his marriage had gained promotion, a peerage, and the patronage and protection of one of the great Whig dynasties, was First Lord of the Admiralty. General Sir John Ligonier, a French Huguenot refugee, was the army's newly-appointed commander-in-chief. He had served with distinction as a soldier of fortune under the Duke of Marlborough. Ligonier became a naturalised Englishman, and his service under five British sovereigns would earn him a monument and burial in Westminster Abbey. He was notorious for his *amours,* as befitted a colonel of a famous cavalry regiment in 18th century London society, sharing, for instance, the favours of the promiscuous actress Peg Woffington with the equally promiscuous Earl of Loudoun. Pitt also used the good offices of the Countess of Yarmouth, the King's mistress, to win over George II to the new appointments, for the King had the legal right to refuse commissions.[1]

To command the Louisbourg expedition, Pitt chose Colonel Jeffrey Amherst, a Guard's officer with a 23-year record of distinguished army service. Jeffrey, Baron Amherst, had as a boy entered the service of the Duke of Dorset as a page, and lived in the magnificent Tudor palace at Knole, a present from Queen Elizabeth I to the Duke's ancestors, the Sackvilles. Instead of following the family tradition of the Law and the Church, he decided on an army career. Thanks to the Duke's patronage and the influence of Ligonier, he obtained an ensign's commission in the 1st Regiment of Foot Guards. Serving on the staffs of Ligonier and the Duke of Cumberland on the continent, his promotion was rapid. On 3 March 1758, Mr Secretary Pitt presented 'his compliments to Major General Amherst, and sends him herewith His Majesty's commission to be commander-in-chief at the Siege of Louisbourg'. He would be supported by a fleet under Admiral Edward Boscawen,[2] 'Old Dreadnought', as his sailors affectionately called him.

Brigadier John Forbes, Ligonier's aide-de-camp, was chosen to capture Fort Duquesne and repair Braddock's failure. Amherst asked for his own regiment, 15 Foot (East Yorkshire Regiment), commanded by Lieutenant-Colonel James Murray, to join him from Maidstone (Kent), and the 58 Foot (Anstruther's) from Ireland. Pitt appointed three new brigadiers. The first, Colonel James Wolfe, fanatically devoted to his country and his military profession, was still only 30. Yet he had already commanded the 20 Foot for seven years, and made a name for himself as an excellent regimental commander. While his fellow officers typically drank, hunted and womanised, he devoted much of his time to mastering the technical skills and studying the tactics of his vocation. He had fought at Dettingen and Fontenoy, and had helped to defeat Bonnie Prince Charlie at Culloden. His Centre Brigade would consist of the 17 Foot, a detachment of 35 Foot, 47 Foot and the 2/60 Foot (Royal Americans) under Colonel Robert Monckton.

Lieutenant-Colonel Charles Lawrence of the 60 Foot, formerly the governor of Nova Scotia, was given command of the Left Brigade, consisting of the 15, 28, 45, 58 and 78 Foot (Fraser's Highlanders). The 78 Foot was raised by General Simon Fraser, son of the 13th Lord Lovat, who had been executed for his part in the 1745 Jacobite rebellion. Six hundred recruits of this regiment came from his confiscated estates, and 800 more from the surrounding countryside. Though not particularly fond of their King, these Highlanders were great fighters and proved excellent soldiers.[3] Colonel Edward Whitmore of the 22 Foot (Cheshire Regiment) was appointed to command the Right Brigade, consisting of the 1 Foot (Royal Scots), 22, 40 and 48 Foot, and the 3rd Battalion, Royal Americans.

Having learned the lesson of Braddock's defeat, a light brigade of 550 irregulars was formed by ordering each regiment that had been 'any time in America' to provide one subaltern and 30 to 40 'resolute men, good marksmen, accustomed to the woods, and able to endure fatigue'. 'They would be dressed in blue, some in green, for the easier brushing through the woods', instead of the traditional red uniforms.[4] As Wolfe would write later, 'our clothes, our arms, our accoutrements, nay even our shoes and stockings, are all improper for this country. Lord George Howe [third Viscount][5] is so well convinced of it, that he has taken away all his men's breeches.'[6]

A powerful fleet with a large convoy of transports was assembled at Portsmouth under Admiral Edward Boscawen, son of Lord Falmouth and grandson of James II and his mistress Arabella Churchill, sister of the Duke of Marlborough. The fleet was joined by Whitmore and Wolfe on 1 February 1758. Wolfe found little satisfaction in the soldiers gathering at 'this infernal den' to accompany him on the expedition. He wrote in a letter of 7 February:

> The condition of the garrison (or rather vagabonds that stroll about in dirty red clothes from one gin-shop to another) exceeds all belief. There is not the least shadow of discipline, care or attention. Disorderly soldiers of different regiments are collected here: some from the ships, others from the hospital, some waiting to embark – dirty, drunken, insolent rascals, improved by the hellish nature of the place, where every kind of corruption, immorality and looseness is carried to excess.[7]

The fleet sailed from England on 19 February but, dogged by unfavourable weather, it did not reach Halifax until 12 May, 11 weeks later. So Amherst's forces struggled into the capital of Nova Scotia a month behind Pitt's April target date. They found the 40, 45 and 47 Foot, which had wintered at Halifax, encamped on the hill close to the citadel, preparing siege materials.[8] On 9 May the 35 and 48 Foot reached harbour, followed 12 days later by 1,100 rangers 'to protect the camps from the insults of the Indians'.[9]

To supplement the British regular regiments for the 1758 campaigns, Pitt had requested the colonial governments to provide 25,000 provincials – five times more than the colonies had ever supplied in any one year. In return Pitt agreed to supply the necessary tents, provisions, arms and ammunition. He also withdrew the regulation giving seniority to British officers over provincials, which had been bitterly resented in the colonies. The provincial assemblies were required to finance the raising, clothing, and payment of their own troops. The southern colonies, however, not being exposed to attacks from Canada, were far less interested in giving support than New England.

'Dull would he be of soul,' wrote Bradley[10] circa 1900, 'who could stand unmoved by that deserted, unvisited surf-beaten shore, where you may still trace upon the turf, the dim lines of once busy streets, and mark the green mounds, which hide the remains of the great bastions of Louisbourg.' Some 15 years later, the great American historian Francis Parkman added to the picture:

> Dotted with a few grazing sheep, the green mounds and embankments of earth enclose the whole space, and beneath the highest of them yawn arches

and caverns of ancient masonry. This grassy solitude was once the Dunkirk of America; the vaulted caverns, where the sheep find shelter from the rain, were casemates, in which terrified women sought refuge from storms of shot and shell, and the shapeless green mounds were citadel, bastion, rampart and glacis [sloping embankment]. Here stood Louisbourg: and not all the efforts of its conquerors, nor all the havoc of succeeding times, have availed to efface it. Men in hundreds toiled for months with lever, spade and gun powder in the work of destruction, and for more than a century it served as a stone quarry, but the remains of its vast defences still tell their tale of human valour and human woe.

At the beginning of June 1758, the place wore another aspect. The circuit of the fortifications was more than a mile and a half, and the town contained about 4000 inhabitants.[11]

It occupied an area of over 100 acres, and had been constructed to the designs of Vauban, Louis XIV's master of fortifications. Since the Peace of Aux-la-Chapelle (1748) vast sums had been spent in repairing and strengthening it, and Louisbourg was the strongest fortress in French or British America. Four great bastions, named from north to south the Dauphin's, the King's, the Queen's and the Princess's, mounted some 220 cannons. The most important, the King's Bastion, contained the governor's residence, the royal chapel and barracks (see illustration). Inside the walls, in addition to the inhabitants, were 4,000 regular troops, two companies of artillery, 24 companies of Canadian La Marine, some militia, some Indians, and 3,000 sailors of the French fleet, all under the command of the governor, Chevalier de Drucour. Taken all together, Louisbourg was nearly as large as all the other Canadian cities and forts combined.

But Louisbourg had two important weaknesses. For France the army always came first. French shipbuilders continued to build ships for the French navy, but there were too few of them. Realising the importance of Louisbourg for the defence of Canada, the French had made a great effort to supply the fortress with ships, men, provisions and munitions. But the superior British navy had limited French efforts by blockading, sinking and turning back many of the ships and reinforcements.

And there were constructional faults. 'The original plan of the works had not been carried out,' concluded Parkman. 'Owing to the bad quality of the mortar [supplied by crooked French contractors!], the masonry of the ramparts was in a poor condition.' Rainwater was seeping into the cracks and, when it froze, splitting the stonework.

Jeffrey Amherst sailed from Portsmouth on 16 March. His brother, Captain John Amherst, was already with Boscawen's fleet. Jeffrey took his younger brother William with him as his ADC but left his wife Jane behind, angry and not a little jealous of his motives, to face yet another long separation.[12] Other officers before had taken their wives or mistresses on expeditions overseas but Amherst knew this would be a hard and dangerous campaign, and he wanted no distractions to jeopardise success. He was anxious, too, to catch up with Boscawen and the fleet, which had already set sail with his brigadiers and a number of the regiments. But he did not reach Halifax until 28 May, after a long and tedious voyage.

According to his journal,[13] Amherst sailed on the *Dublin*, 13 days after receiving his new appointment. He was dogged by delays. A few days out, Rodney, the ship's captain, spotted a French merchant ship and gave chase. He had no intention of losing such a rich prize, even though he had on board the commander-in-chief of an important campaign. The captured enemy ship had to be towed into the neutral harbour of Vigo for safe-keeping, and the £30,000 prize money secured. Buffeted by storms or becalmed in the Gulf Stream, the *Dublin* sailed past Tenerife and Palma, providing Amherst with spectacular views of tropical birds, flying fish and giant turtles. On 17 May, with the ship rolling so heavily in the great swelling sea that 'I was compelled to lie on the floor to write to Mr Pitt,' the *Dublin* rescued,

> all the poor creatures aboard a sinking ship. This ship had been five months out from Bristol, and was bound for Philadelphia. Neither the Master nor any of them knew where they were. The whole crew on a Biscuit a day and a spoonful of Flour were half-starved. A shocking way of sending men to the mercy of the Seas in an old French worn out Ship with an ignorant Master.

Amherst's ship, too, was off course, 'so little Reckonings can be depended on'. On 28 May he met Admiral Boscawen's huge fleet of 157 ships, with 12,000 troops on board, sailing out of Halifax harbour, bound for Louisbourg (Appendix A). Amherst immediately transferred to the admiral's ship, where he met Brigadiers Lawrence and Wolfe, and gave Boscawen a copy of his instructions from Pitt.

On 2 June, Boscawen's fleet sailed into Gabarus Bay, immediately to the west of the tongue of land on which the star-shaped fortress of Louisbourg stood. Peeping above its stone battlements the troops could see the wooden barracks, the blue square tower of the hospital, and the dome-shaped cupola of the citadel. In front of them was Louisbourg's magnificent harbour, some seven or eight miles in circumference, with an entrance less than a mile wide, guarded by two promontories. Midway between these was Goat Island, heavily fortified, with a second battery on the eastern shore at Lighthouse Point. In the harbour Admiral the Marquis des Gouttes's fleet of seven warships and five frigates, with some cargo vessels, rode at anchor, equipped with 540 guns and manned by 3,000 soldiers. Clearly the tasks of Boscawen and Amherst would be formidable, and Pitt's plan of forcing the harbour nigh impossible.

The Admiral's orders for the landing (Appendix B) stated that 'the first body in Gabarus Bay were to carry nothing in the boats but their arms and ammunition, with bread and cheese in their pockets for two days. No women were to be landed, until all the men were ashore, and until their tents, blankets, provisions and necessaries, were likewise landed'. The orders also covered the supply of hospital boats, and light boats to rescue men, 'who may fall into the sea by accident'. Amphibious assaults require detailed preparation, based on reliable information, and swift and determined execution. Even then, the landing of the leading troops on the beaches was a dangerous and complex operation – as all such landings during World War Two demonstrated!

Amherst, Lawrence and Wolfe immediately made a reconnaissance of the coast by boat. They tried to assess the practicalities of landing on a well-defended coast, with the additional hazards of a rocky and surf-bound shore. The shelving beach below Louisbourg was an expanse of broken rocks, much too difficult to attempt a landing. As Wolfe wrote: 'When the Army is landed, the business is half-done. We must get on shore or perish all together in the attempt.'[14]

The curve of the bay below Louisbourg was broken by four small promontories – four possible landing places. As the commanders looked at the four, named Black, White and Flat Points, and Freshwater Cove, they decided the last, on the extreme left, about four miles south of Louisbourg, seemed the most likely. At the mouth of a small river, Freshwater Cove looked comparatively sheltered from the open sea. Amherst decided that, if a landing could be made here, the fortress could be attacked from the rear. A frontal assault on Louisbourg would be suicidal.

At least Amherst would have three decided advantages. He had numerical superiority. He had frigates to provide the landings with covering fire, thanks to the deep water. And he had sufficient boats to carry at least half his attacking force at any one time. These boats, carried on the transports specially for the landing, were of shallow draught, flat-bottomed, carrying 40 to 60 men each, and propelled by 20 oarsmen. But luck might well be needed, and firm leadership.

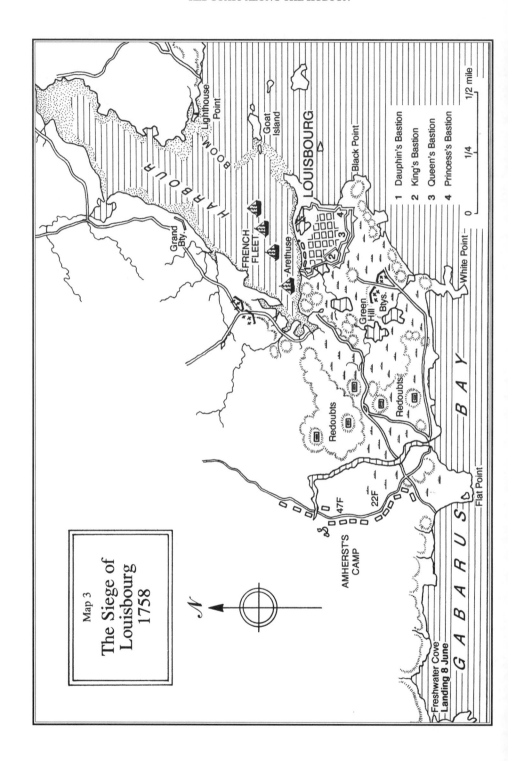

Map 3

The Siege of
Louisbourg
1758

1 Dauphin's Bastion
2 King's Bastion
3 Queen's Bastion
4 Princess's Bastion

0   1/4   1/2 mile

15

THE SIEGE OF
LOUISBOURG

mherst planned to capture Louisbourg by making a beachhead landing, threatening all four possible landing sites simultaneously. From the previous reconnaissance, he decided that Wolfe's brigade[1] would make the real attack, supported by the fleet's fire power, on Freshwater Cove about four miles from the town. The beach was some 350 yards long with rocks at either end. On the shore above it, unknown to Amherst, 1,000 Frenchmen lay entrenched, protected by earthworks. By threatening a two-mile shoreline Amherst compelled the French to deploy these troops accordingly. Once ashore, Amherst aimed to drive the French into Louisbourg, and attack it from the rear.

For five days every attempt to land was frustrated by storms and fog. Finally, at 2am on 8 June, Wolfe's brigade climbed into their boats and rowed towards their objective: the other two brigades followed, moving along the shore to distract attention. The frigates, too, moved shorewards, and opened up supporting fire on the beach. Then Amherst gave the signal 'attack' from his masthead.[2]

So great was the swell that the boats had difficulty in reaching the shore. But the heaving waves proved something of a mixed blessing, for the French batteries, opening up at a range of 100 yards, aimed too high to stop the leading boats.[3] Nevertheless the French, who had remained quiet and well-camouflaged in their trenches, until the landing craft were about 30 yards from the shore, suddenly opened up a devastating fire of grape and musketry. Faced by these difficulties and with his flagstaff shot away, Wolfe signalled to his men to pull away. The signal was either not seen, misunderstood or disregarded by three young subalterns, whose boats were sheltered by a projecting cliff from the enemy's fire. They pulled into a ledge on the left of the cove: officers and men scrambled ashore.[4]

Which boat landed first is hotly disputed by the regiments concerned. The 35 Foot claim Lieutenant Brown; the 60 Foot, Ensign John Grant; 48 Foot, Thomas Hopkins. Others believe Major Scott, who commanded the light infantry, deserves the honour. But Wolfe, seeing the boats landing, sheltered from the firing, quickly countermanded his order to withdraw, and rushed the rest of his boats to the same spot. Nonchalantly landing with only a cane in his hand, he encouraged his men ashore. His coolness, unconcern and indifference to danger bore all the hallmarks expected of an 18th century gentleman officer!

Several of the boats, packed with redcoats, overturned in the surf; others were dashed against the rocks and sank; many men were drowned. But the remainder struggled ashore, scrambling over rocks so rugged and sheer that the French engineers considered them in no need of fortification and beyond the successful attempt of men under arms. Wolfe's troops succeeded in landing on what had been thought 'an inaccessible shore'. Quickly forming up on the firm ground beyond the rocks, their uniforms and powder sodden, the leading troops charged the nearest French battery and captured it with bayonets.[5] Knox believed 'our loss did not exceed 100 men of all ranks killed, wounded and drowned'.[6]

The beach was thus opened up for the landings of the main body. Lawrence's brigade immediately rowed up, and landed virtually unopposed at the western end of the cove. Amherst followed with more troops, and the French, fearing they would be cut off from the town, abandoned their guns and entrenchments and fled. Amherst pursued them, until checked by fire from the ramparts of Louisbourg. The first objective had been secured, after little more than four hours. 'Our landing was next to miraculous,' wrote Wolfe to General Lord George Sackville, who had furthered Wolfe's regimental career. It is difficult to understand how over 1,000 French troops, protected by trenches and breastworks and aided by artillery, could permit a few boatloads of soldiers to land against the odds on so difficult a shore, and then show so little resistance.[7]

Amherst's next task was to consolidate his position and prepare to invest Louisbourg from the land. During the two days following the assault, the weather prevented stores being landed, save for a few tents. On 12 June Amherst sent Wolfe with 1,500 men, including 190 Royal Americans, to Lighthouse Point, which had been abandoned by the French. He planned to install heavy guns to silence Goat Island's formidable batteries, which commanded the entrance to the harbour. Within a fortnight, despite the continual bad weather, the island battery was put out of action, the French warships driven to take shelter under the main fortress, and the harbour opened to the British fleet.[8]

Meanwhile Amherst pitched his camp, which extended for two miles along the banks of a little stream, just beyond the range of the fortress guns and observation from its walls. Stores, guns, and siege equipment were landed, and the camp reinforced with men and materials. Thousands of soldiers laboured with pick and shovel night and day, under enemy fire, to build a road towards Green Hill, from which artillery, under Colonel George Williamson, could be brought to bear on the town. The one-and-a-half mile road consisted of deep mud covered with moss and water weeds. The weather and marshy ground delayed the work and wearied the men, who turned their uniforms inside out as an economy measure. 'Not a man could have a dry shirt on.'[9]

Gradually the British lines drew nearer to the fortress, circling it with a ring of earthworks and steel. Every day saw more guns placed in position, and the artillery fire grew heavier. Enemy sallies were repulsed, the hospital was hit, and the plight of the besieged grew ever more desperate. The houses were built of stone, the streets were broad and regular. The barracks were supposedly bomb-proof, so the women and children took shelter in them. But the constant British shelling brought down the masonry, and no place was safe from shot. There were casualties among military and civilians alike.[10]

On 21 July a lucky shell from the marine battery fell on a French warship and set it alight. The scanty crew left on the ship were unable to check the flames. Cut adrift, it became entangled with two other French ships, which were soon blazing merrily, providing a marvellous pyrotechnic display for the soldiers and sailors of both sides. The two remaining French warships were captured in a brilliant little naval operation a few nights later, when 600 British sailors rowed out silently and boarded them, releasing a number of captured Englishmen.[11] Next day, 26 July, the last gun on the ramparts was silenced.

In the garrison all was now desperate. 'Nearly a quarter of the French were in hospital, while the rest, exhausted by incessant toil, could find no place, in which to snatch an hour of sleep.' And yet, wrote a French officer, 'they still show enthusiasm'.[12] Civilian casualties were mounting, and the garrison was short of food. Their Indian allies, fearing the worst, were deserting them. The rampart walls had been shaken by the concussion of their own guns, and in the Dauphin's and King's Bastions the masonry was being shot to pieces around the ears of the defenders. Gradually the houses, citadel and barracks were being destroyed, the guns knocked out, and the ships in the harbour blown up or captured. Amherst had ordered his gunners to spare the houses of the town, but shot and shells fell everywhere. 'There is not a house in the place that has not felt the effects of his formidable artillery fire,' wrote the French officer in his diary. 'Burning the Town is spoiling our own nests,' wrote Amherst, 'but it will probably be the shortest way of taking it.'[13]

Knox wrote:[14]

The Citadel was soon demolished by fire from the batteries. I saw flames for several hours. A small number of casemates, or rooms in the thickness of the fortress walls of the King's Bastion, are used to shut up the Ladies and part of the women of the town: one casemate is assigned to the wounded officers. All the women with a considerable number of little children came out, running hither and thither, not knowing where to go in the midst of the bombs and bullets, that were falling on every side: also several officers, sick and wounded, were carried on stretchers, without having a safe haven, in which they could be placed.

The governor of Louisbourg, General Drucour, a former naval officer, thought he and the English officers could conduct a campaign under the protection of the medieval code of knightly virtues.[15] In this he was strongly supported by his courageous and theatrical wife, Madame Courserac de Drucour, who daily walked the Louisbourg ramparts in full view of the enemy, and fired three cannons to encourage the French soldiers.[16] Amherst, duly impressed, sent her two pineapples freshly arrived from the Azores, accompanied by an appropriately gallant note.[17] Madame replied with a crate of champagne, which prompted more pineapples and a firkin of butter. General Drucour offered Amherst the services of a noted physician on his staff for any wounded British officers, who wished to accept his services.

But such old world gallantries could not save the fortress. The French were rapidly running out of food and ammunition, and the fortress was falling down around them under the constant bombardment. In addition, there was the threat of a bayonet assault. On 26 July Drucour sued for terms. 'The garrison must surrender unconditionally as prisoners of war, and an answer given within an hour: otherwise, the town will be at once carried by assault,' dictated Amherst. Both knew what happened to a besieged town which refused to capitulate! Drucour tried to bargain but was told 'the time is now half an hour'. At midnight Drucour signed the capitulation papers. After bravely holding out for 52 days, he unconditionally surrendered the town and island.

Next morning three companies of grenadiers, begrimed with smoke and dust, took possession of the Dauphin Gate. The French garrison, drawn up on the Esplanade, flung down their muskets 'and marched from the ground with tears of rage'.[18] One thousand of their comrades lay dead among the ruins. The cross of St George was hoisted on the shattered rampart. 'The Town saluted the British Admiral with 17 guns, as did the ships crowded into the harbour.'[19] So Louisbourg, with the two great islands that depended on the fortress, Cape Breton and Isle St Jean (now Prince Edward's Island), passed to the British crown. The path to the heart of Canada, Quebec and Montreal, had been opened up, claimed Fortescue.[20] But, argued the French, so outnumbered were the defenders, 'anyone else but the English would have taken the place in half the time'.[21] Wolfe agreed:

> An officer and 30 men would have made it impossible to get ashore, where we did. Our proceedings in other respects were so slow and tedious, as this undertaking was ill-advised and desperate. We lost time at the siege, still more after the siege, and blundered from beginning to end of the campaign.[22]

The terms of the surrender were hard. The 5,637 officers, soldiers and sailors[23] captured were to be sent to England in British ships as prisoners of war. The civilians were deported to France; 230 guns and all the stores and munitions were handed over intact. In return, the French sick and wounded were to be cared for, and private property protected from pillage.

On the day of the surrender, 27 July, Wolfe wrote to his mother:

> I went into Louisbourg this morning to pay my respects to the ladies but found them all so pale and thin with long confinement, that I made my visit very short. The poor women have been heartily frightened, as well they might be: but no real harm, either during the siege or after it, has befallen any. A day or two more and they would have been entirely at our disposal – the usual fate of garrisons, which refused to surrender![24]

Drucour and his lady dined with Amherst on board HMS *Terrible*. The governor's gallant defence, lasting from 7 June to 26 July, and Amherst's carefully placed artillery and siege train, gained time and preserved Montreal and Quebec for another season. Wolfe was ordered to lay waste the Gaspé coast – a necessary act of war, as part of the plan to cut off all supplies from Quebec before the final attack upon it.[25] Wolfe did not relish the job. 'Sir Charles Hardy and I are preparing to rob the fishermen of their nets and to burn their huts. When that great exploit is at an end, I return to Louisbourg.' On his return, he wrote: 'Your orders were carried into execution. We have done a great deal of mischief – spread the terror of His Majesty's arms through the whole Gulf: but have added nothing to the reputation of them.'[26] Then Wolfe went home on sick leave, with Boscawen.

Brigadier Whitmore was appointed governor of Louisbourg, and remained there with the 22, 28, 40 and 45 Foot, 'left behind to hold guard over the desolation they had caused'.[27] During the winter, the wife of Lieutenant Colonel Alexander Murray, commanding the 45 Foot, gave birth to a son at Louisbourg, who was named after his godfather, James Wolfe. Ever since, the family has been called Wolfe-Murray.[28] Whitmore, while sailing to Boston in December 1761, drowned off Plymouth, Massachusetts, accidentally falling overboard during the night in a violent storm, and is buried there.[29]

Amherst busied himself with arranging ships to embark the regiments, 'the sooner, the better', settling his accounts, writing his despatches to Pitt, and giving Brigadier Whitmore his orders. In his journal he notes: '11 August: I was obliged to have a Notorious Thief hanged today, to put a stop to Robberies, which began to be frequent in Camp.' On 30 August, 'the wind fair', the transports carrying the 1, 17, 47, 48 and 78 Foot (Fraser's Highlanders) sailed for Boston. 'The Town saluted with 17 guns, which were returned, as soon as we were out of the Harbour.' Boscawen had persuaded Amherst that the plan to attack Quebec would have to be postponed because of the lateness of the campaigning season, especially as news of Abercromby's fate at Ticonderoga had now reached them.[30] Pitt was informed accordingly.

Amherst and the troops reached Boston on 13 September. 'I had desired to have no ceremony but the whole Town was turned out, and I was received by the principal People. I was obliged to walk in procession to the Governor's, where I was to dine.' The troops disembarked the next day, which was declared a Thanksgiving for the success of His Majesty's arms by the taking of Louisbourg. 'Rum was much too plenty in the Town.' On 15 September the troops remained encamped on Boston Common, where thousands of people came to see them.

> They gave them liquor, which made the men drunk, in spite of all that could be done. I sent patrols round the Town all day and night, and when we marched next day I had to leave the Quarter-Guards of every regiment to take care of the drunks, and bring them up, when sober. We marched 10 miles, every man carrying a pound of beef and three pounds of bread for three days.[31]

The men, with the supply wagons and baggage trundling along behind, continued the march to Albany and the relief of Abercromby. *En route* Amherst passed 'a House, where the woman had always lived with two Husbands, one an Irishman and the other a Scotsman: the children were from both Fathers. The woman bedded with them night about – and they never quarrelled or had disputes.' On 3 October he notes: 'I reached Albany – 500 houses in the town, reckoning six in a House.'[32]

Leaving the troops in Albany, Amherst set off for Fort Edward, built by General Lyman in 1755 on the east bank of the Hudson River, 66 miles from Albany. There he met General Abercromby, discussed operations with him – 'no possibility of attempting anything against Ticonderoga' – inspected the camp, and decided on the building of Fort Stanwix (modern Rome). On 6 October he left for Halifax, where Brigadier Lawrence had taken over command, with the 15, 58 and 3/60 Foot. By the end of the year 1758, the troops of the Louisbourg expeditionary force had been dispersed between Halifax, Annapolis Royal, Albany, Philadelphia, New England, the Jerseys and Fort Stanwix.[33]

The end of the 1758 campaigning season was marked by a rash of 'Matrimonial Distemper' among the British officers, succumbing to the fatal charms of prominent American socialites.[34] On 8 December, Colonel Thomas Gage was the first and highest to fall. He had distinguished himself by his gallantry and been wounded when commanding Braddock's advanced column on the march from Monongahela to Fort Duquesne (9 July 1755). Then he raised and commanded the 80th Light Infantry in Abercromby's expedition against Ticonderoga (1758). He married at Mount Kembal, Margaret, daughter of Peter Kembal, president of the council of New Jersey. She would bear him six sons and five daughters: their eldest surviving son became a major-general and the third Viscount Gage, and their youngest an admiral. Thomas Gage would succeed Amherst as commander-in-chief, North America, and become governor of Montreal.

'During the War, we had great intercourse with England,' wrote a citizen of Philadelphia. 'Officers of the Army were continually passing and repassing, many of them sons of the best families, and even Peers of the realm landed on our shores. We paraded our wealth, the wealthier colonial hostesses wined and dined them.'[35] 'Miss Betty Plumstead would marry an ensign in the 17 Foot, and her sister became engaged to a lieutenant in the 35 Foot. The lovely Miss Willing almost married Sir John St Clair, and is now with Colonel Bouquet on the string. Dr. Richard Huck, the Army surgeon, is pursuing her sister' – perhaps unsuccessfully – 'since he later married Jane, the niece and wealthy heiress of Admiral Sir Charles Saunders.' Colonel John Reid married Susanna, daughter of James Alexander of New York and owner of 35,000 acres in the unsettled area east of Lake Champlain. He retired there rather than return to Britain with the 42 Royal Highland Regiment (Black Watch) in 1767. He founded the chair of music at his old university, Edinburgh.[36] Even the Other Ranks caught the disease. 'This afternoon a Lobster (the provincial soldiers' term for a Redcoat, whose women, whether married or single, were always considered 'loose') Corporal was married to a Rhode Island whore'.[37]

General Amherst sent his brother, William, to carry his Louisbourg dispatches to George II. When the 11 pairs of French colours from Louisbourg Fortress arrived in England, the King ordered that they should be carried in procession through London, escorted by the Guards, and deposited in St Paul's Cathedral.[38] The soldiers who took part in their capture were given an advance of pay of one shilling (5p), to drink the health of His Majesty.[39] The army received the congratulations of the King and the thanks of parliament, as the church bells pealed for the first British success in the three years of hostilities. A medal was struck for the naval and army officers, who had displayed such conspicuous gallantry at Louisbourg, but the regiments which took part in the siege had to wait until 1882 for their battle honours to be awarded. Amherst was rewarded with his appointment as commander-in-chief of all British forces in North America. General Abercromby would be recalled.

On 11 August 1758 Wolfe wrote to his mother, setting out his thoughts on the future of America:

> The Colonies are deeply tinged with the vices and bad qualities of the mother country but some time hence they will be a vast empire, the seat of Power and Learning. They have all the Materials ready, Nature has refused them

nothing; and there will grow a People out of our little spot, England, that will fill this vast space and divide this great Portion of the Globe with the Spaniards, who are possessed of the other half.[40]

Unbeknown to him, a year later Wolfe would return to help to fulfil his prophecy.

16

FORTS TICONDEROGA AND DUQUESNE

Wdots hile Amherst's forces were besieging and capturing Louisbourg, General James Abercromby, commander-in-chief in America, was assembling his forces and supplies for the attack on Ticonderoga. Ticonderoga was the Indian name for the French Fort Carillon, a name recalling the sound of water rushing from Lake George into Lake Champlain. This fort, with the magic name, set amid scenery of majestic beauty, was the key to the Champlain front. It was from here that Montcalm launched his army against Fort William Henry. Here, greatly outnumbered, he would make his stand against the British onslaught of 1758.

Abercromby's prospects at the beginning of the campaign must have appealed to him. He had been allocated 7,000 regulars and 9,000 provincials, mostly raw militiamen from Massachusetts, Connecticut, New York and New Jersey, with a train of artillery. His regulars consisted of the 27, 42 (Highlanders), 44, 46 and 55 Foot, and 1,050 all ranks of the 4/60 Royal Americans and 630 men of the 1st Battalion. He also had the newly-raised Light Infantry (80 Foot) of Colonel Thomas Gage, a regiment which modelled itself on Rogers's already famous rangers.[1]

Much of the credit for escorting the convoys from Albany to Fort Edward, via the Mohawk and Hudson Rivers and the three portages, was due to Brigadier Viscount George Augustus Howe, the eldest of three brothers, who would make their mark on British military history. They claimed royal blood through George I and his German mistress, Charlotte Sophia, Baroness Kielmansegge. Pitt had appointed Howe chief of staff at the age of 34, 'to make good the failings which were suspected in Abercromby'.[2] Howe had arrived the previous year as colonel of the 55 Foot, and had spent his time under Robert Rogers learning the art of forest warfare. Abandoning the training and drills of the barrack square, he joined the backwoodsmen in their scouting parties, shared their hardships, and adopted their dress.

The lessons he had learned he introduced to his officers and men. He made them throw off all useless encumbrances ('the officers' apparatus of tables and chairs he thought absurd'),[3] cut the skirts off their coats and the pigtails off their heads, browned the barrels of their muskets to prevent glitter, and clad their legs in leggings to protect them from the undergrowth. The empty spaces in their knapsacks he filled with 30 pounds of meal, to make them independent for days of army supplies. (An early version of today's iron rations!) The officers were restricted to the same ration as their men, instead of the usual ration supplied according to rank, and were even expected to wash their own linen without the help of the regimental women, whom he discharged.[4] Lord Howe set an example by going to the river and washing his own underwear, and sheltering *en bivouac* under a single blanket and bearskin. Termed 'the best soldier in the British army' by Wolfe, he adopted the slogan, 'We must learn the art of war from the Indians'.[5] Not surprisingly, the morale of the troops grew rapidly from his example and methods.

By the end of June 1758 the whole of Abercromby's force was assembled with its supplies at the head of Lake George, near the ruins of Fort William Henry. Eight hundred bateaux, each holding 22 soldiers and their provisions for 30 days, had been hauled by ox teams, and 90 whaleboats pulled by soldiers on low-wheeled trucks over the portage. On 5 July all had embarked with perfect precision. Each regiment marched to its appointed place on the beach, and before the sun was well risen the whole army was afloat.

'The spectacle was superb,' wrote Parkman.[6] The cloudless blue summer sky, the romantic beauty of the scenery, the vast rolling slope of the forest down to the crystal water of the lake, the green summits of the bordering mountains, the countless islets covered with pine, birch and fir; the flash of oars, the glitter of weapons, the banners, coloured uniforms, and the notes of bugle, trumpet and bagpipe and the beat of drum re-echoed by woodland and forest, made an indescribably beautiful scene.

Robert Rogers, most famous of American partisans, with his rangers, and Thomas Gage, second son of the first Viscount Gage in the peerage of Ireland, led the way, with part of the new (80 Foot) Light Infantry. Lieutenant-Colonel John Bradstreet of New England followed next with the boatmen, himself the best boatman among them.[7] Then, in three long parallel columns, came the main body of the army, the blue coats of the provincial troops of New England and New York, the red coats of the English regulars, each regiment marked by its flying colours of green, yellow or crimson. Behind came two 'floating castles' of the artillery, then the bateaux laden with stores and baggage, with a rearguard of both red and blue. So the great army, stretching almost from shore to shore, advanced over the bosom of the lake, until the narrows were reached. The broad front dwindled to a slender procession six miles in length, creeping like some huge sinuous serpent on its errand of death and destruction.

By 5pm the flotilla had advanced 25 miles. Abercromby called a halt for the baggage and artillery to catch up. At 11pm it started again, and at daybreak on 6 July reached the narrow channel, which leads into Lake Champlain by the headland of Ticonderoga.

A French advanced force on the shore was driven back. But thick undergrowth and fallen trees hindered the army's progress: its columns became mixed up, the guides lost the tracks – and their heads – and for a time the force lost its bearings. The centre column, with Howe and some rangers at its head, blundered into the French detachment. In the skirmish which followed, Howe, shot through the heart, was killed instantly, with 300 of his companions. Abercromby's second-in-command and the guiding spirit of the British army had vanished. Abercromby, who felt Howe's loss keenly, had to regroup his forces.

Montcalm had appreciated the importance of the Lake Champlain route, and decided to make a stand at Fort Ticonderoga (Carillon), built on a tongue of land projecting into the twisting river connecting Lake George with Lake Champlain. The fort was surrounded by water on three sides, and protected on the fourth partly by an impassable morass, and partly by a line of fortifications some nine feet high. Montcalm patched up the fortifications and strengthened the breastwork of felled trees, sharpened and pointing towards the enemy, on a ridge in front of the fort itself. He manned his log wall with seven battalions of French regulars (La Reine, Béarn, 1st Berry, Guienne, Royal Roussillon, Languedoc and La Sarre). His force of 3,600, including marines, Canadian militia and native Indians, was small, but he made up for inferior numbers by his audacious and imaginative generalship – qualities Abercromby did not possess!

Abercromby, in planning his attack, could easily have cut the French communications by road or water from Ticonderoga to Fort St Frédéric (Crown Point) by detaching some of his American provincials. He could have pounded the fort into submission by mounting artillery on a hill, Mount Defiance, to the south of Ticonderoga. But he had left almost all his cannon on his barges, and the few he had with him he did not use. Instead, with the misleading advice of an incompetent junior engineer officer, who reported that the works opposite were still unfinished – advice which would cost him his life later in the day – Abercromby decided his overwhelming superiority in numbers was sufficient for an immediate frontal attack. In this worst of options, he would attack with the bayonet without waiting for his artillery to be brought up.[8]

The British regulars approached the defences bravely, but the mass of pointed branches checked their advance, broke their ranks, and exposed them to the very heavy fire of a well-protected enemy able to take deliberate aim without endangering themselves. The French in their white uniforms, with only the tops of their heads visible above the breastworks, poured a deadly cross-fire with muskets and cannon into the struggling mass, as wave after wave of redcoats tried to move forward.[9]

It was more than flesh and blood could stand. Men who had fought at

Fontenoy declared that battle was child's play compared with the assault on Ticonderoga.[10]

Parkman vividly described the scene:

> Masses of infuriated men could not go forward and would not go back; straining for an enemy they could not reach, and firing on an enemy they could not see, they were caught in the entanglement of felled trees. Shouting, yelling and cursing, they were assailed all the while with bullets, which killed them by scores, stretched them on the ground, or hung them on jagged branches, in strange attitudes of death.[11]

Held back in reserve were the 42 Foot (Lord John Murray's Highlanders, now the Black Watch) and 55 Foot. The 42 Foot had been formed by a Royal Warrant of 25 October 1739 addressed to John, 20th Earl of Crawford, 'a veritable knight – errant of the 18th Century'. He had served as a volunteer in the imperial army on the Rhine (1735) and fought with the Russians against the Turks in 1738, being severely wounded at the siege of Belgrade. The regiment he formed was of pure Highlanders of standing, so family and personal pride were the salient characteristics of both officers and men of this famous regiment.

In the current battle, the regimental records[12] relate:

> Then the Highland soldiers of the 42nd could endure no longer. Impatient of their position in the rear, they rushed forward, hewed their way through the obstacles with their broadswords, and, since no ladders had been provided, made strenuous efforts to carry the breastworks, partly by mounting on each others' shoulders, and partly by fixing their feet in holes, which they had excavated with their swords and bayonets in the face of the work. The defenders were so well prepared that the instant an assailant reached the top, that instant he was thrown or shot down.

At length, after great exertions, Captain John Campbell, one of the two soldiers presented to George II at Whitehall in 1743, and a handful of valiant followers forced their way over the breastworks. They were instantly despatched by the bayonet. The struggle lasted for six hours, under desperate and disadvantageous conditions. General Abercromby, seeing no hope of success and completely demoralised, ordered a withdrawal. But the soldiers, exasperated by the physical opposition and the loss of so many comrades, could be recalled only with difficulty. The Highlanders, in particular, seemed more anxious to avenge the fate of their fallen friends than careful to avoid a similar death. Not until the third peremptory order from Abercromby could their commanding officer, Lieutenant Colonel Grant, prevail on the Highlanders to retire.[13]

Abercromby was able to retreat from Ticonderoga unmolested by the

French, who expected him to resume the attack next morning, this time with his cannon. He had lost 23 officers and 567 other ranks killed, and 65 officers and 1,178 other ranks wounded. The 42 Foot suffered terrible losses. Eight officers, nine sergeants and 297 men lay dead on or before the fort's breastworks; 17 officers, ten sergeants and 306 men were wounded. With 647 of its total strength *hors de combat*, the Black Watch was reduced almost to a skeleton.[14] Before the tidings of that 'glorious though unfortunate' battle had reached the public, the King conferred on the regiment the title 'Royal' for its extraordinary courage, loyalty and exemplary conduct.[15]

Montcalm lost 106 killed and 256 wounded. Among the wounded were his two generals, Bourlamaque and Bougainville. Montcalm was full of admiration for the bravery and tenacity of his British opponents, but even more so for the courage and skill of his own troops. 'The too small army of King Louis XV has beaten the enemy,' he wrote. 'What soldiers are ours! I have never seen the like! Why were they not at Louisbourg?'[16] This victory proved to be France's high point in the 1758 campaign!

French manpower and economic resources were becoming stretched to the limit, thanks to the shortsighted policies and European-orientated priorities of Louis XV and his court. Montcalm had to content himself with strengthening the defences of Ticonderoga, and sending out parties of irregulars to harass Abercromby's communications with his base at Fort Edward. For his part, Abercromby was demoralised, and remained throughout July and August at Fort Edward, losing many of his men from dysentery. Just at this moment, the resourceful Lieutenant-Colonel John Bradstreet turned the scale. Whilst others almost despaired of a successful defence, Bradstreet persuaded Abercromby to allow him to lead a counter-offensive expedition against Fort Frontenac (modern Kingston). Frontenac commanded Lake Ontario, and formed a starting point and supply depot for Montcalm's attack on Oswego.

On 12 August Bradstreet set out with a force of about 3,000 men, mostly provincial militia, except for two companies of the Royal Americans (4/60 Foot). Twelve days later his flotilla of bateaux landed near the fort. He found it occupied by barely 100 men, with a few women, children and Indians, because of Montcalm's need to maintain Ticonderoga at maximum strength. Once Bradstreet had positioned his artillery, the French commander, vastly outnumbered, surrendered. Bradstreet captured an enormous quantity of munitions, stores and provisions, and seven armed ships – the whole French naval force on Lake Ontario. New France was cut in two: Fort Duquesne was left isolated, and the Six Nation Indians once more looked towards England. After setting fire to the fort, Bradstreet returned in triumph to Albany.

The fall of Frontenac was greeted with great satisfaction in New York. 'The taking of Frontenac,' wrote one of Bradstreet's officers, 'gave more joy to the inhabitants of Albany than even the taking of the more distant Louisbourg.'

It also gave pleasure to Intendant Bigot, who could claim that the accounts he had falsified had gone up in the flames.[17]

Brigadier John Forbes, a former medical student turned scholar and an expert in the basics of 'backwoods fighting', had been ordered to 'annoy the Enemy, and to remove all future Dangers from the Frontiers of any of the Southern Colonies on the Continent of America'.[18] He decided to attack Fort Duquesne. Born in 1710, he began his military career as a cornet in the Scots Greys. At the age of 47 he was given command of the 17 Foot and attached to Loudoun. He knew the country, got on well with the colonials and, having acted as deputy Quartermaster for the army, was thoroughly familiar with the problems of supply. Now in his 60s, he was a sick man, and for the most part had to organise his campaign from a litter.[19] Previous expeditions against Duquesne had failed for lack of a siege train, and maintaining a supply of food and ammunition.

Forbes decided on a methodical advance, first making a usable track along which to bring up his artillery and supplies. His force numbered upwards of 6,000 men, including 1,200 men of the 77th Montgomery's Highlanders. The Regiment had been raised in 1757 by the Honourable Archibald Montgomerie, son of the Earl of Eglinton. The following year it embarked at Greenock for Halifax, and this was its first campaign. The rest of Forbes's force were provincials from Virginia, Maryland, North Carolina and Pennsylvania, for whose military inefficiency Forbes had nothing but contempt. New England, he said, sent stalwart yeomen and men trained in the whale industry, ill-disciplined but physically capable, miserably armed with old fowling pieces. The southerners were 'the scum of Virginia': many had never fired a gun, and their officers were 'an extremely bad collection of broken innkeepers, horse-jockeys and Indian traders'.[20] The force included four companies of the 1st Battalion Royal Americans under Colonel Bouquet.

But military experience and discipline were seldom important factors with provincial volunteers. Increased status in his community and a sense of adventure might have motivated the volunteer officer, but the private soldier's reasons 'for risking gunshot, gangrene, smallpox and scurvy' were more complex. They might be simply an admiration for the man who asked him to enlist, hatred of Catholicism, a chance to escape from parental supervision or indentured servitude, or the prospect of getting rich. Others joined for bounties, high pay, freedom from impressment for a number of years, permission to keep issue clothing and muskets, or the chance to obtain a large piece of land or plunder a captured French garrison.

Nevertheless, an army needed to function as a disciplined body. Provincial commanders issued instructions reminding their officers to wear their insignia of rank and to refrain from querying orders given to them on parade. 'Soldiers were told they could not dress to suit themselves, sleep or cook or defecate where they pleased, sing, halloo or gamble late into the night.' But trying to produce order out of chaos proved difficult.[21]

Brigadier Forbes set off from Philadelphia at the beginning of July, after a long delay in assembling his provincial contingents. Then came an argument over the route. Virginia did not want a trading road opened between Pennsylvania and the Ohio: the young George Washington, being a Virginian, recommended the route followed by Braddock. But Forbes cared nothing for colonial squabbles, and took the advice of Bouquet to cut a shorter route to Fort Duquesne from Pennsylvania via Fort Carlisle[22] – a distance of 324 miles. Warned by Braddock's failure, Forbes was determined to avoid an unwieldy wagon train, and to establish fortified posts at 40-mile intervals.

Colonel Henri Bouquet of the 1/60 Foot was in command of the road-building operation, establishing the first of the fortified posts at Fort Bedford (modern Bedford). Slowly Forbes's road through Pennsylvania moved forward, over mountain range and through dense forests, the men 'hewing, digging and blasting, or worming their way like moles through the jungle of swamp and forest'.[23] Toil was incessant, rations spartan, and disease rampant: forage was scarce, defiles and flooded rivers abounded. 'A few petty skirmishes resulted in the taking and losing of a few scalps, amid the uninhabited wilderness, overgrown with trees and brushwood, so that no one can see 20 yards,' Forbes wrote to Pitt.[24] Adverse weather added to the difficulties. Heavy rain destroyed Bouquet's new road; the horses, underfed and overworked, died in numbers; supplies faltered.[25] In October things got worse:

> Dejected Nature wept, and would not be comforted. Above, below, around, all was trickling, oozing, pattering, gushing. In the miserable encampments, the starved horses stood steaming in the rain, and the men crouched, disgusted, under their dripping tents. The rain gave place to snow. The wheels of the wagons sank to the hub in the trench of half-liquid clay, that was called a road. To advance or retreat was impossible.[26]

But patience and determination surmounted all difficulties.

The French, cooped up in Fort Duquesne with their Indian allies, and faced with this slow, methodical advance, made repeated forays. On 27 August Fort Frontenac's capture by Bradstreet deprived them of its supplies and decided their fate. In November intelligence was brought to Forbes, now a dying man and confined to a litter, that the French garrison had been so weakened as to be almost defenceless. On 18 November Forbes set out on his litter, at the head of 2,500 men and a few light guns but without tents or baggage, to attack the fort. During the night of 24 November, within a few miles of his objective, Forbes and the British camp were aroused by the sound of a heavy explosion. The French had blown up Fort Duquesne and retired to Venango. When the troops reached Duquesne next day, they found it in ruins. Forbes renamed it Fort Pitt (modern Pittsburgh), in honour of England's chief minister. By destroying the fort the French had relieved the western borders from the scourge of Indian war, and had abandoned all hope of controlling the forks of the Ohio, the gateway to the lands of the west.[27]

'If Forbes's achievement was not brilliant,' wrote Parkman,[28] 'its solid value was above praise. From southern New York to North Carolina, the frontier populations had caused to bless the memory of this steadfast and all-enduring soldier.'

When the British troops entered Fort Duquesne, the only signs of human habitation were the heads of Highlanders, who a few weeks earlier had been captured during a reconnaissance on the fort, stuck on poles, and the charred bodies of five of their comrades. They had been ceremonially burned at the stake, their kilts hung in derision around them. Forbes left a garrison of 200 provincial soldiers behind, all he could spare, to brave the winter and the almost certain return of the French from Venango, further up the Allegheny River. Carried on a litter between two horses, the dying Forbes set off with the remainder of his troops on the return journey to Pennsylvania, living from hand to mouth without tents, shoes or clothing.

During the journey a detachment made a detour to bury the bones of the soldiers who had died with Braddock. Major Halket, on Forbes's staff, found two skeletons lying together under a tree on the battlefield. One he identified from its teeth as his father, Sir Peter Halket of the 44 Foot, and the other as his brother, who had fallen by his father's side. The detachment wrapped the remains in a Highlander's plaid shawl, and buried them in one grave.

Sutlers, many army widows, followed the troops in the baggage train. They sold liquor and provisions (except bread, which was an army ration) to the soldiers, often at prices fixed by commanding officers. On this expedition their wagons also contained 'luxury' items, such as Madeira, spirits, sugar, soap, candles, cheese, chocolate, coffee, tea, butter, condiments, tobacco and writing paper, as well as shoes, cloaks and blankets. Sutlers also ran the officers' messes, drew the army's rations, and charged each officer sixpence per day for their messing.[29]

Forbes lingered on at Philadelphia until the following March, when he died – a tired old soldier of forty-nine – his heroism recognised by the city and the British army. George Washington, also on the expedition, was elected to the Virginia House of Burgesses, married a rich widow, and retired from soldiering for the next 17 years. He would reappear as commander-in-chief of the American forces in the War of Independence (1775–83).[30]

The 1758 campaigning season was now over. Although Pitt had not achieved all the results he wanted, either in Europe, India or North America, nevertheless he was reasonably well satisfied. Hanover had been cleared of

1. Women join the male settlers at James Town, c. 1612. Bettmann Collection. *Courtesy of Range Pictures.*

2. Madame de Pompadour. François Boucher, 1757. *National Gallery of Scotland.*

3. Solomon in All His Glory, 1738. George II and Madame Wallmoden with Portrait of Queen Caroline on the Wall. *The Trustees of the British Museum.*

4. A Fleet Wedding. A sailor weds his landlady's daughter, 1747. *The Trustees of the British Museum.*

5.   British soldier of the 43 Foot in front of Windsor Castle. Copyright Levinge.
Courtesy of Curator (Oxford) Regimental Museum, The Royal Green Jackets.

6. Young Washington. *The Trustees of the British Museum.*

7. The French Invasion, 1756. William Hogarth. *The Trustees of the British Museum.*

8. British Hutted Camp, Dyckman Farm, New York City. John Ward Dunsmore. Officers of the 28 Foot (Gloucestershire Regiment) and 42nd Highlanders are in the foreground: the men train, carry out fatigues and sentry duty around the camp. *Courtesy of the Secretary of the New York Historical Society.*

9. Anti-French Feeling, 1755. *The Trustees of the British Museum*

10. Louisbourg Fortress, King's Bastion. *Courtesy of Eric Krause and Mrs Heather Gillis, Fortress of Louisbourg National Historic Site.*

11. Louisbourg Fortress, soldiers of the Compagnies Franches de la Marine. *Courtesy of Eric Krause and Mrs Heather Gillis, Fortress of Louisbourg National Historic Site.*

12. Louisbourg, view of fort. (L to R) Soldiers' barracks rooms: Chapel with spire:Officers' rooms and Governer's Wing.*Courtesy of Eric Krause and Mrs Heather Gillis, Fortress of Louisbourg National Historic Site.*

13. Louisbourg Fortress, soldiers of the Compagnies Franches de la Marine on parade. *Courtesy of Eric Krause and Mrs Heather Gillis, Fortress of Louisbourg National Historic Site.*

14. Attack on the French Fleet at Louisbourg, 1758. Engraving after R Paton. *National Maritime Museum.*

15. View of Quebec, 1740. The Heights of Abraham on the left. *The Trustees of the British Museum.*

16. The capture of Quebec, 13 September 1759. *Peter Newark's American Pictures.*

I. J. M^{quis} DE MONT-CALM.

17. Death of Montcalm. *The Trustees of the British Museum.*

the French; Ferdinand of Brunswick had crossed the Rhine and inflicted enormous damage on the ill-disciplined French army. Germany was proving a colossal drain on French resources, and Pitt's raids on Cherbourg and St Malo diverted troops from the main theatres, while the Navy blockaded the French fleet bases at Rochefort, Toulon and Brest. In India, Clive was consolidating his achievements after his success at the Battle of Plassey.[31] In America, though the plan to attack Quebec and Montreal had to be abandoned, Louisbourg, Duquesne and Frontenac were in British hands.[32] The pressures on French Canada were beginning to reveal her weaknesses. She had lost control of the Ohio Valley and her positions between the Great Lakes and the St Lawrence settlements were threatened. Her agriculture was barely sufficient for her own needs, and quite inadequate to support large bodies of troops, many drafted into the army instead of working in the fields. The harvests of 1756 and 1757 had been bad, and the Canadians had been placed on low rations. Supplies from France were denied by the British navy, so Vaudreuil and Montcalm were starved of regular reinforcements, provisions and munitions.

As the prestige of the British and colonial forces increased, so the support of France's Indian allies waned. The strategic advantages of central control, interior lines of communication, terrain, and the ability to call on the entire manpower and resources of New France, once the prerogative of the French, were beginning to succumb to the pressures of Britain's superior numbers, improved military organisation and tactics – and the dominance of the British navy.

'It is a beautiful sight to see English noblemen in North America,' wrote the French Abbé Desenclaves, a loyalist Acadian priest, 'going to face all the terrors, hardships, and even dangers of roads and weather, sacrificing their pleasures and their interests for the service of their Prince and their country.'[33]

Pitt, firmly in control of parliament, promised vigorous operations for 1759 against the French. The King, once his enemy, now became his most ardent supporter. Pitt was ready to apply the *coup de grâce* to his great design for the destruction of French power in Canada.

17

GENERAL
JAMES WOLFE

In November 1758 Wolfe was on sick leave in London, fêted everywhere for his exploits at Louisbourg. In December Pitt offered him the command of the 1759 expedition he was planning to capture Quebec, and promoted him major-general. He was not yet 32! Newcastle immediately complained to George II about the rapid promotion of this eccentric brigadier, who had never commanded an army. The King, admiring Wolfe's military energy and dash and soured by the string of British defeats, replied: 'Mad, is he? Then I hope he will bite some of my other generals.'[1]

Wolfe was born in 1727 at Westerham in Kent, the son and grandson of army officers of Irish extraction. About 1737 his family moved to Greenwich, where he was educated at a school for the sons of officers. His father, one of Marlborough's officers in the 3rd Foot Guards, married, when over 40 and a lieutenant-colonel, a young beauty of 24 from the Yorkshire landed gentry but without any money. He therefore chose to reside near the court, the source of military patronage and promotion. There he obtained for his son in 1741 a commission in his regiment of marines, the 44 Foot, and could watch over his future career. As an ensign in the 12 Foot, Wolfe fought at the battle of Dettingen, aged 16, as acting adjutant. At 19 he fought at Culloden (1746), which finally ended the Jacobite rebellion and the aspirations of the Young Pretender, Bonnie Prince Charlie, to regain the Stuart throne.

In 1750 Wolfe was promoted lieutenant-colonel in command of Lord George Sackville's 20 Foot. Sackville, a friend of the Duke of Cumberland, the army's commander-in-chief, advised Wolfe to cultivate the social graces at an age and rank, when the lieutenant-colonel, as 'the father of the regiment', was usually married. But love and women came a very poor second to Wolfe's army aspirations. In 1752, aged 25, he wrote to his mother, the dominant influence in his life: 'There is a great probability that I shall never marry. I shall hardly engage in an affair of that nature purely for money. Unless some gentle nymph persuades me to marry, I had much rather listen to the drum and trumpet than any softer sound whatever.'[2] But like many others of his generation he saw nothing immoral in seeking a good match to advance his career.

His mother cast around to find a suitable heiress. Her choice fell on a Miss

Hoskins of Chelsea, plain but with a dowry of £30,000 a year. However, Wolfe preferred Elizabeth Lawson, the eldest daughter of Sir Wilfred Lawson and the niece of his brigade commander in Scotland, General Sir John Mordaunt, who had considerable influence at the Horse Guards. Miss Lawson, too, was maid of honour to the Princess of Wales, mother of George III, and 'a beauty'. Wolfe's parents decided she possessed an inadequate fortune, and at the end of four years' frustration, he gave up hope.

Instead, he spent the winter of 1750–1 in London in wild dissipation, 'committing more imprudent acts than in all my life before'. 'I lived,' he told his army friend Rickson, 'in the idlest, dissolute, abandoned manner,' which injured his health and weak constitution. It was the age *par excellence* of the rake, gambler and winebibber, commented Beckles Willson, but profligacy and idleness offered few attractions to the youthful colonel, and vice was not in his nature.[3] Miss Lawson died in 1759, six months before Wolfe, boasting many suitors but still unmarried.

Wolfe's leave of absence also took him to Paris, to further his military and social education. In October 1752 he arrived, armed with letters of introduction to persons of influence, including the Earl of Albermarle, the British ambassador to the court of Versailles. 'Paris is full of people, and an abundance of genteel persons of both sexes,' he wrote, and his letters are full of gossip about the court, French manners and women. Albermarle introduced him to Louis XV and the royal family, and he had an intimate interview with Madame Pompadour in her boudoir. He found her extremely handsome, and thought she must have 'a great deal of wit and understanding'. How strange to reflect, wrote his biographer, Beckles Willson, that a few years before the fall of Canada, Pompadour's small apartment at Versailles should have contained the real ruler of France, seated before her mirror, while her coiffeur arranged her hair, and the man who was to wrest from Old France its finest jewel.[4]

With his regiment in Scotland, Wolfe had studied mathematics and Latin; in Paris, he improved his French, riding, fencing and dancing – a skill he later commended to his officers to 'soften their manners and make them civil'. In Paris he became good friends with a young Guard's officer, Ensign William Hamilton, who would become for over 30 years British minister to the court of Naples. He is remembered in history as the husband of Emma, famous for her adulterous relationship with another British hero, Admiral Nelson.[5] Wolfe would have liked a longer stay on the continent to increase his knowledge of foreign armies, but the Duke of Cumberland refused permission for a commanding officer to be so long away from his regiment. So Wolfe returned to duty, with the conviction that 'the English are not favourites in France; they can't help looking upon us as enemies. And I believe they are right.'[6]

During these formative years with the 20 Foot, Wolfe was learning his professional duties as a regimental officer and practising his skills in the management of his officers and men – and their women. He was becoming a marked man through the excellent peacetime training he gave his regiment; the Prince of Wales, for instance, specially inspected the 20 Foot to see how ordinary officers and men could reach such high standards of efficiency.[7]

Wolfe was especially critical of the officers, the future leaders of British armies, as 'an effeminate race of coxcombs ... In general, they have little application to business and have been so ill-educated that *a man of common industry* is held in high esteem amongst them ... There are young men amongst us, who have great revenues and high military stations, that are discontented at three months' service with their regiments, if they go 50 miles from home. Soup, Venison and Turtle are their supreme delight and joy.'[8]

He told his mother he hoped to learn some civility and mildness of bearing 'by discoursing with the other sex – but better a savage of some use, than a gentle, amorous puppy, or a perfect Philanderer'.[9] He blamed drink, debauchery and defective methods of training for such defeats as Braddock's at Fort Duquesne. 'We are lazy in time of peace and our military education is by far the worst in Europe.'[10]

Most of Wolfe's pre-American army experience came from home service – in Scotland, which he left in September 1753. He marched his 20 Foot southwards 'with drums beating and colours flying' to Dover and garrison duty in 'that vile castle dungeon, haunted with the spirits of our restless Saxon forefathers and their wives, for here are ghosts of both sexes'.[11] Then he served in Exeter, chafing at his enforced inactivity and lack of prospects for promotion. War was imminent, and he would have only a few years in which to achieve fame!

Sixteen months after the beginning of the Seven Years' War in Europe, Wolfe was in September 1757 appointed quartermaster-general of the ill-fated expedition commanded by his friend Sir John Mordaunt against Rochefort. He returned indignant at the blundering – 'no zeal, no ardour, no care and concern for the good and honour of the country'.[12] But as a result of this expedition he came to the notice of Pitt, who summoned him to London on 7 January 1758 and offered him command of a brigade in the force sent against Louisbourg. Wolfe accepted, 'though I know the very passage threatens my life, and that my constitution must be utterly ruined'.[13]

The Rochefort expedition also taught Wolfe lessons about combined army and naval operations. An admiral should enter an enemy port, he wrote, as soon as he appears before it: anchor the transports and frigates as close to land as possible, and after a quick reconnaissance, disembark the troops on shore according to previously-given instructions to the appointed leaders as to the order of disembarkation and disposition of the boats. Generals should decide their plan of operations, so that time was not lost in idle debate and consultations, especially when quick action was required; 'and in war, something must be allowed to chance and fortune, seeing that war is in its nature hazardous and an option of difficulties'.[14] Armchair critics (and professional historians) do well to bear these principles in mind when assessing Wolfe's plans before Quebec, and his method of operation!

In 1757 come the first references to Wolfe's 'pretty neighbour' at Bath, one of the most fashionable women of the day: Miss Katherine Lowther, sister of the immensely rich first Earl of Lonsdale and daughter of Robert Lowther, a former governor of Barbados. Katherine was wintering at one of England's most fashionable spas, where the hot water heated the passions and dissolved social distinctions. Peers and commoners mingled round the gaming tables, at concerts, dances and the theatre, and jostled fortune-hunters, quacks and charlatans in the streets. Katherine's name will always be linked with that of James Wolfe. But just as his thoughts were turning to romance, his military duties carried him off to Rochefort; the same thing happened again when he accepted his commission for Louisbourg. His heart may have been in Bath, but his thoughts were on arrangements for his imminent departure. 'Of late, no thought of matrimony ... Being of the profession of arms, I would seek all occasions to serve: the business of a divan or seraglio are unknown to me.'[15]

This conflict between Cupid and Mars, love and war, has bedevilled military men down the ages, even to the present day.[16] In a letter to his father, Wolfe wrote:

> There is a fit time, and 'tis commonly later with us soldiers than with other men, for two reasons. The first is that in our younger days we are generally moving from place to place, and hardly have leisure to arrange matters. The second reason has prudence and necessity to support it – we are not able to feed our wives and children till we begin to decline. [Many a modern soldier would agree with these two statements]. But the almost natural consequence of not marrying is an attachment to some woman or other that leads to a thousand inconveniences. The French Marshal Saxe died in the arms of a little whore, that plays upon the Italian stage – an ignominious end for a conqueror![17]

When commanding the 20 Foot, Wolfe issued regimental orders following the army policy on marriage.

> The officers are to discourage Matrimony amongst the men as much as possible. Clandestine marriages,[18] or those soldiers neglecting the public ceremonies of the church, will be punished with vigour, as will those who do not first obtain their commanding officer's permission, prior to a marriage, so that the woman's character may be enquired into.[19]

Troublesome and lazy women could be a nuisance to a regiment, and unsettling for the men, hence the warning in the November 1751 orders:

> The Commanding Officer further recommends to the soldiers not to marry at all: the long March and Embarkation that will soon follow must convince them that many women in the Regiment are very inconvenient, especially as some of them are not so industrious nor so useful to their husbands as a soldier's wife ought to be.[20]

The women following the regiment had to be regularly inspected to ensure they were 'clean'. Wolfe commanded:

> If any woman in the Regiment has a Venereal Disorder, and does not immediately make it known to the Surgeon, they shall upon the first discovery be drum'd out of the Regiment, and be imprisoned in the Tolbooth, if ever she returns to the Corps.[21]

When Wolfe returned to England in November 1758 for some leave after the capture of Louisbourg, and to recuperate from 'gravel and rheumatism', he went to see his old regiment, the 20 Foot, and the 67 Foot, of which he was currently colonel. He also wanted to see his parents, especially his father, who had only a few months to live. But he also wanted to see Miss Lowther, whose family could hardly object to an officer whose praises all England were singing. So the couple became engaged and exchanged portraits. Wolfe wore Katherine's miniature on his last campaign; on his death it was returned to her, set in diamonds his estate could not afford and paid for by his friends. At Christmas 1758 Pitt was once again the arbiter in Wolfe's game of love and war when he posted him to command the expedition to Quebec. Katherine never saw him again; six years afterwards, she married Admiral the Duke of Bolton.

Although Wolfe was to have full responsibility for the expedition against Quebec, he would be under Amherst's command for other operations.

> **Secret Instructions for Our Trusty and Well beloved James Wolfe Esq., Brigadier-General of Our Forces in North America, and Major-General and commander-in-chief of a Body of Our Land Forces, to be employed on an Expedition against Quebec, by the way of the River St Lawrence. Given at Our Court of St James the Fifth of February, 1759, in the Thirty Second Year of Our Reign. George R.**
>
> **Whereas, We have appointed You to be Major General and commander-in-chief of a considerable Body of Our Land Forces directed to Assemble at Louisbourg in our Island of Cape Breton, in**

order to proceed, by way of the River St Lawrence, as early as the Season of the Year will admit of operations, by Sea and Land, in those Parts, to attack and reduce Quebec.

And whereas We have appointed Rear-Admiral Saunders to be commander-in-chief of a squadron of our ships to act in Conjunction, and co-operate with our said Land Forces, in the execution of the above most important service.

We have thought fit to give you the following instructions for Your Conduct. And it is Our Will and Pleasure that you do carry into Execution the said important operation with the utmost application and vigour.

Whereas the success of this expedition will very much depend upon an entire Good Understanding between Our Land and Sea Officers, both Wolfe and Saunders were strictly enjoined and required to maintain and cultivate such a good Understanding and Agreement.[22]

The entire direction and strategy of the Quebec expedition was Pitt's masterpiece. The execution and tactical decisions were to be left to the commanders on the spot.

Besides giving Wolfe his instructions for the mission and campaign in New France, Pitt gave him freedom to select two of the three senior military commanders. Command of the 1st Brigade Wolfe gave to the Honourable Robert Monckton, son of the first Viscount Galway. Monckton, six months older than Wolfe, was already in America as colonel of the 2nd Battalion Royal Americans (60 Foot).[23] He had previously served six years with distinction in Nova Scotia, where his tactful handling of the expulsion of the Acadians had been warmly commended. He was the senior brigadier, and would be Wolfe's second-in-command.

For the 3rd Brigade Wolfe chose James Murray, a son of Lord Elibank. He had served almost continuously abroad in the 15 Foot, and shown his capability at Louisbourg. He was six years older than Wolfe, who had a high opinion of him, singling him out for the most hazardous exploits of the campaign. He, too, would become a general, and the first British governor of Canada.

Command of the 2nd Brigade was given by Pitt to the aristocratic Colonel George Townsend, grandson of a great Whig minister and brother of another, a nephew of the Duke of Newcastle. He was superior to Wolfe in both birth and years, and the reversal in their status was little to his liking. Townsend had been a lieutenant-colonel in the First Foot Guards at the age of 21, but had left the army some years previously after quarrelling, when ADC, with the Duke of Cumberland. He had a malicious tongue and a talent for drawing offensive caricatures, which he used on the Duke, Wolfe and others. Horace Walpole said he was of 'a proud, sullen and contemptuous temper', and he was to prove a sore trial to Wolfe, whose reputation he did his best to denigrate after Wolfe's death. Nevertheless, he was a very competent soldier.

Wolfe chose for his two senior staff officers Guy Carleton and Isaac Barré. Carleton, Wolfe's friend of his Paris days, was appointed quartermaster-general. He had fought at Louisbourg under Amherst, and was destined to become a highly popular governor of Quebec, a general, and, in recognition of his long and distinguished services, the first Lord Dorchester. Barré, another old friend, was the son of a French Huguenot refugee, who emigrated from La Rochelle to Dublin. He was to be Wolfe's adjutant general; later he entered parliament and became, with Edmund Burke, one of the staunchest champions of the rights of the American colonies. Both officers were severely wounded at Quebec.[24]

To command his artillery, which would play an important part in the siege, Wolfe selected Colonel George Williamson. He later became a general and officer commanding Woolwich, home of the Royal Artillery. The chief engineer was Major (later Colonel) Patrick Mackellar, who had served with Braddock making roads and bridges in advance of the army's march from Alexandria in Virginia across the Allegheny Mountains to Fort Duquesne. As chief engineer of frontier posts in 1756, he constructed Forts Ontario and Oswego. He was captured there, and held a prisoner of war in Montreal and Quebec before being exchanged. His maps of the Quebec fortifications were of great help to his commander. Wolfe also had a number of excellent regimental commanders, like Lieutenant-Colonel William Howe, who commanded the Light Infantry battalion; and William Delaune of Wolfe's own 67 Foot. These two would lead the assault troops up the cliffs at the Anse au Foulon. With such leaders, it is no wonder that the military historian J F C Fuller should conclude: 'Wolfe was supported by probably the finest body of English officers, which has ever taken the field of battle.'[25]

Wolfe realised from the start that he would not receive an army of the 12,000 first promised. Regiments from Guadeloupe could not be spared, owing to their wretched condition, and, as at Louisbourg, he found that more than a quarter of the authorised regimental establishments were non-effective. The embarkation return for 5 June 1759 (Appendix C) gives 8,628 all ranks. These were nearly all regulars, and as good as any the British army could then supply. There were about 900 American rangers present during the siege, including 100 who joined on the way to Quebec, and 300 others who joined after the siege began. Wolfe, somewhat hastily and unjustly, condemned these men in unfavourable terms:

> The Americans are in general the dirtiest, most contemptible cowardly dogs that you can conceive. There is no depending upon them in action. They fall down dead in their own dirt and desert by battalions, officers and all. Such

rascals as those are rather an encumbrance than any real strength to an army.[26]

The 13 colonies were very slack in their military organisation, always at loggerheads with the home government, and unwilling to send large bodies of troops away from home on distant operations. Most were raw recruits, unaccustomed to a disciplined, military life. However serviceable they may have been in bush-fighting, they were less efficient in a regular campaign of siege warfare.

The force was divided into three brigades under Monckton, Townsend and Murray respectively.[27] In addition, Wolfe had three companies of 100 men each, drawn from the 22, 40 and 45 Foot, known as the Louisbourg Grenadiers; 200 light infantry, 300 Royal Artillery, and six companies of provincial rangers – not militiamen provided by colonial governments, but long-service professionals raised under the Crown.

The fleet which Pitt assembled for the expedition was formidable, though none too large for the task. There were 39 men-of-war and ten auxiliaries, mounting nearly 2,000 pieces of ordnance, 76 transports and 162 miscellaneous craft, manned by 13,750 naval personnel, and 5,000 mercantile marine – twice as many as the landsmen under Wolfe. It was a difficult task to keep this motley collection of ships of all sizes and conditions together. Fortunately there was fine weather as a rule, and favourable winds for a good part of the way.[28]

Command was given to Sir Charles Saunders, one of Admiral Lord George Anson's favourite officers, who had accompanied Anson on his famous voyage around the world (1740). He put patriotism before any professional jealousy he may have felt as the head of the senior service. Much of the success of the combined amphibious operation was due to Saunders and the Royal Navy. Philip Durrell, his second-in-command, was also a competent officer, who had served with distinction as commodore under Boscawen at Louisbourg. Charles Holmes, third in command, was a very good seaman and commander, who would co-ordinate the timings and movements of the ships engaged in the landings.

Many of the ships' captains in the fleet were also men of distinction. James Cook, a farmhand's son who would become famous as one of the world's greatest navigators, was sailing master of the *Pembroke*. His soundings helped the fleet to navigate the hazards of the St Lawrence River. Lord Colvill of the *Northumberland* commanded as a rear admiral the North American squadron, which would see the final surrender of New France the next year. Captain John Jervis, later Admiral Earl St Vincent, commanded the gallant little *Porcupine* of 14 guns at the age of 24. He would gain even greater fame with Lord Nelson.

The most friendly spirit prevailed between the two Services. This rendered possible the decisive action, which immediately led to the fall of Quebec and the conquest of Canada. The brilliance of this little battle, with Wolfe's glorious death, caught the popular imagination, and has prevented many from seeing that, it was but the crowning incident of a long series of operations, all based on the actions of the fleet, which alone rendered them possible.[29]

On 17 February 1759 Wolfe set sail from Portsmouth on board the flagship *Neptune*. Although he was under the overall command of Jeffrey Amherst, the commander-in-chief, Pitt had given him a free hand at Quebec. Before he sailed, Wolfe wrote to his uncle in Dublin, 'I shall do my best and leave the rest to fortune'.[30]

18

BEFORE QUEBEC

'Art had conspired with Nature
To render the place impregnable'. Wolfe's monument.

Pitt's plan for 1759 in North America was to strike two great blows at
Canada, in an all-out assault on the St Lawrence Valley from the newly-
won bases. Starting from Louisbourg, General Wolfe was to attack Quebec
through the mouth of the St Lawrence River. He would be supported by a
powerful fleet under Admiral Saunders, with a force of about 12,000 embarked
troops. The commander-in-chief, General Amherst, with the main army of
12,000 regulars and provincials, would start from Lake George. He was to
travel down the Richelieu River, via Ticonderoga and Crown Point (the Lake
Champlain route), and capture Montreal. A third expedition, under Brigadier
Prideaux, was ordered to attack Fort Niagara from the west. This force would
be mainly composed of colonials, with a few regiments of regulars and Sir
William Johnson's Indian warriors. After capturing Niagara, the force would
march on Montreal and co-operate with the combined forces of Amherst and
Wolfe.

The rendezvous for the great armada, which left Spithead on 17 February
1759 under Admiral Saunders, was Louisbourg. The date for the warships,
frigates, fire-ships, transports, ordnance vessels and supply ships to assemble
was 20 April. But the armada made slow progress in bad weather, and arrived
off Cape Breton ten days late to find Louisbourg still choked with ice and
blanketed with fog. Unable to enter the harbour, the fleet made for Halifax,
where Wolfe learned of the death of his father. On the voyage, Wolfe had
suffered sea-sickness and was in constant pain from his rheumatism and bladder
complaint.

Waiting for Wolfe in Halifax were the troops from the American garrisons.
One of these regiments was the 43 Foot (the Monmouthshire Light Infantry),
with the diarist Lieutenant Knox, looking forward to some active service after
20 months' confinement in a backwoods fort. Joining the troops assembling at
Louisbourg were Fraser's Highlanders (78 Foot) from New York, bringing
Lieutenant (later Colonel) Malcolm Fraser, who kept a journal of the Quebec
operations.[1] Almost his first entry recorded that 'A lieutenant on board one of
the men of war has shot himself, for fear, I suppose, the French should do it.

If he was wearied of life, he might soon get quit of it in a more honourable way.'[2]

The fleet, which included 74 American ships and 3,000 American sailors, set sail for the Gulf of St Lawrence on 4 June with 8,600 regular soldiers on board (Appendix C), and double that number of sailors and marines. American waters had never before seen such an armada. Wolfe realised that his army, however excellent in quality and morale, however well led and equipped, would have to attack one of the strongest fortresses in the world, defended by an army nearly twice as large as his own, and Canadians fighting for their home and country. To preserve the health of his men on the voyage, Wolfe instructed them to keep in the open air and take as much exercise as possible, to eat on deck, and to keep their berths and bedding clean.[3] Day after day, spread out for 50 miles along the coast, the vast fleet steadily approached Quebec.

Wolfe distributed his troops under the three brigadiers as follows (see Appendix C for details):

1st Brigade (Monckton)15, 43, 58 and 78 Foot Regiments
2nd Brigade (Townsend) 28, 47 and 2/60 Foot Regiments
3rd Brigade (Murray 35, 48 and 3/60 Foot Regiments.[4]

The French could command 6,000 regulars, 1,500 colony marines and 14,000 militiamen, though Vaudreuil had left a mixed force of 3,000 regulars and 4,000 militia and marines to protect the rest of New France. Wolfe had considerably less than the 12,000 troops promised. Nevertheless, 'if valour can make amends for want of numbers, we shall succeed,' he wrote to Pitt.[5]

The regiments were allowed to take married women with them on a scale of four per 100 men, since they would provide useful services in the field. The normal active service allowance was six per 100 men, but a commanding officer would often look the other way when soldiers smuggled aboard the transports wives who had been unlucky in the ballot at the quayside.[6] It was also customary for a number of female sutlers, usually army widows, to be attached to the force travelling in separate transports, most of whom acted abroad as part-time prostitutes.

Early in May, Admiral Philip Durrell, second-in-command to Saunders, had been sent ahead with ten ships to block the entrance to the St Lawrence. Unfortunately, he arrived four days too late to prevent three French frigates and 18 transports from slipping into Quebec with 340 recruits, 1,500 sailors, and much-needed provisions to reinforce the garrison. On board one of the frigates was one of Montcalm's ablest generals, Louis de Bougainville.[7] Montcalm had sent him, after the fall of Louisbourg, to represent to Louis XV the desperate plight facing the French colony, once the 1759 campaigning season began.

'The situation of the colony is most critical,' Montcalm wrote to the minister of war. '*La paix est nécessaire ou le Canada est perdu.*'[8] Though only 30, Bougainville was an accomplished diplomat as well as a soldier, and had once been a secretary at the French embassy in London. He was a favourite of Madame de Pompadour, and discussed his mission with her. 'The King is nothing: Pompadour all powerful,' he noted.[9] Unfortunately, king, court and courtesan had less interest in the fate of the colonies than in France's war in Europe.

Bougainville found France preparing to invade England with 65,000 men, and assembling the necessary transports at Brest, Le Havre and Dunkirk. The attack never materialised, after the French escorting fleets were defeated by Boscawen at Lagos, and by Hawke at Quiberon Bay. Bougainville realised that French priorities were troops for Europe and help for Maria Theresa; Canada was regarded as an endless source of expense. Moreover, the extravagance of the court, the inefficiency of the administration and the prosecution of the European war had exhausted the treasury.

To Bougainville's requests for infantry reinforcements, artillery, ammunition and food, the Minister of Marine, de Berger (who had succeeded Machault, sacked by Pompadour), replied: 'The King cannot send all you need. You must confine yourself to the defensive. When the house is on fire, one doesn't bother about the stables.'[10] Canada must rely on its own resources.

In fact, Vaudreuil had already undermined the mission by duplicity.[11] To put his own case he had sent Major Péan, the corrupt husband of Bigot's mistress. Outwardly he had warmly commended Bougainville to the Minister of Marine. 'Bougainville is in all respects better fitted than anyone else to inform you of the state of the colony. I have given him my instructions, and you can trust entirely in what he tells you.' At the same time, he wrote under confidential cover: 'I have given letters to Bougainville but I have the honour to inform you that they do not represent the colony, and to warn you that he is a creature of M. de Montcalm.' Bougainville did return with some assistance, as we have seen. He also brought back promotion for Montcalm, Lévis, Bourlamaque and Bougainville himself, and instructions for Vaudreuil from Berger to defer to Montcalm in all matters concerning military operations and army administration. At least Berger, another of Pompadour's appointments, did begin to probe the corruption in Canada, and to reprimand Bigot.

More importantly, Bougainville returned to Quebec with a copy of Amherst's letter to Pitt detailing the whole British campaign plans, which had been intercepted at sea. This intelligence, that the main British attack would be directed on Quebec by sea and not via Lake Champlain, and the news of Durrell's squadron blocking the entrance to the St Lawrence, meant a re-casting of the French plans, and spurred Montcalm to the task of fortifying the Beauport heights.[12]

Back in Quebec, Bougainville found relations between Vaudreuil and Montcalm growing ever more strained over the strategy to meet the expected British attacks, and the deployment of French troops. Despite the quarrels, steps had been taken to prepare the colony for the coming campaign. Vaudreuil had mobilised every able-bodied man to support the French regulars and their Indian allies. But the French firmly believed that Quebec was unassailable by water, since no foreign ships would dare navigate the 500 miles of strong currents, small islands, reefs, shoals and fogs from the mouth of the St Lawrence to Quebec.[13]

Saunders had been asked to accompany Wolfe with his entire battle squadron to the very walls of Quebec, and wonderfully well he performed his task, despite the many obstacles and the French belief that such a feat was impossible, without the help of experienced pilots. Using a chart drawn after the capture of Louisbourg by a talented engineer of the Royal Americans,[14] the British naval captains Jervis and James Cook[15] safely navigated the river. They anchored the smaller ships on the ebb tide, took soundings, and left marker buoys to guide the main fleet. It is also claimed that French Canadian pilots were shanghaied aboard the British ships and forced to assist the navigation, under threat of being hanged from the mainmast.[16] Thus Saunders and his intrepid captains successfully dealt with every hazard and brought the fleet unscathed to Quebec – a masterly feat of seamanship!

On 26 June 1759 the whole fleet dropped anchor off St Laurent, four miles from Quebec. That night a small party of rangers landed virtually unopposed on the Isle of Orleans, followed at daybreak by the rest of the army. Vaudreuil, later tried in France with Bigot for negligence over the passage of the St Lawrence, was horrified. 'The enemy has passed 60 ships of war, where we hardly dared risk a vessel of 100 tons,' he wrote – a fitting tribute to the British navy![17]

As soon as his troops had landed, Wolfe, with his chief engineer MacKeller, crossed the island to inspect his objective more closely. Before leaving England MacKeller had given Wolfe an excellent map of Quebec and a detailed account of its defences from his own personal observations. But the situation now looked very different. Quebec, the ancient capital of Canada, lay across the river before him – a noble setting for the coming drama! It stood proudly on a lofty ridge on the north bank of the St Lawrence River, protected from assault on every side. In the Upper Town, 180 feet above the river, was the residence of the governor (Chateau Frontenac now occupies the site). Westward from the city the ridge falls nearly sheer into the river for several miles, strengthened by every defensive device imaginable. Watched by a mere handful of men, it was considered by the French to be safe against any form of attack.[18]

The other side of Quebec was guarded by the St Charles River, joining the St Lawrence immediately below its walls. A pontoon bridge over the St Charles enabled French troops to cross from the city to the Beauport Lines. Here, Montcalm had built his main defences on the ridge, stretching for nearly six miles in an almost straight line along the northern shore. The harbour was protected by a boom and a floating battery of 12 guns. Opposite the town, the St Lawrence River suddenly narrows to a width of three-quarters of a mile, so Quebec's batteries could fire on ships trying to pass. The few French warships were lying dispersed as far away as Sorel, 120 miles above Quebec.[19]

The garrison of 2,000 men under Commandant de Ramezay mounted more than 100 guns, while 14,000 soldiers and 1,000 Indians were entrenched along the Beauport Lines. Quebec is impregnable, Vaudreuil had assured Versailles.[20] But its real defensive strength was due to nature rather than to man. To Wolfe, picking out the fortifications and gun positions through his glasses, Quebec must have seemed less of a fortress than a cathedral city, with its spires, roofs and pinnacles silhouetted against the western sky.[21]

The Beauport ridge ended in a gorge, where the Montmorency River rushes into the St Lawrence over a waterfall more than 100 feet (30 metres) higher than the Niagara Falls – one of the most beautiful sights in a landscape teeming with natural beauty! Leaving the 2,000 town militia and sailors to hold Quebec, Montcalm concentrated his five regular regiments, Canadian militia and Indians in entrenched positions along this ridge. Two hundred and fifty picked men were converted to mounted infantry, as a small mobile observation force. In the middle of the Lines, at the house of Monsieur de Vienne, Montcalm established his headquarters in the village of Beauport.[22] His deputy, Lévis, was in command of the troops on the French left flank along the Montmorency River. Bougainville, his aide-de-camp, guarded the high cliffs between Quebec and Cap Rouge, seven miles upstream towards Montreal, made practically impregnable by a corps of observers posted on the cliffs, and always on the alert.[23]

Wolfe established his main camp and hospital on the Isle of Orleans. He quickly realised the importance of Point Lévi and Pointe aux Pères on the rocky heights opposite Quebec. Here the river narrows to some 1,000 yards, and Vaudreuil's failure to secure it was a serious mistake. Wolfe sent Monckton's brigade to occupy the heights and drive off the small number of Canadian troops, settlers and Indians in the area. Guns were hauled up, batteries constructed, and they opened fire on 12 July, inflicting heavy damage among the buildings of the Lower Town. The area also provided a safer anchorage for the fleet, exposed to the elements on the south side of the Isle of Orleans. These measures were Wolfe's initial steps towards controlling the river both above and below the town.[24]

On 28 June, the day after he landed, Wolfe issued his first proclamation as 'Commander-in-Chief of his Britannic Majesty's Forces in the River St Laurence at Laurent, on the Island of Orleans':

The formidable sea and land armament, which the people of Canada now behold in the heart of their country, is intended by the King, my master, to check the insolence of France, to revenge the insults offered to the British colonies, and totally to deprive the French of their most valuable settlement in North America. The King of Great Britain wages no war with the industrious peasant, the sacred orders of religion, or the defenceless women and children; to these, in their distressful circumstances, his royal clemency offers protection. The people may remain unmolested in their lands, inhabit their houses, and enjoy their religion in security.[25]

In return, Wolfe expected the Canadians to take no part 'in the great contest between the two crowns'. If they did, they must expect 'their habitations to be destroyed, their sacred temples exposed to an exasperated soldiery, their harvests utterly ruined, and the only passage for relief stopped up by a most formidable fleet'.

Even as this manifesto in French was being placed by Monckton on the door of the village church of Beaumont, and Saunders was moving to the safer anchorage to protect his ships from the squalls of the open bay, the Governor of Quebec made his first offensive move,[26] launching a night attack of seven fireships against the British fleet. But 'these engines of destruction' were ignited prematurely. As 'explosion after explosion rent the midnight air', the British sailors coolly rowed out and towed the fireships to the shore, where they blazed harmlessly till dawn. 'They were certainly the grandest fireworks, that can possibly be imagined,' wrote Knox.[27] There was little the French could do to prevent the build up of Saunders's fleet, as a steady stream of ships manoeuvred to anchor before Quebec. On the night of 18 July, Holmes managed to sail the *Sutherland* and six other ships past the menacing French batteries to anchor off Cap Rouge, thus blockading Quebec on both sides of the river – one of the decisive achievements of the siege.

Wolfe's plan, before he had seen Quebec for himself, had been to force the St Charles River and reach the weaker side of Quebec.[28] But seeing Montcalm's army entrenched on the Beauport Lines convinced him that the plan was impracticable. So on 9 and 10 July he transferred his 2nd and 3rd Brigades (Townsend and Murray) across the river from the Isle of Orleans to establish a camp on the eastern side of the Montmorency Falls.[29] Here his guns could enfilade some of the French positions. During July and August he probed, reconnoitred, and wrestled with the problem – whether to make a frontal water-borne assault from the Basin, or attack Montcalm's left flank across the Montmorency River, or both! But though he tempted the French to attack him by a dubious division of his forces, Montcalm declined. 'While they are there,' he said, 'they cannot hurt us. Let them amuse themselves.'[30]

Captain Robert Stobo, one of the two hostages taken by the French when

Washington surrendered Fort Necessity, was transferred to Fort Duquesne, where he made a plan of the fort and sent it, signed, to Braddock. The signed plan was found by the French army among Braddock's documents. Stobo was sent to Quebec, court-martialed and sentenced to death. The sentence was sent to Louis XV for confirmation. In the meantime he was lodged in a house on the ramparts, where he was given a certain amount of freedom of movement. According to Stobo's *Memoirs*, the daughter of a French officer 'took pity on the unfortunate Captain, and ministered to his wants'. In 1759 he escaped to Louisbourg, and the governor sent him to Wolfe in Quebec. He gave Wolfe useful information about the town, its surroundings and inhabitants.[31] General Mahon[32] claims he may have provided information about possible landing places on the Cap Rouge side of Quebec before he left to join Amherst on 7 September. Whatever his information and methods, the British were sufficiently grateful to him to reward him with a commission in the 15 Foot.[33] Others might argue he was a disgrace to the Service, repaying French generosity by breaking his parole.

Besides carefully probing the Beauport defences, seeking a weak spot, Wolfe sent out armed patrols to lay waste all the settlements around Quebec. His earlier proclamation had produced little effect, so he decided to provoke desertions amongst the provincial militia and destroy the harvest and cattle, hoping to starve them into submission.[34] Colonel Fraser, with a detachment of 350 Highlanders, marched down the river during the night of 24 July, and returned two days later with 'three women and one man prisoners and about 200 head of cattle. At the same time, the Light Infantry went up the river on the same errand, and returned with about 200 prisoners, mostly women and children, and about 30 Canadian men, with 300 head of cattle, horses, cows, sheep etc.'[35]

Fraser also records[36] that on 18 July Wolfe dispatched Colonel Guy Carleton with a fighting patrol of Royal Americans (3/60 Foot) and grenadiers (15, 48 and 78 Foot) on board a group of armed ships. 'They passed the Town without receiving any hurt', and anchored opposite St Augustin, the troops continuing in boats to Pointe aux Trembles, 14 and 22 miles respectively from Quebec. This raid was the first menace to Montcalm's rear and lines of communication, and caused him to send 600 men from Beauport to Cap Rouge, eight miles above Quebec.

On 22 July hostilities were suspended for a time, while a party of French ladies, captured the previous day, were sent to Quebec in charge of Wolfe's ADC, Captain Hervey Smith. A French journal reported:

All the women, though of different rank, spoke well of the treatment they had received from the English officers. Several of them had supper with General Wolfe, who joked about the caution of the French generals. He told the ladies he had afforded very favourable opportunities for an attack, and had been surprised that no advantage had been taken of them. Several gentlemen had been captured with them, including one M. Lacasse, who, making the excuse of an injured leg, had left Quebec to spend the night with a Madame Landry. [37]

The soldiers hated going into the woods on reconnaissance patrols or to search for food, because they were likely to be killed and scalped by the Indians. Quartermaster John Johnson of the 58 Foot described the Indian methods in his *Memoirs*,[38] written in retirement at Chelsea Hospital (designed by Sir Christopher Wren and opened in 1692 by Charles II 'for such aged and maimed officers and soldiers, as might have to be discharged as unserviceable'; Louis XIV's equivalent in Paris, Les Invalides, was opened in 1674).

> The person, who unhappily falls a victim into their barbarous hands, is first disabled and disarmed. If there is any resistance, they take a cool and deliberate aim and throw their Tomma Hawk, which they throw with great certainty for a considerable distance and seldom miss. Then they spring up to him with their scalping knife, rip him open and sometimes take out his heart. After all, they cut round the top of the crown, to the Skull bone, and raising up one side of the Skin, with the Knife, with a jerk they tear it off by the hair, and the work is done: upon this they set up the Indian Whoop, as a signal that the work is finished, and also as a shout of Triumph.

Wolfe protested to Montcalm against this barbarous practice, but without effect. On 23 July 1759 Wolfe issued an order that scalping was forbidden, except when the enemy were Indians or Canadians disguised as Indians.[39] He also ordered five guineas to be given to the sentries of the 35 Foot for taking alive an Indian, who had crept up intending to assassinate them.[40]

The season was wearing on, noted Fortescue, and Wolfe was no nearer to his object than at his first disembarkation. Spurred on by his lack of success, he decided on 31 July to carry the Montmorency Heights by storm. The brigadiers did not approve of Wolfe's plan, which involved a frontal attack in broad daylight by 5,000 men, engaging a force twice their strength, entrenched in a very formidable position.[41] Wolfe held the Canadian militia in such contempt that he was not afraid to pit against them, at whatever odds, the valour of his own disciplined soldiers. His plan was simple: he would distract the enemy as much as possible by feints and bombardments in different places, while concentrating all available forces on the mile of entrenchments on the French left, commanded by Lévis, to the west of the Montmorency Falls.[42]

Monckton's brigade made the frontal attack from Point Lévi, supported by the guns of three armed vessels. Townsend and Murray left the camp on the north shore, forded the Montmorency below the Falls, and marched along the beach to join Monckton.[43] To distract Montcalm's attention, one of Townsend's regiments, with a detachment of light infantry, marched up the Montmorency in full view of the enemy, as if intending to ford the river above the Falls. Another regiment from the Lévi batteries marched along the south shore and threatened a landing at Sillery.[44]

The attack, though bravely attempted, failed with the loss of 33 officers and 450 men. A violent thunderstorm turned the slopes into mud and dampened the priming of the soldiers' muskets. Wolfe, perhaps unjustly, blamed much of the failure on the impetuosity of the grenadiers and Royal Americans. 'Such impetuous, irregular, unsoldierlike, proceedings destroy all order, and put it out of the General's power to execute his plans.' So impatient were these untried troops to engage in battle that, without orders and formation, and without waiting for support, they rushed at the enemy 'thinking they alone could beat the French army'. Inter-regimental rivalry doubtless had much to do with it.[45] Wolfe at least recognised it was 'a hazardous plan, which depended on the successful working of many combinations. A man sees his error often too late to remedy it.'[46]

This staggering reverse was a terrible blow to Wolfe, who pictured himself as being seen at home as yet another failed British general. Twice wounded himself with gun splinters, he went from tent to tent visiting his wounded officers and men, consoling himself with the belief that the defeat could be repaired, 'if the men will show a proper attention to their officers'. Vaudreuil called it 'a mad enterprise, certain to fail'; Montcalm realised it was but a small prelude to something more important. Meanwhile, 'their savages came down to murder such wounded, as could not be brought off, and to scalp the dead, as their custom is,' concluded Wolfe in his account of the battle to William Pitt.[47]

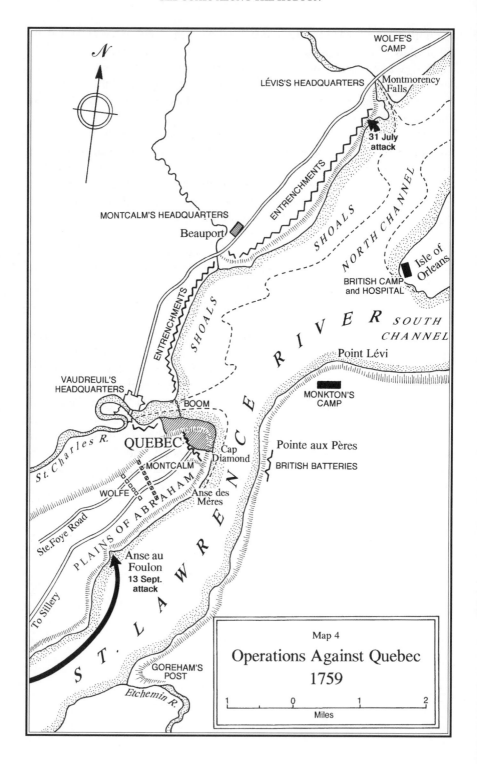

Map 4

Operations Against Quebec
1759

19

WOLFE FINDS THE KEY

'In War something must be allowed to chance and fortune'.[1]

T he month of August was a time of severe trial for both sides. Although the French had lost very few men in action, the British guns at Pointe aux Pères left the whole of the Lower Town, the richest and most thickly populated part of the city, and half the Upper Town in ruins, as shot and shell rained down on Quebec and overwhelmed the city batteries.[2] Houses, churches and monasteries crashed to the ground. The great cathedral was gradually reduced to a skeleton of charred walls; the church of Notre Dame de la Victoire, erected in gratitude for Quebec's deliverance from a previous attack 60 years earlier,[3] became one of the first victims.[4]

More and more British ships ran the gauntlet of the French guns and began to interrupt the river line of communications for 20 to 30 miles upstream, preventing French supplies reaching Quebec from Trois Rivières and Montreal. Murray was sent up the river with a commando force of 1,200 men and a naval squadron under Holmes to seek out the French ships, reconnoitre French defences, and destroy the large depots of food, clothing and ammunition established at Deschambault by Vaudreuil. Leaving by night on 6 August, the expedition reached Pointe aux Trembles two days later. Two attempts to land were anticipated by Bougainville and driven back. In spite of this, the expedition was reasonably successful: apart from the destruction of the stores and ammunition, much useful information was obtained. At Deschambault, Murray destroyed the house in which Madame Cadet had taken refuge, and captured letters giving full accounts of the fall of Niagara and Crown Point.[5]

The shore was clearly fortified at every accessible point. However, according to General Mahon, a descendant of Murray and his biographer,[6] Murray reported to Wolfe that the tides were suitable for a landing attempt on the north shore from Cap Rouge and Deschambault, 14 miles above Quebec, 'but the assault must be made at night, and at high tide'. This report was of great significance, because in the second half of August Wolfe's health confined him to bed and prevented him from executing 'my plan'; his brigadiers were asked to formulate a plan of their own. They were unanimous in proposing operations around Pointe aux Trembles, but not at night.

After Murray returned to camp on 25 August, the only tangible result of his expedition was to force Montcalm to detach 1,500 men from his camp at Beauport to reinforce Bougainville, who dug himself in at the mouth of a small stream at Cap Rouge. Montcalm also had to deplete his forces further by sending Lévis to Montreal with another 1,500 men, to oppose Amherst's steady advance after the fall of Ticonderoga and Niagara.[7]

In Quebec the garrison grew short of food, and the army was put on half rations. The British ships had cut the supply line by river, and food had to be sent from Montreal over bad roads in country carts, loaded and driven by old men, women and children. Sickness was rife; hospital accommodation was limited and of poor quality.[8] The only hope for the French was to hold on, until winter came to release the stranglehold on Quebec by the British fleet. The crops in the fields were unusually heavy but could not be harvested without further depleting Montcalm's forces; and Canadian militiamen were already deserting daily.

To encourage more defections among the Canadians, Wolfe resumed his tactic of laying waste the countryside, 'burning houses, felling the fruit trees, cutting the wheat' and taking prisoners.[9] Vaudreuil, fearing for the morale of his troops and the local inhabitants, wrote to Wolfe warning him that, if he persisted in this tactic, he would hand over all the English prisoners to the mercy of his Indian allies. 'Do as you like with them,' Wolfe replied. 'But you will know that we have captured a number of fair hostages. The very instant you carry out your threat, all the French ladies, without distinction, will be given up to the delicate embraces of the English marines.' In a postscript Wolfe added: 'We have at least three, if not four, transports, full freighted with French females, some of them of the first rank in this country.'[10]

Ensign Knox provides us with a glimpse of the British army in camp before Quebec. Wolfe had ordered the soldiers to keep their camp 'sweet and clean'. 'But,' wrote Knox, 'the swarming flies, short rations [the troops were eating mainly horse-flesh], dysentery and scurvy, were as big a plague, as the painted Red Indians, prowling around the sentry posts with tomahawks and scalping knives.'[11] Complaisant farm-girls were almost non-existent, and hopeful soldiers or sailors usually ended up as scalped bodies, if they strayed on the forest tracks. Deserters dreamed of 'the well-equipped brothels and wine cellars'[12] awaiting them in Quebec, and risked certain execution by their regiments, if caught outside the camp. 'The only relief', according to Knox, 'was to be found in the almost lethal spirits, provided by the women sutlers [mostly army widows], whose petticoats and leather stays, hanging up between the trees, drove Wolfe to fury.'[13]

Wolfe's own frustration at the siege's lack of progress, and his continuing ill-health, were perhaps responsible for the threatening series of general orders he published.

All Orders relating to women must be read to them by the sergeants of their respective companies, so that they may not plead ignorance. Only those women with specific authority to sutle in the camps are to be allowed to do so. Women refusing to serve as nurses in the field hospitals are to be struck off the victualling roll. Camp followers are to be chased out of camp by the Provost staff. No rum or spirits of any kind are to be sold in or near the camp. Soldiers, who give away their rum allowances or sell them, risk being struck off the rum Roll and being court-martialed. Any soldier found outside the camp lines, or with plunder in his tent, is to be sent to the Provost in irons to be tried for his life.

On 14 July his general orders permitted regiments to send to the encampment on the Pointe of Orleans for 'one woman per company' – much to the delight of the soldiers![14]

On 20 August Wolfe was laid low with fever, exhausted by the heat, hard work and anxiety. Desperately he begged his surgeon to patch him up, so he could 'do his duty for the next few days'.[15] He was compelled to delegate the planning of operations to a council of his brigadiers, but he was unwilling to delegate responsibility for any important operations he could not direct himself. Knowing he would probably not outlive the campaign, Wolfe was determined to retain the glory for himself, argue historians. 'Sure of being well seconded by the Admiral and the Brigadiers, you may be assured,' Wolfe wrote to Pitt on 2 September, 'that the small part of the campaign, which remains, shall be employed, as far as I am able, for the honour of His Majesty, and the interest of the nation.'[16]

Historians have criticised Wolfe's reluctance to abandon his idea of an attack on the Beauport Lines. Clearly, he wished to engage Montcalm's army and destroy it before investing Quebec. But that meant fighting Montcalm on his own terms. To his mother, on 31 August, Wolfe wrote:

The enemy puts nothing to risk, and I can't in consequence put the whole army to risk. My antagonist has wisely shut himself up in inaccessible entrenchments, so that I can't get at him, without spilling a torrent of blood, and that perhaps to little purpose. The Marquis de Montcalm is at the head of a great number of bad soldiers, and I am at the head of a small number of good ones, but the wary old fellow avoids an action, doubtful of the behaviour of his army.[17]

Time was pressing: Wolfe had either to strike a decisive blow in September, or abandon Quebec for that year. Saunders and the brigadiers were impatient. Wolfe suffered a relapse, and was again confined to bed. But on 28 August he was well enough to dictate a letter to his army commanders asking them for their advice. To Wolfe this must have been a bitter blow, since they had made no secret of their criticism of his conduct of the campaign. Until then Wolfe had made his own plans, kept his own counsel, and taken full responsibility for his actions.[18]

The brigadiers advised bringing the troops to the south shore from the Montmorency camp; then,

> To carry out operations above the Town, forcing Montcalm to fight on our terms, and putting us between him and his provisions, and between him and the Army opposing General Amherst. If he gives us battle and we defeat him, Quebec, and probably all Canada, will be ours. Whatever you determine to do, you will find us most hearty and zealous in the execution of your orders.

Their plan meant transferring the army from Montmorency to a new camp on the south shore, between the Etchemin and Chaudière Rivers. The object was to land on the north shore at any convenient spot between Cap Rouge, nine miles, and Pointe aux Trembles, 22 miles up the river. Some troops would be left to defend the Isle of Orleans and the guns at Point Lévi.[19]

Wolfe accepted the plan to assault above the town, but the exact landing place had been left to him. He ordered the Montmorency camp to be abandoned on 31 August. This difficult and dangerous operation took four days, and the necessary staff work was ably managed by Carleton.[20] On 2 September Fraser reported the regiments crossing the St Lawrence River at night to the camp at Point Lévi, 'without molestation from the French, though they must have known some time ago, that we intended to abandon that post'.[21] On the last night a feint attack was launched from Point Lévi to deceive the French, while the last of the troops were brought off from Montmorency by the fleet, and successfully passed above the town with the baggage and stores.[22]

Next day, the Light Infantry under Colonel William Howe,[23] with the 28 and 35 Foot, and the Louisbourg Grenadiers, marched overland from Point Lévi and embarked with Wolfe himself on Admiral Holmes's ships. By this redeployment the centre of operations had moved from Beauport to the French coast, opposite the Etchemin River. Soon Monckton and Townsend joined Murray with the 15, 43 and 78 Foot, leaving small detachments to guard the base at Orleans and the artillery at Lévi. The army of some 4,000 men was now in the upper river, ready to launch an attack on the north bank. The 48 Foot, some 700 strong, was left under Colonel Burton near Point Lévi to await orders.[24]

Montcalm's answer was to leave his main army strongly entrenched in the Beauport Lines, but to reinforce Bougainville with another 3,000 men. He directed them to watch the movements of the ships with the utmost vigilance.

Bougainville's headquarters was at Cap Rouge, with fortified detachments at Sillery and Samos, and a large 'flying column' under his personal control. Montcalm remained at Beauport, convinced that the main attack, when it came, would be on his front.

For four days, from 7 to 10 September, Wolfe began a game of deception to conceal his real intentions – a very necessary precaution, when captured soldiers or deserters on both sides were ready to talk, often under duress. Making use of the river's tidal ebb and flow, its velocity of four knots, and its known movements, Wolfe's men drifted or rowed up and down, as if searching for a place to land, closely followed on shore by Bougainville and his flying column. On the morning of 7 September, for example, Holmes's squadron of 22 ships weighed anchor and sailed up to Cap Rouge with 3,600 sailors, followed by Bougainville's men.[25] Fraser confirmed this in his diary: 'The Army above the town, being about 4,000 strong, continue on board the ships, most of the men above deck, though it is very rainy weather. The same next day, Sunday 9th. Because of the overcrowding on the ships, about 1,500 men were ordered on shore at St Nicholas on the south side of the river, "to refresh themselves".'[26]

On 10 September more troops were landed to dry their clothes and accoutrements. Fraser continued, 'We hear we are to land soon on the north shore. We see a number of the French entrenched there, on a beach, where they have got some floating batteries.' Saunders also used his fleet to make feint attacks opposite Beauport, to keep Montcalm and his main army guessing, while the batteries on Lévi bombarded the Quebec garrison opposite.

The French were now on the alert everywhere along a 30-mile stretch of the north shore from the Montmorency Falls to Pointe aux Trembles. Montcalm was convinced that the steep cliffs stretching along the north shore above the town made a landing in force impracticable much below Cap Rouge. Bougainville's mobile force and fixed defences, guarding the difficult terrain, would prevent that. By the time any opposed landing could gain a foothold, Montcalm could transfer his army across the St Charles bridge to cover Quebec, and throw back the assault with his superior numbers. If the main attack came on the Beauport front, his main army, skilfully entrenched, could repel it.[27]

But Wolfe, by re-embarking his army every evening on board the ships in the upper river, and using the flowing and ebb tides in succession, now had the mobility to strike whenever and wherever he chose. For the first time in the campaign he dominated the battle-front. The continual movement accustomed the British soldiers to the boats and the river; it also led Bougainville and Montcalm to believe that the manoeuvres on 12 September were only a variation on what they had witnessed for the past several days.[28]

Wolfe had already issued his landing orders in great detail. Each regiment had been told, on 7 September, its place in the order of landing and in the distribution of boats. But the orders contained no hint of the exact landing place.[29] The next day, Wolfe took his brigadiers on a reconnaissance up river to Pointe aux Trembles. Two days of bad weather followed. On board HMS *Sutherland* Wolfe sent a situation report (9 September) with his last despatch to England, addressed to Lord Holdernesse, Secretary of State for the Northern Department:

> If Montcalm had shut himself in the town of Quebec, it would long since have been in our possession, because the defences are negligible, and our artillery formidable. The town is totally demolished and the country in a great measure ruined. Our fleet blocks up the river, both above and below the town, but it can give no kind of assistance in an attack upon the Canadian army. We have continual skirmishes: old men of 70 and boys of 15 fire on our units, and kill or wound our men from the edges of the woods. Every man able to bear arms, both above and below Quebec, is in the camp at Beauport. The old men, women and children are retired into the woods. The Canadians are dissatisfied, but forced by the Government to man the trenches, and terrified by the savages posted around them.
>
> Our poor soldiers have worked, without ceasing or grumbling, to protect themselves with entrenchments, and have repulsed all attacks by their valour. But scarce a night passes, without the enemy watching for an opportunity, to surprise and murder. There is very little quarter given on either side.
>
> The natural defences of the town and countryside are formidable, and the river, particularly here, so strong, that ships often drag their anchors by the mere force of the current. Storms and extreme heat hinder us, and make us inactive.[30]

He ends his despatch on a note of pessimism, bordering on despair. He was in terrible pain, and near mental collapse. 'For myself, I am so far recovered, as to do business, but my constitution is entirely ruined, without the consolation of having done my considerable service to the State, or without any prospect of it.'

The same day, 9 September, Wolfe resumed his search for a suitable landing place. He disembarked from a ship's boat just below the Etchemin River, and surveyed the opposite shore through a glass. He saw the tents of the enemy on the top of the cliffs – scarcely more than a dozen at one point, in charge of Vergor, whom he knew to be a true product of the Bigot regime.[31] While his brigadiers continued to believe that he would land at the Pointe aux Trembles, Wolfe's chief engineer, Major MacKeller, who accompanied Wolfe on his reconnaissance, was certain he had another place in mind.[32] Wolfe had written to Saunders on 30 August: 'My ill-state of health hinders me from executing my own plan: it is of too desperate a nature to order others to execute.'[33] Beyond this, he kept his thoughts to himself.

The next day Wolfe again set off down river on reconnaissance, escorted by an officer and 30 men of the 43 Foot. This time he took with him Holmes, Monckton, Townsend, Carleton, MacKeller, Captain Chads of the *Vesuvius,* who was to be in charge of the landing craft, and Captain Delaune of the Light Infantry, who would command the landing party. Murray was left behind, in charge of the troops. Wolfe took the reconnaissance party to Goreham's Post, a hillock near the mouth of the Etchemin, from where they had a clear view of the Anse au Foulon Cove. It was early afternoon and, despite their efforts to disguise themselves 'in grenadier coats', the vigilant French officer commanding the post at Sillery watched them through his telescope. He reported their activities to his superior, Bougainville, without causing any alarm in the French camp. The party spent three hours carefully examining the area, but, as is clear from the brigadiers' later request for more exact information, Wolfe kept the details of his plan to himself, with two exceptions. The only officers who knew the exact landing place in advance were Admiral Holmes, in executive command of the covering squadron, and Captain Chads, the naval officer in charge of the landing boats.[34]

Before returning to the *Sutherland,* Wolfe gave Carleton and Burton orders to have their detachments ready to start from the Isle of Orleans and Lévi in good time on 12 September. It is certain that Saunders would also have been informed of his plan, since the naval support was vital.

For some time Wolfe had been searching the cliffs above Quebec with his telescope, hoping to find a weak spot in the defences. At the Anse au Foulon, now called Wolfe's Cove, one-and-a-half miles from Quebec, he had spotted a narrow path running from the shore across the face of the 175-feet-high cliffs, protected by an abattis of felled trees. Nearby was a steep spur, which a determined storming party might scale, overpower the small guard at the top, and cover the ascent of an attacking party up the path. The ascent was so steep and rugged that the French thought the cliffs impossible to scale.[35]

So audacious was the plan that historians have speculated on its origin. Had Wolfe made the discovery with his telescope? Did he learn of the path from Stobo?[36] Montcalm believed the cliffs were so high and steep that '100 men posted there would stop the whole British army'. Why was the post so lightly defended, and how did Wolfe learn of this? Did Wolfe simply take a calculated risk, hazarding the fate of his army and the success of his campaign on such a stroke of luck?[37] Did he receive this vital piece of information from a deserter?[38] Traditionally the Canadian Captain Louis de Vergor, tried for cowardice after the surrender of Beauséjour (1755), is blamed for the failure. He commanded the small picket at the cliff-top, having replaced a French regular officer, only a day or two previously on Vaudreuil's own orders. Had this cowardly and incompetent officer sent his locally-enlisted militia to gather in the harvest on their farms, or work on his own farm in the neighbourhood?[39]

General Mohan provides another possible and plausible explanation for some of the mysteries and inconsistencies surrounding the landing.[40] On 5 September Montcalm had ordered the Guienne Regiment to be deployed on the Plains of Abraham outside Quebec, between the town and the Anse au Foulon, ready to assist either. Two days later Vaudreuil ordered the Regiment to withdraw, countermanding Montcalm's order at the suggestion of Bigot and Cadet, with disastrous results for the French. Mahon suggests that these two rogues were now hoping for a French defeat, to cover up their years of swindling the French government. He suggests it was an informer in their pay who gave Wolfe the vital information he needed. Furthermore, Mahon sees their hand in some of the other puzzling events which follow, including Vergor's conduct.

On 11 September Wolfe issued orders for the re-embarkation of the troops at St Nicholas, repeating their instructions 'to hold themselves in readiness to land and attack the enemy'. They would be expected 'to go into the boats about nine tomorrow night, or when it was pretty near high water'. The first wave would consist of 30 flat-bottomed boats, and five ships, containing about 1,700 men of Howe's Light Infantry and the 28, 43, 58 and 47 Foot, with a detachment of Monckton's 2/60 Foot and 200 Highlanders. The rest of the army would follow in the four ships of the line and the armed transports, save Burton's 1,200 men, who were to be ferried across from Goreham's Post when the main body had landed, making an assault force of 4,600.[41] The signal for the assault would be 'two lights on the main top-mast shrouds' of HMS *Sutherland,* wrote Knox, when the leading boats were to drop down the river on the ebb-tide. The definite point of attack had still not been given.[42]

On 12 September, as Wolfe was making his final dispositions, he enjoyed a piece of real good fortune. Two deserters from Bougainville's camp disclosed that Cadet had written to Bougainville to arrange for a convoy of much-needed provisions to pass down the river at night to Quebec on the ebb tide. Bougainville warned his outposts to let the convoy pass, despite the presence of the strong British squadron at Cap Rouge.[43] Wolfe used this vital piece of information, with disastrous consequences for the French.

Throughout the day Bougainville watched the ships lying motionless off Cap Rouge, while the British troops busied themselves cleaning their weapons and checking their equipment and ammunition. Montcalm remained at his headquarters, confident that no attack could be made below Cap Rouge and that, if an attack were made, the vigilant Bougainville could contain it, until Montcalm could arrive with reinforcements from his main army at Beauport. According to the Abbé Recher, Montcalm on this day again ordered the Guienne Regiment, encamped in reserve at the St Charles bridgehead, to Foulon; but once more Vaudreuil revoked his order, adding to the confusion and unrest in the army.[44] After the battle, Vaudreuil would try to dissociate himself from the blame for losing Quebec, spinning an intricate web of lies to damage the reputation of the military commanders, and, in so doing, to cloud the evidence of corruption and incompetence in his administration. But there is no evidence that Vaudreuil was a party to a betrayal of Quebec – he loved his native Canada too much!

Wolfe, on board HMS *Sutherland*, issued his last written orders to his army – a call to battle!

> The enemy's force is now divided; great scarcity of provisions in the camp, and universal discontent among the Canadians. A vigorous blow struck by the Army at this juncture may determine the fate of Canada. The troops will land, where the French seem least to expect them.
>
> The officers and men will remember what their country expects from them, and what a determined body of soldiers, inured to war, are capable of doing against five weak French Battalions [La Sarre, Languedoc, Béarn, La Guienne and Royal Roussillon], mingled with a disorderly peasantry.[45]

During the day the brigadiers, in a letter signed by all three, angrily asked for more precise details, 'thinking ourselves not sufficiently informed, particularly to the place or places we are to attack'. Wolfe quickly replied, dating and timing his letter for 8.30 that evening. He reminded them of the reconnaissance to show them 'the situation of the enemy and the place, where I meant they should be attacked – the place is called the Foulon, where you remember an encampment of 12 or 13 tents, and an abattis below it'. He explained the orders he had given to the others in the reconnaissance party concerning the order and stationing of the boats, and the composition and duty of the landing party. 'I shall be present myself to give you all the aid in my power.' Then he rebuffed their implied criticism of failing to provide sufficient information by reminding them that:

> it is not usual to point out in General Orders the direct point of an attack, nor for any inferior Officer, not charged with a particular duty, to ask for instructions upon that point. To the best of my knowledge and abilities, I have fixed upon that spot, where we can act with the most force, and are most likely to succeed. If I am mistaken, I am sorry for it, and must be answerable to His Majesty and the public for the consequences.[46]

The landing place had still not been revealed publicly, and this secrecy was fully vindicated when that same evening a soldier from the Royal Americans deserted to the French.[47] Deserters had little option but to talk!

Then, on the last evening of his life, Wolfe settled down to compose his own affairs. He had a presentiment of his fate. He sent for his old schoolfriend, Commander John Jervis (afterwards Lord St Vincent) of HMS *Porcupine,* and handed him, with his will, a miniature of his fiancée, Katherine Lowther, asking him in the event of his death to deliver it to her.[48] This same feeling of the brevity of life and the vanity of fame prompted him to recite, or listen to (which and exactly when are hotly debated by military historians), lines from Gray's *Elegy in a Country Churchyard* –

> The boast of heraldry, the pomp of pow'r,
> And all that beauty, all that wealth e'er gave,
> Awaits alike th'inevitable hour.
> The paths of glory lead but to the grave.[49]

As he sat in the boat, visiting some of the posts where the troops sat silent, before their boats drifted quietly down the river to their allocated places, he murmured: 'Gentlemen, I would rather have written those lines than take Quebec.'[50]

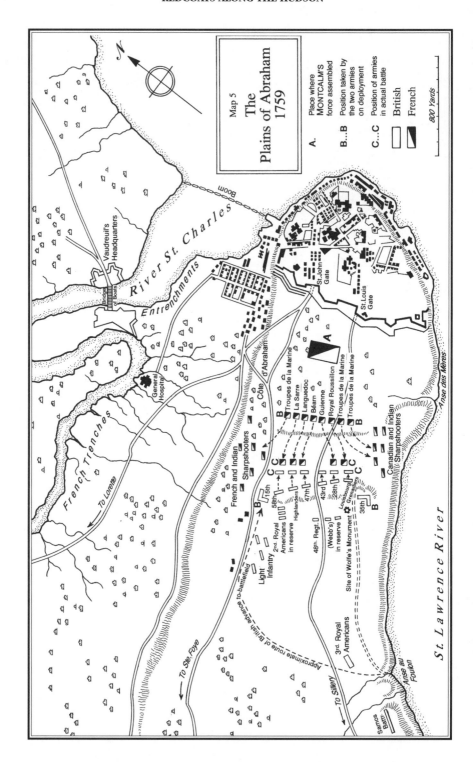

Map 5

The
Plains of Abraham
1759

A.   Place where
     MONTCALM'S
     force assembled

B...B Position taken by
      the two armies
      on deployment

C...C Position of armies
      in actual battle

     ☐ British
     ◆ French

800 Yards

20

WOLFE VERSUS MONTCALM
– THE FINAL GLORY

'What storms of Battle swept these crags of yore!
What fateful thunder shook them to their base.'[1]

At 9pm the troops began to embark in their appointed boats, scattered over a long stretch of the river. Fortunately the weather was fine, with no moon to reveal the activity to the French sentries on the shore. Silence was essential, as the boats were rowed with muffled oars down river, hugging the safety of the south shore.[2] At 1.30am a single light shone from the masthead of the *Sutherland,* lying off Cap Rouge: the signal for the boats to assemble between the headquarters ship and the south shore. Here they were marshalled by Captain James Chads into their proper order. Wolfe joined the foremost boat, with 24 volunteers of the Light Infantry, under the command of Captain William Delaune of the 67 Foot, who were to be the first to scale the cliff. Half an hour later, two lamps from the *Sutherland* signalled the line of boats to turn slowly across the stream of the river and head towards the north shore.

Meanwhile, Admiral Saunders had moved out of the basin of Orleans after dark with his ships, manned by marines, sailors and a few soldiers from the regimental hospitals on the Isle of Orleans. He ranged his ships along the whole length of the Beauport camp. At the appointed time they would open fire, as if to cover an assault landing, to keep Montcalm occupied during the night. The British batteries at Pointe aux Pères opposite Quebec kept up a constant furious bombardment. The French army spent a sleepless night, as Montcalm, booted and spurred, with his black charger saddled at the door of his Beauport headquarters, awaited the attack, which he still firmly believed would be launched on his side of Quebec.[3]

The plan for the assault ships was simple and effective. With Wolfe in the lead, the first eight boats of Light Infantry under Colonel William Howe of the 58 Foot formed the vanguard, closely followed by 28, 43, 47 and 58 Foot, and a detachment of Highlanders and Royal Americans. Captain Chads marshalled the boats, as they arrived in strict order.[4] Monckton was in charge of the first landing, some 1,700 men, and Murray was his second-in-command. One by one the sloops and frigates followed, the flotilla commanded by Vice Admiral Holmes to give artillery support – for the assault was to be a wonderful example of combined operations. After half an hour's interval the second wave approached under command of Brigadier Townsend, who described it:

> the most hazardous and difficult task, I was ever engaged in. For the distance of the landing-place, the impetuosity of the tide, the darkness of the night, and the great chance of exactly hitting the very spot intended, without discovery or alarm, made the whole extremely difficult.[5]

Wolfe ordered that, after the first wave had successfully landed, the boats would bring the troops waiting on the ships, and then ferry across Colonel Burton's 48 Foot and the 3rd Battalion Royal Americans – some 1,200 men, waiting on the south shore opposite the Cove. Wolfe wanted every man he could obtain for the coming battle.

As the leading craft approached the north shore, the chance of discovery was acute. The boats had to pass Sillery, within a few yards of the guns and French outposts, where the sentries were straining their eyes and ears for any sign of the enemy. Suddenly, out of the darkness came the clear challenge of a French sentry. '*Qui vive?*' Captain Simon Fraser, a French-speaking Highlander, who had been waiting in the first boat for such an eventuality, satisfied the challenger that they were a provisions convoy. The ships glided on, and in a few minutes the first boat slipped into Wolfe's Cove (Anse au Foulon). The time was just after 4am.

A mystery surrounds this episode.[6] The provisions convoy had, in fact, been cancelled (perhaps because of the British naval activity in the area), but the sentries had not been notified – again, with fatal consequences. Mahon accuses Cadet of cancelling the convoy without telling the military. Other historians believe Cadet was a rogue but never a traitor!

Dawn was just breaking, as the assault group of 24 volunteers, led by Captain Delaune, began to climb the steep spur, rising 175 feet above them. They hoped to take Vergor and his picket from the rear. Wolfe was among the first to leap ashore, encouraging them up the difficult climb. The leading group was quickly followed by Colonel William Howe and the three Light Infantry companies. Scrambling up on hands and knees, the roar from the Lévi batteries helping to drown any noise of the ascent, the storming party reached the top. They were challenged again. A reply in French created a moment's hesitation, enough for the leading climbers to attack the sentries with bayonets. Surprise was complete, and the picket put to flight. Vergor was captured in his shirt, wounded in the foot; others were taken prisoner. From these, Wolfe obtained useful information.[7] 'The difficulty of the ascent,' wrote Saunders to the Admiralty, 'was scarcely credible.'[8]

The other posts around Sillery and along the top of the cliffs were quickly eliminated, and the landing place secured. The Light Infantry, reinforced by the 58 Foot, captured and silenced the Samos battery, several hundred yards away and protected by a deep gully, which had begun to fire on the last boats of the first wave.

The firing and cheers of the men at the top gave Wolfe the signal to send up the rest of the troops. Soon a long file of redcoats swarmed on to the plateau, stumbling and cursing in the darkness, silence no longer necessary, as they cleared the obstacles from the path. Wolfe joined the first 1,600 at the top, as the boats smoothly disembarked their soldiers and sped back to collect Townsend's brigade from the ships, and Burton's 48 Foot waiting on the opposite shore.[9] By 6am Wolfe had his whole force of some 4,500 men on the heights, each man carrying 70 rounds of ammunition. But the task of dragging the guns up the cliffs was onerous, and by the time of the battle only one cannon was available.[10]

While the men were grouping into their regimental formations, Wolfe went forward to reconnoitre. He took the 58 Foot and most of the Light Infantry to the Ste Foy road, and was astonished to find no signs that the alarm had been raised. He returned to the cliff-top and, leaving the 3rd Battalion Royal Americans (60 Foot) to guard the landing place and his rear, marched his regiments as far as the Ste Foy road before wheeling right towards Quebec.[11] Wolfe selected a fairly level piece of ground less than a mile wide, known as the Plains of Abraham (named after Abraham Martin, a French pilot who had some land there in the early days of the settlers), to deploy his troops within a mile of Quebec. The grassy tract, patched here and there with corn and studded with clumps of bushes, formed good cover for marksmen. There he formed his battalions in line of battle on either side of the Quebec–Sillery road (see diagram).[12] 'Weather showery', reported Knox,[13] laconically.

On the extreme right, at the edge of the cliffs, Wolfe stationed the 35 Foot on a small knoll to protect his right flank. Next, from right to left, he placed the Louisbourg Grenadiers under Guy Carleton, the 28 Foot and the 43rd Regiment – all commanded by Monckton. Across the Sillery road, under Murray's command, were the 47 Foot, the Highlanders, the 58 Foot, and the 15 Foot protecting the left flank. The Light Infantry under Howe he deployed in a wood far in the rear, facing north, to repel the expected attack from Bougainville; in reserve, commanded by Townsend, were Webb's 48 Foot under Colonel Burton, and the 2nd Battalion Royal Americans.[14] When they arrived, he sited two brass cannons,[15] dragged up the cliffs by sailors, between the two halves of his army on the Sillery–Quebec road. Waiting on the beach were several strong landing parties of marines and seamen, in charge of guns and siege material for use after the battle on the cliffs above had been won.

Wolfe was able to deploy 3,265 men in the firing line, but about 1,000 of these were needed to protect his vulnerable flanks.[16] He had only some 2,000 men in the six regiments facing Quebec to cover the half-mile battle-front and bear the shock of the French attack. Thus, for the first time, the British army was drawn up by Wolfe in its famous 'red line', two deep instead of three, 50 years before such a formation was officially authorised. Having deployed his troops, Wolfe ordered them to load with double shot and lie down to await the appearance of the enemy. The time was just after 8am. Wolfe had gained complete surprise; it only remained now to crush Montcalm and his army.

Meanwhile, Montcalm was spending a sleepless night expecting an attack on the Beauport lines. About midnight, reports of the movements of Saunders's fleet seemed to confirm this. Around dawn he could clearly hear the firing from the Samos battery; but as no news arrived from Vaudreuil in Quebec, where he had stationed Marcel, one of his ADCs, to keep him informed, he was not alarmed.[17] Vaudreuil, in fact, had received news of an attack at the Anse au Foulon from one of Vergor's men at about 5am, and other reports were coming in of attempts to land at the Anse des Mères. But all was confusion at his headquarters. It was not until 6am that Montcalm, riding with Chevalier Johnstone, another of his ADCs and a Scottish Jacobite who had escaped from Culloden, to see Vaudreuil, received the astounding news that the British army had not only landed in strength but was forming up on the plateau behind the city. 'There they are, where they have no right to be,' he cried. 'This is a serious business.'[18]

Quickly Montcalm collected all the troops nearby. He ordered the Guienne Regiment forward, and dispatched his ADC to bring up the whole of his army from Beauport. When Johnstone arrived at Beauport he was told that Vaudreuil, not yet convinced of the strength of the landing, had only an hour earlier ordered the army left wing to stay where it was. Eventually the ADC was able to impress on Montcalm's deputy at Beauport the desperate urgency of the situation. Soon the troops from Beauport began to stream across the bridge of boats, towards the city and the slopes beyond.[19] Here, outside the St John and St Louis Gates of the city, Montcalm began to deploy his forces up the slopes and on to the Plains of Abraham beyond.

First, Montcalm sent groups of grey-clad Canadian militiamen, 'whose all was at stake, faith, country and home', and Indians in scalp-locks and warpaint to harass the flanks of the British army.[20] An estimated 1,500 'sharpshooters' took up positions in the copses, scrubland and cornfields which fringed both sides of the battlefield. They caused great annoyance and many casualties, before British rifles and bayonets 'obliged these skulkers to retire,' wrote Knox.[21] Next Montcalm deployed his five regiments of Old France, from right to left, La Sarre, Languedoc, Béarn, Guienne, in their white uniforms, and Royal Roussillon in blue. On either flank were blue-coated *troupes de la Marine* from Montreal, Quebec and Trois-Rivières. Counting the Indians, Montcalm had about 4,500 men: thus in numbers the two armies were of similar strength, but very different in quality.[22] The French had only 2,500 regulars to oppose the British all-regular army on a battlefield of Wolfe's own choosing. Montcalm believed Bougainville, with 3,000 men, including cavalry, would threaten the rear of Wolfe's army. In fact he remained six miles away, in ignorance of what was happening until too late.[23]

Montcalm was faced with an agonising decision. Should he attack at once or await the arrival of Bougainville to assail the British army from behind? Vaudreuil would also be bringing reinforcements: should he place his troops within the protection of Quebec's walls and guns? If he waited for two or three hours, he would have almost 10,000 men at his command, with strong artillery support. But he had no idea of Wolfe's numbers, nor whether he too would be reinforced: Wolfe might dig in, cutting across the French lines of communication and supply with Montreal. Montcalm, having consulted his commanders, was never in doubt. He had to attack, as soon as possible.

For an hour the British watched Montcalm manoeuvring his troops on the skyline, extending his front and moving his regular battalions closer to the enemy. Captain York fired one brass cannon with grapeshot at a range of 300 yards, to good effect, as the sharpshooters kept up a lively fusillade on both flanks. Wolfe, resplendent in a new uniform, strode up and down the ranks, chatting to his troops and repeating his orders not to open fire, until the French were within 40 paces, and then only when ordered. He seemed buoyant in mood, and confident of victory.

At about 10am Montcalm, 'dressed in the full uniform of a Lieutenant General of the French King, wearing his cuirass and mounted on his black charger', unsheathed his sword and ordered the advance.[24] The drums rolled, the French cheered, and the mixed formations of regulars and militiamen moved forward at a trot, with bayonets fixed. Knox says the French opened fire at 130 yards, uncontrolled, the regulars firing and halting to reload on one knee, the colonial marines lying prone to fire, as was their custom.

The British stood motionless. Wolfe had advanced them 100 paces, when he saw the French forming up, and now stood at their head, between the Louisbourg Grenadiers and the 28 Foot. The troops, magnificently disciplined, obeyed him nobly, according to the records of the 47 Foot.[25] They held their fire, as ordered, until the French were within 40 paces of the British line. Then Wolfe gave the order to fire. The shattering double volley of several thousand musket balls at close range that followed, 'the most perfect volley ever fired on a battlefield,' wrote Fortescue,[26] was devastating in its precision and effect. The French called it 'un coup de canon'. A dense cloud of smoke blotted the French from sight: when it cleared, nearly every man in the French front rank had fallen, like corn before a sickle. The British, as on the parade ground, at once reloaded and advanced another 20 paces. Another series of volleys followed. Hardly any of the two front ranks of the French were left standing. The confused mass of dead, dying and wounded were incapable of further resistance, as Wolfe gave the order to advance. The scarlet line strode forward with bayonet, sword and claymore to complete the rout. Montcalm rode through his broken ranks trying to rally them, but in vain. The French fled for their lives – a mob of panic-stricken men. The engagement had lasted barely ten minutes.

Wolfe, at the head of the 28 Foot, was hit twice and fell. He was helped to his feet again, as the regiments swept on, until stopped by the city gates and cannons firing from the ramparts above. Wolfe was hit a third time, supported as he fell. 'Let not my brave soldiers see me drop,' he said. Mortally wounded, he was carried to the rear. It was clear that he was dying, and appeared to be in a coma. Many claims have been made for the honour of having helped Wolfe in his last moments, and several may have assisted him.[27] Certainly officers of Bragg's regiment (28 Foot) and the Louisbourg Grenadiers would have been nearest to him. Ensign James Henderson of the 28 Foot, who joined the Louisbourg Grenadiers as a volunteer, wrote:

> When the General received the shot, I caught hold of him, and carried him off the Field. He walked about 100 yards, and then begged I would let him sit down. Then I opened his breast, and found his shirt full of blood, at which he smiled. And when he saw the distress I was in, he said, don't grieve for me. I shall be happy in a few minutes. Take care of yourself, as I see you are wounded.

Mr Watson, a surgeon's mate of the 48 Foot, attended him. A cry went up. 'They run! See how they run!' 'Who runs?' Wolfe asked. 'The enemy, sir. Egad, they give way everywhere.' With the victorious cheers of his men bringing him back to life again, he gave his last order. 'Go, one of you, to Colonel Burton: tell him to march Webb's regiment to Charles's river, to cut off the retreat to the bridge.' Turning on his side, he murmured: 'Now, God be praised. I die content.' From that instant the smile never left his face till he died. He had found the hero's death he wanted, dying in the arms of his beloved soldiers.[28]

Brigadier Monckton was also wounded beside his old regiment, the 47 Foot.[29] Major Isaac Barré, his adjutant-general, had half his cheek shot away, his eyeball hanging out of its socket. Guy Carleton was badly hurt. Only a few minutes after Wolfe, Montcalm was mortally wounded, as he retreated on horseback near St Louis Gate, three soldiers holding him in the saddle. The French regular battalions, protected by the local Canadian militia fighting from cover in their traditional way, escaped across the St Charles River bridge to their Beauport camp; the British regiments 'chasing them vigorously all the way to Quebec,' wrote Knox.[30]

Townsend was told of Wolfe's death and Monckton's injury, and took over command of the British army. He ordered the pursuing regiments to return from the walls of Quebec and regroup. All afternoon he made the men dig in, secure their positions, fortify the houses nearby, and bring up the cannon from across the river. Burial parties toiled to bury the dead before nightfall, when the Indians would come to scalp them. At dusk scores of British soldiers scavenged the battlefield, looking for loot and souvenirs, turning over the wounded and the mangled corpses, friend and foe alike.[31]

The British casualties were 664, of whom 58 were killed. The French lost 500 killed and 1,000 wounded or prisoners – half their officers and nearly a quarter of their army! According to Knox, the 78 Highlanders, who had had about 500 men on the battlefield, 'suffered in men and officers more than any three regiments in the field'.[32]

As Townsend expected, Bougainville had appeared at 11am with 3,000 French regulars and Canadians to attack the British rear from the south-west. At 6am he had been at St Augustin, 15 miles from Sillery, marching towards Cap Rouge, eight miles away. Told of the British landing by Vaudreuil's note, he hastened towards Quebec. Near Samos he was fired on by British troops and, making a detour, approached the Heights of Abraham from the Ste Foy road. Finding Townsend's 48 Foot, 3/60 Foot, and the Light Infantry waiting to receive him, and the French army nowhere to be seen, he had prudently withdrawn to Ancienne Lorette, seven miles away.[33] Vaudreuil and Bigot, believing all was lost, deserted the army and fled towards Jacques Cartier, followed by the rest of the leaderless troops from the Beauport Lines. Before he fled, Vaudreuil left a note for the governor of Quebec, Jean de Ramezay, authorising him to surrender the city 48 hours later. To the city governor's credit, he did not capitulate until 17 September, and only when faced with imminent assault by the British.[34]

The late arrival of Bougainville on the battlefield is one of the unsolved mysteries of the campaign. On the night of 12 September he was expected to be at his headquarters at Cap Rouge, with his flying column of 1,100 men. The rest of his forces were distributed in fortified posts along the cliffs above and below Cap Rouge. Foulon was only four miles from Cap Rouge, and the Samos battery firing on the British ships at 4am on 13 September could be heard at distant Beauport. Montcalm said, 'Is it possible that Bougainville did not hear the firing at Samos?' Yet it was not until seven hours later that Bougainville arrived on the battlefield, only six miles from Cap Rouge.[35]

Mahon claims that Bougainville was not at his headquarters at Cap Rouge that night but at Jacques Cartier, nine miles further from Quebec, visiting a certain Madame de Vienne, 'an attractive lady of notoriety and charm', wife of one of Cadet's officers, whose house outside Quebec Governor Vaudreuil was using as his headquarters. Her favours were much in demand, and Mahon suggests that the youthful Bougainville was arranging for her safe conduct with her luggage from the danger zone to Montreal. Contemporary accounts suggest that several gentlemen were caught in this way, 'conquering their mistresses rather than fighting the English'.[36] Any man can fall for a pretty face, but there is no evidence to show that Bougainville spent the night in question with her, nor that he was a party to Cadet's machinations over the convoys. In a letter to Bourlamaque, Bougainville claimed he was at Pointe aux Trembles, following Holmes's ships up the river, and knew nothing of the landing until 8am. Given Bougainville's character, this is a more likely explanation.

So Quebec fell to Wolfe's amphibious force. It had been a hazardous operation, only brought to success by the superb seamanship of the naval commanders and the brilliant leadership of Wolfe, whose calculated risk was fully justified by the result.[37]

After the battle, with all their senior officers dead or dying, confusion reigned among the French. Knox says[38] that many of the captured French officers were still haunted by fears of vengeance for the Fort William Henry massacre. Earnestly protesting their innocence, they 'piteously sued for quarter'.

Montcalm, shot through the abdomen, lay dying in agony in the ruined town.[39] When told he had only 12 hours to live, he dictated a generous note to Townsend – 'it is a great consolation to me to be vanquished by so brave and generous an enemy'.[40] Begging for clemency for the French and Canadian prisoners, he asked Townsend 'to be their protector, as I have been their father'.[41] Finally, he said to those standing around him he had no more orders to give for the defence of Quebec. 'My time is short. I have far more important business to attend to.'[42] With his strength failing fast, he sent a farewell message to each member of his beloved family at Candiac. He was then given the last rites, and died just before dawn.

This great and gallant soldier, in his 48th year, wrote Parkman,[43] escorted by a few officers of the garrison and a troop of weeping women and children, was borne to the Ursuline Chapel.[44] There his remains were buried in a grave made by a bursting British shell. 'There was no tolling of bells nor the firing of cannon, only the tears and sobs of this small party. But his funeral was the funeral of New France.' One hundred years later, on 14 September 1859, he was given a State funeral in the Ursuline Chapel, draped in black, with all the religious pomp and ceremonial, which had been lacking on the earlier occasion. 'Destiny, in robbing him of victory, compensated him with a glorious death', reads his monument on the Heights of Abraham.

The loss of Montcalm robbed his successors of their senses, wrote Parkman.[45] A council of war was called, at which Vaudreuil urged a retreat up the river of the whole army. Panic-stricken, the French leaders agreed. Vaudreuil, Bigot, and the senior French officers, together with the remnants of their defeated army, streamed away that night, in disorderly flight up the east bank of the St Charles River to Jacques Cartier, 30 miles away. The Beauport lines were abandoned, just as they stood – tents, ammunition and food supplies, left behind, through lack of time and transport, to be looted by the country people and the Indians.[46] The militiamen deserted to their homes. Left behind, too, was the small Quebec garrison of 600, 'half starved old men and boys, with a few soldiers and sailors, to stiffen up the 2,600 women and children, and the 1,000 invalids, on half-rations, which could not last the week'.[47]

Knowing the retribution that would follow the loss of Canada, the gang of corrupt officials was quick to put as much blame as possible on Montcalm. As soon as he was safe in Montreal, Vaudreuil led the chorus with a letter to the Minister of Marine:

> From the moment of M. de Montcalm's arrival in this Colony down to that of his death, he did not cease to sacrifice everything to his boundless ambition. He sowed dissension among the troops, tolerated the most indecent talk against the Government, attached to himself the most disreputable persons, and used means to corrupt the most virtuous. He wished to become Governor-General, and told his friends he would succeed in his aims. If I had been sole Master, he concluded, Quebec would still belong to the King.[48]

When Madame de Pompadour learned of the fall of Quebec, she is alleged to have said, almost certainly without any foundation: 'It makes little difference. Canada is useful only to provide me with furs.'[49] Like so many others of France's failures, the blame for the loss of Canada was laid on her fair shoulders!

On 17 September, the Chevalier de Lévis, summoned from the Montreal front by Vaudreuil, arrived at Jacques Cartier, to take over command of the disorganised French army. Lévis considered the retreat an error, and set off immediately to prevent the capture or surrender of Quebec, or at least to destroy the city, to prevent the British wintering there. He arrived too late. Townsend, criticised by some historians for not seizing the opportunity to capture Quebec and destroy the demoralised French army, had, instead, dug in close to the city walls, after restoring discipline among his troops. He moved up his batteries of artillery to breach the fortifications, while Saunders positioned his warships to bombard the Lower Town. The Chevalier de Ramezay was offered capitulation or storm. With the almost unanimous agreement of his senior officers, the commander hoisted the white flag, and capitulated. Townsend gave the garrison the honours of war – repatriation to France, property to be safeguarded, and the inhabitants allowed freedom to exercise their Catholic religion.[50]

On the 18th, the British took possession of the fortress: the Louisbourg Grenadiers mounted guard on the gates. The keys of the city were presented to Townsend. The Union Jack was raised on the Citadel. The Royal Marines took possession of the Lower Town, and the Royal Navy formed its ships into one unbroken line from Montmorency to Sillery. By the 27 September most of the British troops had moved into the city, and preparations were begun to improve its defences, and to make the accommodation suitable for the winter. A couple of days earlier, Wolfe's body, embalmed in a barrel of rum, and escorted by Captain Bell, his ADC, and Captain Delaune, who had served with Wolfe in his regiment, the 20 Foot, and led the ascent of Anse au Foulon, sailed on the *Royal William* for Spithead.

The news of the victory was greeted in Britain with national rejoicing. In London special editions of newspapers were printed, to broadcast the success to the people. The King issued a proclamation, setting aside the 29 November, as a day of thanksgiving. As the guns of the Tower of London thundered, Horace Walpole wrote: 'Our bells are worn threadbare with ringing for victories.' The people triumphed, and wept, for Wolfe had fallen in the hour of victory. Knox added the Army's tribute – 'joy inexpressibly damped by the loss of one of its greatest heroes'. Only Townsend failed to do full honour in his dispatches to his dead rival – though he gave full credit to the soldiers, and to the Royal Navy, which had so loyally and successfully supported the campaign.[51]

On 17 November, Saunders and the Royal Navy brought home Wolfe's body to Portsmouth. The naval guns fired in salute, the muffled bells tolled, and the vast concourse of spectators stood in silence. The funeral cortège set off on the long journey to London and Greenwich for burial in the family vault in the parish church. Parliament passed a vote of thanks, and gave Wolfe a monument in Westminster Abbey.[52] Like other regiments in the campaign, the 47 Foot, The Loyal North Lancashire Regiment, did not receive recognition for its services in the capture of Louisbourg and Quebec, until 125 years later. In 1882 these regiments were authorised to inscribe Louisbourg and Quebec on their Colours.[53]

Collections were made for the wounded soldiers, the widows and orphans. Those who contribute, declared one editor,[54] 'join in a cause to perpetuate their country's glory'. In a flight of romantic fancy and seasonal good cheer, the editor pictured himself seated, 'with such honest neighbours and their wives' round his Christmas roast, 'banqueting with Queen Elizabeth's Dames of Honour, or smoking tobacco with Walsingham and Sir Francis Drake'.

Mrs Wolfe saw to the setting of Katherine Lowther's miniature in diamonds. Six years later Katherine married the Duke of Bolton. Mrs Wolfe left the residue of her estate (£3,000) to the Royal Hibernian School, Dublin, founded in 1769:

> For the great number of boys and girls of soldiers serving in Ireland, and of Irish soldiers overseas, left destitute and without any support; to preserve

such objects from Popery, Beggary and Idleness, and to train them to become useful, industrious Protestant subjects.[55]

Posterity has always had an affection for the gallant Montcalm, and it is fitting that a shared monument has been erected on the Plains of Abraham above Quebec. It is dedicated jointly to the memory of both Wolfe and Montcalm:

Mortem virtus, communem famam historia, monumentum posteritas dedit.
    Valour gave them a common death, history a common fame, posterity a common monument.[56]
    Parkman provided another epitaph:

'With the fall of Quebec began the history of the United States'.[57]

21

AMHERST'S OPERATIONS
– ROGERS AND THE RANGERS

W hile Wolfe was capturing Quebec, the British commander-in-chief,
General Jeffrey Amherst,[1] was carrying out his orders to capture
Montreal. His plans were directed upon three different points. He
would command one column by way of Fort Edward, Ticonderoga and the
shores of Lake Champlain. Another under Brigadier Prideaux[2] was to advance
westward along the Mohawk to seize Niagara. A third column under Brigadier
Stanwix was entrusted with the relief of Pittsburg, to capture the forts which
barred the road to Lake Erie, and then push on to Niagara and release Prideaux
for operations on the St Lawrence towards Montreal.[3]

Amherst assembled his army at Albany during May 1759. His force of
11,500 consisted of six British regular regiments; the remainder provincials.[4]
He also had a body of Rangers and a corps of Indians under Sir William
Johnson, from whom he had to keep his operations secret. 'If the Indians
know them,' Amherst wrote,[5] 'the French will have it: it is their business to
give intelligence on both sides.' Among the General's orders were 'No women
will be permitted to go with the Regiments, or to follow' and 'The General is
determined not to show any mercy to any man that can be such a scoundrel,
as to desert his King and country during the campaign'.[6]

Albany was selected to be the chief hospital centre for the forward area,
although it was 100 miles behind Amherst's headquarters at Crown Point. The
plan[7] of the director of hospitals and chief surgeon in North America, James
Napier, was to provide regimental hospitals at the rear of the administrative
and baggage column, which followed the vast flotilla of river craft conveying
the army on Lake George to Ticonderoga. The sick and wounded would be
evacuated from these small regimental hospitals to Albany: the more serious
cases would then be sent from Albany to New York, carried entirely on the
lakes and rivers by boat. The general hospital at New York had only 150 beds,
but when Napier visited it in November 1759 he found 531 patients, including
292 wounded. Part of the troops' barracks in New York had been taken over
as additional accommodation.

On 6 June Amherst arrived at Fort Edward, and immediately surveyed the
area 'to fix the Camp for the Troops'.[8] Once known as the Great Carrying

Place, Fort Edward had become an important strategic garrison for the British, and a base for supplies brought up the Hudson river and then carried (portaged) across to Lake Champlain. In 1755 Fort Edward saw the build-up of many thousands of soldiers for the expeditions against Ticonderoga (Carillon) and Crown Point. Leaving Thomas Gage at Albany to bring up the remainder of his infantry, artillery, stores and provisions, Amherst set about organising the camp and his troops:

> 7 June 59. The Royal Highland Regiment (42 Foot) arrived this day, half drowned. I sent them under cover to the great blockhouse and sheds on the Island, opposite the Fort (Edward). Two days later the 77 Foot rowed in, 'greatly fatigued', 'I wish the Regiments were up. 'Tis time I should get forward.'
>
> On 11 June Amherst ordered 600 men to repair the roads over the 15 mile stretch between Fort George and the southern end of Lake George to carry artillery and vehicles. During the next few days he was busy moving forward guns and stores.[9]
>
> On 12 June Amherst ordered:
>
> that no scouting parties or others in the Army under his command shall (whatsoever opportunities they may have) scalp any women or children belonging to the enemy: they are to bring them away, if they can: if not, they are to leave them unhurt. The General is determined, if the enemy should murder or scalp any women or children, who are subjects of the King of Great Britain, he will revenge it by the death of two men of the enemy for every woman or child murdered or scalped by them, whenever he has occasion.[10]

This order did not seem to have much effect, for the scalping continued on both sides.

Knox[11] described the camp at Fort Edward as 'the great rendezvous of the Army', and, as the provincial troops arrive, great pains were taken over their training in musketry, wood-fighting and the work of scouts. The men were also employed cutting down trees, building boats and repairing roads. Once more, wrote Bradley,[12] the rough forest road from Fort Edward on the Hudson to Lake George was beaten hard by a steady stream of marching troops, guns and wagons. Once again the scene was gay with tents and colourful uniforms, and the bay dark with boats. On 21 July a pageant no less gorgeous than Abercromby's the previous year crossed Lake George, and landed next day without much opposition near the saw-mill at Ticonderoga.[13]

Here Bourlamaque was in command of 3,000 but, under orders from Montcalm to keep his army intact and positioned between Amherst and Montreal, he slipped away to Isle aux Noix during the night. His orders were to withdraw slowly and abandon Ticonderoga and Crown Point successively as each fort was threatened with encirclement. Isle aux Noix, in the centre of the Richelieu river, was more easily defensible and there, with his force intact, he could block the English advance on Montreal.[14]

Suddenly, on the night of 27 July, a tremendous explosion rent the air at Ticonderoga. A rearguard left by Bourlamaque to light the fuses had blown up the fort. A British sergeant cut down the French colours flying amongst the flames, and was rewarded by General Amherst with ten guineas. Four days later Crown Point (St Frédéric), 14 miles down the lake, was blown up in its turn. This fort, built in 1731 and the chief seat of French power on Lake Champlain, fell without striking a blow.[15]

Amherst consolidated his gains. He carefully repaired Ticonderoga; beside the dismantled walls of St Frédéric he built Fort Crown Point. In his journal for 17 August[16] he entered '1,600 men at work on the Fort today: built barracks for the winter, and gathered oxen, wood, and spruce beer. If I left the provincials, growing homesick, to themselves, they would eat fried pork and lie in their tents all day.' The French had four gunboats on Lake Champlain which delayed his advance, so Amherst built more and better boats.

By the time he was ready to assault Isle aux Noix, the 1759 campaigning season had slipped by.

> 30 September. Mohawks chose to return home. They say Wm. Johnson lets them do what they will, and don't like to be ruled as I order them. They seem to be like the rest, drunken and idle. Number of sick increasing. Sent them back to Fort Edward and Albany.

Amherst decided to return to Crown Point and finish building the fort there.

Amherst's plodding advance, and his failure to create a diversion for Wolfe, have been criticised. 'How General Amherst will excuse himself to his Court, I don't know,' wrote one of the French generals.[17] His grip when fastened, however, was that of a vice. He did much useful work in fortifying posts and improving communications, and his unspectacular advance formed links in a chain of triumphs, which would bear fruit the following year. His decision to build a strong fort at Crown Point, for instance, was not only of military importance, but allowed settlers, driven from their homes by fear of the Indians, to return and colonise the country between Fort Edward and Lake George.[18]

While Amherst had been carrying out his campaign, Brigadiers Prideaux and Stanwix of the Royal Americans had been pursing their plans for the reduction of Niagara, the last of the French fortresses on Lake Ontario, and for the relief of Fort Pitt, respectively.

Prideaux was the first to take the field, assembling his force of 5,000 at Schenectady on the Mohawk River – the 44, 46 and 4/60 Foot (Royal Americans) and 2,500 provincial troops from New York. On 15 June he marched upstream to Oswego, where he left nearly half his force under Colonel Haldimand to secure his communications. Then he embarked with the rest upon Lake Ontario for Niagara.[19]

Like Bouquet, Haldimand was an able Swiss officer, who had been imported to recruit and train the motley collection of colonials into the now efficient 60 Foot (Royal Americans). He immediately set about building a fort. While his men were felling timber, they were attacked by 1,200 French Canadians under their French partisan leader, de la Corne, and the notorious Abbé Piquet with some of his so-called Christian Indians, whom he exhorted to give no quarter to the British heretics. The Royal Americans hurriedly got under arms, killed de la Corne and put his men to flight. Thereafter Haldimand was left in peace to erect a new fort at Oswego on the site of Montcalm's first Canadian victory by Lake Ontario. In later years this fort became familiar quarters for many British regiments.[20]

Prideaux, in the meantime, with Sir William Johnson and his Indians, was hugging the 70-mile southern shores of Lake Ontario to Niagara, in boats and bateaux mounted with guns. They had to take care to avoid a French warship cruising on the lake. The fort at Niagara was situated in the angle formed by the Niagara River and the lake, and garrisoned by 600 men. In command was Captain Pouchot, an excellent officer of the Béarn Regiment. For once, Pouchot was let down by his Indian allies and taken by surprise. He hurriedly sent for reinforcements, and prepared to hold the fort. Prideaux laid siege to the fort, but his engineers were not very skilful and delayed the opening attack. When he did open fire, Prideaux was killed by the premature explosion of a shell from one of his own guns.

Johnson took over, and pressed the siege with vigour. After two or three weeks' artillery fire the fort was in dire straits, when suddenly a party of 1,300 French and Indians appeared on the scene, intent upon relieving it. Leaving one-third of his men to occupy the trenches, and another third to guard the boats, Johnson sallied forth on 24 July with the rest – fewer than 1,000 men – and completely routed the French in a brisk engagement.[21]

Day after day the besieged Pouchot and his men had bravely watched and waited. When they learned of the defeat of the reinforcements, Pouchot hauled down the French flag and surrendered. They were given the honours of war. 'The French ladies with their children, and those women who chose not to follow their husbands, were sent with the chaplain to Montreal.'[22] Fort William Henry was once again in the minds of the captured garrison, but Johnson had his Indian allies firmly under control, and the prisoners of war were sent unmolested to New York. The fort, with its 40 guns, ammunition and stores, was quietly occupied by the British.[23]

With the British in possession of Niagara and Oswego, the French flag finally disappeared from Lake Ontario and its shores. When Brigadier Stanwix eventually occupied every fort to Presqu'île on the shore of Lake Erie, the whole region of the upper Ohio had been cleared of the French and their posts in the west hopelessly cut off from Canada. Only Montreal now remained to be captured.

News reached Amherst in August of the capture of Niagara and the death of Prideaux. He immediately sent Gage to take command at Crown Point. Before the war the garrison there, then called Fort St Frédéric, had led an idyllic life in this romantic spot, reasonably paid and admirably fed, amid woods full of wild game and beside a lake full of fish. French soldiers were committed to serve, until they were 40 or 50 years old, when the French king presented them with a farm and food for the first two or three years, and sometimes even provided them with a wife. War had changed this peaceful life; but Amherst's garrison now witnessed 'one of the most sensational pieces of daredevil enterprise than even Robert Rogers ever achieved'.[24]

One hundred and eighty miles north of Crown Point, near Montreal and far in Bourlamaque's rear, was a large settlement of Abenakis Indians on the St Francis River. They were under French protection and outwardly Christians, but they were invaluable to the Canadians and the scourge of the New England and New York frontier. They burned the farmhouses and small hamlets of the New Englanders, killed their men, women and children, and carried off others to their villages to face ritual tortures around the scalps of their parents and friends.[25] Rogers set out on 13 September with 230 picked men on his famous raid to teach a lesson to these bloodthirsty savages. 'Take your revenge for their barbarities,' Amherst instructed them.[26] 'But though these villains have promiscuously murdered our women and children of all ages, it is my order that none of theirs are killed or hurt.'

Rogers and his party stole along the western shore of Lake Champlain in whale boats to Missisquoi Bay, 90 miles to the north. There they hid their boats, watched over by some friendly Indians. For the next 90 miles, Rogers marched his party through the trackless forest, beset on every side by enemies. His friendly Indian watchers soon overtook him with the information that a party of 400 French had discovered his boats, and were in hot pursuit. They decided to outmarch their pursuers, push straight for the Indian settlement at St Francis, and then make for the New England frontier. Rogers sent back a message to Amherst to forward provisions to a certain spot on the Connecticut River.[27]

For ten days Rogers and his men, including some volunteer British soldiers, toiled on through dense forest and swamp, until they reached the St Francis River. The current was swift and the water chin deep. Linking arms, they waded across to the further bank in safety. Climbing a tree, Rogers saw the Indian village three miles away, unaware of its impending fate. Creeping closer to the edge of the settlement, they watched the whole village 'dancing one of their characteristic orgies'. Waiting till dawn, Rogers and his men rushed the sleeping Indians in their cabins and wigwams. All 200, mostly women and children, were slaughtered: about the same number of men were absent on an expedition. Five English female captives were released 'and 600 English scalps of both sexes found nailed to the doors of the houses as trophies'.[28] On 7 November Amherst noted: 'Received letter from Major Rogers. Took 20 women and children, 15 of which he let go. Brought away two Indian boys and three girls.'[29]

Rogers burnt the whole village to the ground, including the Catholic church. Then these courageous men, eluding Bourlamaque's army and his pursuing Frenchmen, and on meagre rations, slogged for eight days through tangled swamps and wooded heights, until they reached the broad waters of Lake Memphremagog. The officer Amherst had sent with the food to the Connecticut River waited two days, and then returned with the provisions. (For this outrageous conduct he was cashiered.) The 90 or so survivors, in despair and starving, knew the vast distances still to be covered. They split up into small groups, the better to find the game they desperately needed before the survivors reached the British lines and safety. Many were killed, many taken prisoner to face torture and the stake in Indian villages. A French contemporary said, 'they became victims of the fury of the Indian women, from whose clutches the Canadians tried in vain to save them.'[30]

Rogers made a raft of pine logs, and with two companions decided to drift down the river, brave the rapids, and try to bring help. He reached Charlestown in five days and the promised relief was quickly sent. Most of the men were saved, though starvation and exhaustion carried off a number. The expedition had covered over 400 miles, and Amherst thanked them warmly. Their adventures and sufferings are among the thrilling tales of border warfare,[31] but all in a day's work for these fearless and resourceful rangers!

The provincials thanked Amherst for the success of his campaign. The grateful colonists of Massachusetts, New Hampshire and Virginia named three towns in his honour; but historians have sometimes tended to damn him with faint praise:

> In planning campaigns he displayed considerable ability, but in executing them he was frequently a hindrance rather than a help. Painfully elaborate in his preparations, he spent weeks in brewing spruce beer, as a health-giving elixir for his troops, with the same gravity that he planned his military strategy.[32]

By now winter was approaching: the weather had broken and storms were lashing the surface of the lake into a fury. The garrisons at Crown Point and Ticonderoga fired salvoes, cheered and drank bumpers of rum to celebrate George II's birthday on 10 November – his last! Two days later, the provincial regiments handed in their tents, arms and ammunition, and set off home; Amherst and his army went into winter quarters.

But the war was not yet over. The French were preparing a counter-attack on Quebec. Montreal had still to be captured. A Cherokee revolt would threaten South Carolina. And soon Amherst would be ordered to send every available British regular soldier to the West Indies, where most would die of sickness and the climate.

22

THE FRENCH
STRIKE BACK

Following the surrender of Quebec, General Monckton left on sick leave for New York, of which he would become governor and commander-in-chief. Brigadier Townsend sailed for England and a new command in January.[1] On 19 September Brigadier Murray wrote in his diary: 'This day I marched into Quebec, or more properly the ruins of it, with the battalions of Amherst (15 Foot), Bragg (28 Foot), and Otway (35 Foot).'[2] Two days later, at the age of 39, he was left in command of the troops remaining in the city (Wolfe's ten battalions and a company of New England rangers), and appointed governor of the province, with Colonel Burton of the 48 Foot as his deputy. A Strength Return of 29 October 1759 showed 7,317 effectives,[3] including the 2nd and 3rd Battalions Royal Americans.

Quebec had indeed been reduced to a shapeless mass of ruins. A third of the houses had been destroyed, the rest made uninhabitable, and streets were impassable through fallen masonry. The officers drew lots for quarters in the ruined houses. The population was thoroughly demoralised and given over to theft and pillage. Liquor was abundant and the British soldier was thirsty.[4] It would need all Murray's firmness to restore order. Winter was approaching, and the effects of bad quarters, poor food, insufficient and unsuitable clothing, and a poor supply of fuel would become apparent.

Parkman described the scene very graphically:

The fleet was gone: the great river was left in solitude: and the chill days of November passed over Quebec in alternations of rain and frost, sunshine and snow. The troops, driven by cold from their encampment on the Plains of Abraham, were all gathered within the walls. Their own artillery had so battered the place, that it was not easy to find shelter. The Lower Town was a wilderness of scorched and crumbling walls. Even in the Upper Town few of the churches and public buildings had escaped. The Cathedral was burned to a shell. The bombshells, which had fallen through the roof of the Récollet's church, had thrown up the bones and skulls of the dead from the graves beneath.[5]

The standing orders for the garrison[6], issued by Murray on 4 November 1759, show the extent of his problems and his methods of handling them. He complained of the many desertions, thefts and plunderings, as well as the drunkenness. He ordered that no liquor should be sold, so the men had only the official allowance served out regularly by the officers. To discover the source of the drunkenness, he ordered that 'those found drunk to receive 20 lashes every morning, till the man acknowledged, where he got it, and to forfeit his allowance of Rum for six weeks'. Seventeen days later, two pairs of army women were whipped through the streets for selling rum contrary to orders.

The gallows and whipping triangles were set to work. Desertion or incitement to desert were serious offences under the Mutiny Act. On 17 November a Frenchman (although not subject to the Act) was hanged 'for enticing our men to desert'. 'An active officious Priest' who was 'supposed to have caused our men's base desertion' had thought fit to abscond, recorded Knox. A soldier received 1,000 lashes for absenting himself from duty, and using language to excite mutiny and desertion. A second soldier received 300 lashes for being disguised with an intent to desert, and for being out of his quarters at night.

For desertion or trying to persuade others to desert, a soldier was ordered to suffer death by shooting on a parade before his fellows, as a deterrent. The whole regiment was drawn up on three sides of a square. On the fourth side was a post, to which the condemned man would be tied and blindfolded. He was marched round the regiment, accompanied by his coffin, to a slow drumbeat. One man in the firing squad drew a blank, to salve the consciences of those detailed to carry out the sentence. Sometimes a man was ordered to dig his own grave, and occasionally, when two or more were sentenced to death, one man was selected by the throw of a dice to suffer for the rest. Last minute reprieves enhanced the drama and provided 'volunteers' for military graveyards, like the lethal West Indies.

As supplies arrived from New York, Murray drew up a table of provisions[7] 'for one man for seven days', which included bread, flour, beef and pork, pease, oatmeal, butter or cheese, suet or fruit, and cooking oil. With the provisions, he issued a warning:

> Every soldier is receiving 2lbs of provisions more than ever was allowed in any of the King's garrisons before, in addition to the gill of rum, which is provided gratis. So every Officer, Sergeant, Corporal and faithful Soldier is asked to discover any man, who shall presume to complain of the said allowance, so that the offender may be brought to trial for sedition, and receive the punishment, which such a notorious crime deserves.[8]

THE FRENCH STRIKE BACK

This memorandum was posted up in every barrack-room and read by an officer at the head of each company every day for a week, so that no soldier could plead ignorance.

The standing orders of 4 November made clear that the women had previously been entitled to the same rations as the men. Now their rations were reduced to two-thirds of the men's allowance. Murray reminded the officers:

> For this purpose, the women are to be mustered tomorrow by the Town-Major. Those, who are sick and cannot appear, are to be certified by their commanding officers. The King victuals the women, in order to render them useful to the men, either by attending hospitals or by washing for them and the officers.[9]

But henceforth women who sutled were not to be enrolled, 'nor will any provisions be issued to those, who do not reside in the men's quarters'.

Quebec swarmed with troops, wrote Parkman.[10] There were guard-houses at 20 different points; sentinels paced the ramparts; squads of armed men went the rounds; soldiers off-duty strolled the streets; everywhere there was the sound of rolling drums, bugles and the rigid observance of military etiquette. While some of the inhabitants left town, others remained, having nowhere else to go. They were civil to the victors, but angry with their late rulers; the citizens, especially the women, cursing Vaudreuil upon every occasion:

> They bear misfortunes in a way we would find insupportable. Families, whom the calamities of war have reduced from the height of luxury to the want of common necessaries, laugh, dance and sing, comforting themselves with the reflection that it is *the fortune of war*.

A lieutenant of the 78th Highlanders wrote: 'The Canadian ladies take the utmost pains to teach our officers French: why, I know not, unless it be that they may hear themselves praised, flattered, and courted without loss of time.'[11]

One of Murray's early priorities was dealing with the civil population. The colony was still at war, and Quebec could be attacked at any time. The provincial militia had to be disarmed; the oath of allegiance to George II had to be administered to the colonists of the conquered districts; the embarkation of French troops under the capitulation terms had to be arranged. Food was short and fuel scarce, so the number of inhabitants within the city walls had to be reduced, and the Jesuits expelled, because they were suspected of giving information to the French enemies, who lurked in the neighbourhood.[12]

His major problem was, naturally, the defence of the city. Murray kept his 6,000 troops busy, according to regimental records,[13] filling in entrenchments, repairing the fortifications, mounting guns, constructing billets and storing provisions. Their military duties were especially heavy. Every day 25 officers and 930 other ranks were required for guard duties alone: rumours of a French counter-attack were rife, and skirmishes near the outposts a frequent occurrence. Lieutenant Fraser (78 Foot) in his journal relates that, at the beginning of November, a detachment of 700 men under Colonel Welsh of the 28 Foot marched to Cap Rouge, about nine miles from Quebec, and attacked the enemy post at Pointe aux Trembles. On their return they set up outposts at Lorette (seven miles from Quebec) and Ste Foy. The purpose of the latter, he said, was to protect the wood-cutting at Ste Foy and 'hinder the enemy from insulting the garrison by their Indians or other parties'.

On 1 December the governor ordered two weeks' firewood to be issued to the garrison. Previously the troops had been tearing down damaged houses to provide their fuel – much to the anger of the local inhabitants. Murray arranged for a regular supply from the Canadians, and ordered that 'no person whatever shall pull down houses or fences or carry off any timber belonging to the inhabitants'. But, commented Fraser, 'it is thought we shall have great difficulty in supplying ourselves with fuel this winter. The winter is now very severe.'[14]

Knox, commenting on Murray's orders, wrote:

> Our brave soldiers are growing sickly: their disorders are chiefly scorbutic [scurvy], with fevers and dysenteries. This is hardly surprising, when we consider the severe fatigues and hardships they undergo. With unsuitable clothing, uncomfortable barracks, worse bedding, and confinement to a diet of salt meat and no fresh vegetables, the men are subjected to conditions, sufficient to reduce or emaciate the most robust constitutions in this extremely frigid climate.[15]

Each regiment had to send the commissary a ration return of their effectives every Monday morning, 'including officers, women and servants, who are not soldiers and, who came with the Army from Louisbourg'. These women were those 'officially recognised': women living with the men and 'not recognised' were not to be included, nor were French servants or boys hired since the army took the field to be victualled. At the bottom of the returns, 'the number of women, with their names of servants and their masters, are to be specified' (see the victualling return for February 1760 on page 210 for numbers).

Both Knox and Fraser[16] report in December that the winter had become almost insupportably cold.

> Cases of frostbite increase and our soldiers grow numerous in the hospitals. Scarce a day passes without two or three funerals. Some, who died within

these few days, are laid in the snow, until the spring thaw. By then 700 bodies awaited burial. Despite this, the men are obliged to continue to drag all the wood used in the garrison on sledges from Ste. Foy, about four miles distance. This is a very severe duty: the poor fellows do it, however, with great spirit, though several of them have already lost the use of their fingers and toes by the incredible severity of the frost. The country people tell us the winter is not yet at its worst.

Fraser tells us his Highland regiment (*les sauvages sans culottes* to the French) suffered in particular from the indifferent clothing general in the garrison. 'The Philibeg [filibeg or kilt] is not all calculated for this terrible climate – and is no substitute for breeches, which Colonel Fraser is doing all in his power to provide'. The nuns in the Ursuline Convent in Quebec knitted homespun stockings for them.[17] Regulation dress was set aside: the soldiers cut up blankets, donned mittens, leggings and moccasins – anything, in fact, to keep them warm.

The cold weather even affected the governor's punishments. Four men were found guilty of deserting their posts, and breaking open and robbing the king's stores.[18] Two were sentenced to death, two to receive 1,000 lashes each.

Because of the extreme severity of the season, his Excellency is pleased to reduce the corporal punishment to 300 lashes each.[19] The other two have thrown the dice for life, the Governor having been generously pleased to pardon one of them. Eleven was the lucky number, which fell to the lot of a soldier of the 48 Foot. The other poor fellow was instantly executed and behaved with great decency.

During December it was ordered that 'one woman per regiment from the 35 Foot, 47 Foot, 48 Foot, 2/60 Foot, and 3/60 Foot (Royal Americans), to join as soon as possible the wood-cutting parties at the forest of Ste. Foy, in order to wash for them'. The firewood had to be cut and brought back a distance of four miles in sleighs, each drawn by eight men. Nine of these sleighs were issued to each regiment, and the wood-cutting parties were protected by strong guards against prowling Indians. Every man worked with his musket slung over his shoulder, and Ste Foy itself was protected by a strong outpost.[20]

In February 1760 the regimental victualling return contained the following remarkable statement: 'Not one of the regimental women has been lost in the whole course of this severe winter, nor have they even been sickly.'[21] Yet on 24 April, Murray was reporting 2,299 sick in the 11 regiments, and a fall in the effective strength of the garrison in one month from 4,800 to a little over 3,000 fit for duty.[22] The general's orders for March 1760 read:

> As the King victuals the women in order to render them useful to the men, they are ordered, for the future, to attend the sick at the hospitals (each regiment provided its own), instead of the healthy men hitherto employed at that service. These nurses will receive full allowances of provisions, and be paid by their regiments for their trouble: such women as refuse are to be struck off the victualling roll.[23]

The February 1760 victualling return for Quebec gave the following numbers of women per regiment authorised to draw rations: 15 Foot (37); 28 Foot (65); 35 Foot (73); 43 Foot (63); 47 Foot (42); 48 Foot (82); 58 Foot (53); 2/60 Foot (35); 3/60 Foot (38); 78 Foot (58); Artillery (20); Rangers (3). Total 569 – one for every 13 soldiers. They were to receive now four full rations for six women, instead of the customary half a man's ration each – a modest but welcome increase, considering the severity of the climate, and the increased difficulty of washing and drying clothes in frosty weather!. 'The Sergeant, who brought me this Return,' said the commissary, 'reported all the women well, able to eat their allowance, and *fit for duty both by day and night.*'

In August 1759 General Wolfe had written to the Abbess of the Augustine convent, founded in 1637, thanking her for her care of the British wounded. One of Murray's first acts after the capitulation was to place a guard round the hospital, and he took every precaution to protect the property of the nuns ('the ladies of the General Hospital are of the best families in Canada,' he wrote).[24] The soldiers supplied them with fuel and provisions, cleared the snow for them, and repaired their houses.

Knox was quartered in a small stable, with a hay-loft above and a manger at one end – a lodging better than most of his brother officers! By means of a stove and a carpenter, he made himself reasonably comfortable. He fared better when he was ordered for a week to the general hospital a mile out of town, where he commanded the guard stationed to protect the inmates and watch out for the enemy. The hospital tended the sick and wounded of both armies, nursed by the nuns with equal care. 'Our poor soldiers were delighted', when they were moved from their 'odious regimental hospital' to a place where each patient had his own bed, with curtains, and a nurse to attend him, he wrote. Every sick or wounded officer had an apartment of his own and was looked after by one of the religious sisters, who 'in general are young, handsome, courteous, rigidly reserved, and very respectful'.[25]

The nuns for their part were well pleased with the behaviour of their new masters, 'most moderate of all conquerors'. Knox dined with the French officers and their ladies, played cards with them, and passed the days so pleasantly that his stay at the hospital seemed an oasis in his hard life of camp, garrison and campaigning.

All winter long the French made no secret of their intention to recover Quebec, and they occupied St Augustine, only three miles away. Active patrolling and French deserters confirmed this. During February, for instance, the Light Infantry, 28 Foot and Colonel Fraser's Highland regiment marched over the frozen St Lawrence to attack a French force, which had landed at Point Lévi, and returned with prisoners. The following month an armed patrol attacked St Augustine and brought back 80 prisoners.

As spring approached and the ice melted, Murray grew ever more certain that Lévis, the ablest officer left in the French army, was busily assembling a very strong force to attack Quebec. On 17 April, although scurvy was raging in the garrison and he had barely 3,000 men fit for duty, Murray occupied the mouth of the Cap Rouge River to prevent a French landing there. Four days later he ordered all Canadians, except the nuns, to leave the city, giving them three days' notice to comply, and facilities to store their property. He could not risk an active fifth column inside Quebec, with such depleted forces at his command.

On 26 April Lévis arrived at Pointe aux Trembles with his ships, supplies and men from Montreal – 4,000 regulars, 3,000 militia and 200 Indians. He set off for Ste Foy and Quebec. By a chance in a million, Murray learned of his landing. During a storm that night, a French soldier was washed overboard and carried downstream, clinging to an ice-float and expecting every minute to be his last. The tide turned and washed him back to where HMS *Racehorse*, the only British ship to winter in the river, was anchored in the calmer water below the town. His feeble cries were heard by the watch, and the exhausted Frenchman was picked up more dead than alive. It was two hours before the soldier had sufficiently recovered to reveal that he was a sergeant in Lévis's army, at that very moment marching against the city, backed by a French fleet.

Murray immediately put the garrison on the alert, and decided to meet the French army in the open. Despite his numerical inferiority of at least two to one, he formed up his 3,000 men on the Buttes-à-Neveu outside Quebec, which Montcalm had occupied when opposing Wolfe on the Plains of Abraham. Many were unfit to fight, 'a poor pitiful handful of half starved, scorbutic skeletons,' Quartermaster-Sergeant Johnson called them. 'Many of them had laid by their crutches, and would not be prevailed upon to stay behind. They followed us to the gates in the rear, and fell in, when we formed line of battle.' 'When I considered that our little army was in the habit of beating the enemy, and had a very fine train of artillery,' Murray afterwards wrote to Pitt that 'it seemed better to go out boldly and attack the French, than to await attack behind the wretched fortifications of Quebec'.[26]

In the Battle of Ste Foy which followed, Murray was forced to withdraw to the city after two hours of bloody fighting, the troops and guns slithering and slipping in the mud and snow-drifts. Both sides each lost about 1,000 killed and wounded. The British soldiers, carrying as many of their wounded comrades as possible, retreated to the temporary safety of the walls. Knox said the greater part of the wounded left behind were murdered and scalped by the Indians.[27] Fraser confirmed that 'the French allowed the savages to scalp all the killed and most of the wounded, as we found a great many scalps on the bushes'.[28]

The position now was critical: the city had to be defended at all costs. Murray mobilised every fit man, and put them to work making embrasures and platforms for the guns – 'even the officers were yoked in the Harness, dragging up Cannon from the Lower Town, at work on the Batteries with Barrow, Pick-axe and Spade'.[29] Convalescents filled sandbags, the hospitalised rolled bandages and made wadding for the guns. 'The women,' wrote Knox[30] 'are all ordered to cook for, and attend the men at work with their victuals: also to nurse the sick and wounded: 10 women per regiment to join the artillery to sew up sandbags and make wads from old junk for the guns: the officers to keep the men sober and to water their rum' (which almost caused open rebellion, one man being hanged as a deterrent). The provost were given orders to hang all stragglers and marauders; the insubordinate were sentenced to 1,000 lashes or shot out of hand.

Lévis, too, worked tirelessly, preparing the investment of the city. Guns were mounted, trenches dug and scaling ladders constructed, all the time harassed by the guns of the British garrison. Both commanders knew that Quebec was untenable against a regular siege, and all anxiously watched the river, now beginning to thaw. The fate of Quebec hung in the balance. Which fleet would succeed in reaching the city first, to force a surrender or lift the siege?

Murray had sent HMS *Racehorse* to Halifax with news of the critical situation.[31] Admiral Colvill was cruising in the area with a strong fleet, and hastened up the St Lawrence. A deafening cheer from the ramparts greeted the sight of the red Cross of St George as the first ship, HMS *Lowestoft*, raised her colours and gave the British garrison a 21-gun salute.[32] She was quickly followed by the battleship *Vanguard* and the frigates *Diana* and the *Lawrence*. Quebec was saved!

On 16 May Lévis raised the siege: his last chance had gone. He abandoned his trenches, guns, baggage and stores, and left his dead and wounded behind. 'We found ourselves entirely freed of very disagreeable neighbours,' duly commented Fraser.[33] Jean Vauqueline, the French squadron commander with Lévis, fought his ship to the last: the rest offered little resistance, and departed. Lévis, having conducted a most arduous six-week campaign with considerable skill and valour, withdrew to Montreal. Vauqueline, severely wounded, was captured and sent to France, where his gallantry was rewarded with a dungeon and an early death.[34]

It is commonly said that Wolfe's victory decided the fate of Canada. The Battle of Ste Foy shows how precarious was the British hold on Quebec – the city was saved by Britain's sea power. But as long as Montreal remained in French hands, the conquest of Canada was not complete.

23

THE CAPTURE OF
MONTREAL

M ontreal was the final objective. Pitt, confident of the ability of his commander-in-chief, left the strategy and tactical details to Amherst. Amherst's plan was to invade Canada simultaneously from east, west and south, and converge on the capital and jewel of the French crown in North America from three widely-separated points.

The Commander-in-Chief would lead the main army of 10,000 men[1] (5,300 regulars and 4,200 provincials), starting from Oswego (Fort Ontario). The physical difficulties would be immense: whilst he realised the rapids would prove an obstacle, he had no idea of their fury. Brigadier Haviland, with 3,400 regulars, provincials and Iroquois Indians,[2] was to make his way from Ticonderoga and Crown Point up Lake Champlain to the Isle aux Noix and Montreal. Murray's sickly battalions, restored by the return of spring and a supply of fresh provincials, soon became an army fit for service in the field. But his whole Quebec force had to be re-equipped, clothed and provisioned. Ships arrived by every tide with stores, liquor and provisions of all kinds. He was to ascend the St Lawrence River to meet Amherst before Montreal, with all the troops he could spare after providing a garrison for Quebec. Supported by Colvill's excellent fleet, he would have the easiest task of all. The now useless fortress of Louisbourg would be demolished, freeing its garrison to supplement his small army, daily increasing, as the soldiers were restored to health. Colonel Fraser was left with 1,700 troops to garrison Quebec.

This three-pronged pincer attack was finely conceived but its success demanded the most careful calculations and timing. Starting from points hundreds of miles apart, with little possibility of inter-communication, it would be difficult for the three commanders to arrive at their goal together. With the enemy holding interior lines, it was possible for the French commander, Lévis, to concentrate his forces and attack each British force separately. For Lévis, the principal French posts for barring the British lines of advance were Isle aux Noix at the head of Lake Champlain, Sorel on the eastern side of Montreal, and La Galette at the head of the St Lawrence rapids.

Before the campaigning season began, Amherst had to detach a force of some 1,300 to South Carolina, to suppress a rising of Cherokee Indians.[3] The

Cherokees, distantly related to the Iroquois, were a loose federation of some 10,000 Indians inhabiting the southern end of the Appalachians. In 1730 representative chiefs went to London, where they visited Westminster Abbey, the Tower, playhouses and the Bedlam lunatic asylum. George II received them at Windsor Castle, and a treaty of eternal friendship was signed. To protect them against the French, the British built Forts Prince George and Loudoun close to their capital Chota (1756–7). Cherokee women, who enjoyed much personal freedom, were soon living with soldiers in the garrisons.

But friendly relationships deteriorated during the war. French agents spread discord, smallpox decimated the population through contact with Europeans, and Braddock's defeat caused a loss of confidence in the British. Border raids broke out, and South Carolina appealed to Amherst for military help. The 17 and 22 Foot each sent two companies, and eight companies of independents joined them from New York. The Cherokees besieged Fort Loudoun and reduced the garrison to eating dogs and horses. Capitulation terms were agreed, but once the soldiers and their families had left the fort they were ambushed and massacred. Amherst's troops arrived under Colonel James Grant, systematically destroyed the Indian towns and countryside, and drove 5,000 refugees into the mountains to starve. The Cherokees were no longer able to wage war.

French morale, both of the army and of the Canadian population, had suffered by the capture of Quebec and Lévis's retreat from Ste Foy. Ill-discipline, drunkenness and theft beset the army, and the Canadian militiamen's one thought was to return home. Vaudreuil had staked all his resources on the attack on Quebec, stripping the country bare in the process. Now he tried to reassure his countrymen with the news that, although French arms had suffered reverses in North America, Great Britain would soon be compelled to sue for peace.[4] In Europe, Frederick the Great had suffered reverses, and the demands of war on his manpower and finances were beginning to cripple his efforts.[5] Britain, despite her victories, was also feeling the strain of the war, and the threat of a French invasion hung over the country. Pitt, never strong, had suffered from the demands of office and political opponents, and his constant gout. France had won victories over the English and the Prussians, and Louis XV was in Holland at the head of 200,000 men. According to Vaudreuil, Canada was 'reaching the end of her suffering and misery'. By August, at the latest, Canadians would have 'news of peace, provisions and all else they needed'.[6] Lévis had 8,000 troops, their Indian allies, and a strong base at Montreal. But it would take more than inaccurate and bombastic reports to remedy the desperate French situation in North America.

Murray was the first of the three British commanders to take to the field. On 12 July he reviewed his troops, which he divided into two brigades[7] of five composite battalions, each of nine officers and 161 men, and commanded by Colonel Ralph Burton (Right) and the Honourable William Howe (Left) respectively. One battalion of grenadiers, formed from the different regiments, was attached to each brigade.

Two days later Murray set sail, moving slowly up the river, skirmishing with small parties of the enemy and disarming the inhabitants as he passed. He issued a proclamation promising protection to all who remained peacefully in their homes, and threatening to set fire to every house from which men were absent. This quietened the countryside and caused a large number of the Canadian militia to desert, despite Vaudreuil's threat to put to death every deserter or militiaman, who neglected to join the army.

By 28 July Murray had successfully negotiated the rocks and shallows, and his army arrived at Point Champlain, where the two battalions from Louisbourg (40 and 22 Foot) under Colonel Rollo arrived as reinforcements. A schooner also brought Captain Stobo, with dispatches from Amherst, to join his regiment, 15 Foot. On 4 August Murray reached Les Trois Rivières and, ignoring the French detachment there, passed on to Sorel, about 50 miles from Montreal, where Bourlamaque and 4,000 French troops were entrenched on both sides of the river.

Here, 'by severity towards the recalcitrant and gentleness towards the submissive,'[8] Murray put into effect his proclamation, persuading half of Bourlamaque's militia to surrender their arms and take an oath of neutrality. Pushing on, by 27 August he had reached Isle St Thérèse, just below Montreal. There he encamped to await the arrival of Amherst and Haviland. He did not have long to wait. On 3 September an officer of the American Rangers (60 Foot), in disguise, brought a message that Haviland and his 3,500 men had passed all the French posts between Lake Champlain and Montreal, and were within easy march of the capital.[9] When Haviland reached the Isle aux Noix, Bougainville abandoned the island and joined Bourlamaque on the banks of the St Lawrence. Now outnumbered, Haviland halted, consolidated his position, and awaited Amherst's arrival.

Amherst, in his journal,[10] traces the progress of the main army (4,000 British regulars and 6,000 provincials, with Johnson and his 700 Indians) under his personal command:

16/17 July. Colonel Williamson arrived at Oswego with the Artillery stores, and seven companies of the Royal Highlanders Battalion [42 Foot, the Black Watch]. Indians come in every day: we have now 212 men, squaws and children. By some means got at Rum. A squaw was drowned, and another had entertained herself so often with the soldiers, that she was almost dying. In their frolics the Indians cut a horse to pieces, which belonged to a Sutler. They are devils when drunk: when sober quiet enough.

5 August. 1,330 Indian men, women and children in camp.[11] The last two Sir William Johnson is getting rid of, as fast as he can.

> 10 August. With the 80th Light Infantry as advance guard, the expedition set off from Oswego, after executing five notorious deserters and pardoning nine others.

Leaving 259 sick in hospital, Amherst and his army boarded a flotilla of nearly 800 small craft. 'The lake was rough and several men were as sick as if they were at sea.' Five days later he reached La Galette (Ogdensburg). At the head of the rapids stood a French post named Fort Lévis, commanded by Captain Pouchot, the defender of Niagara. When the British troops recognised him, they greeted their former prisoner with a resounding cheer, wishing him good luck. He stood on the rampart, hat in hand, returning their good wishes, though the French didn't stop firing at them.[12] The fort was invested, and after three days surrendered (26 August). 'Monsieur Pouchot (who had resisted gallantly with his little garrison of 384 men) dined with me,' wrote Amherst,[13] 'while the Indians scratched up the dead bodies and scalped them.' Amherst renamed the fort William Augustus.

Then came the most difficult part of the expedition – the descent of the seven great rapids. 'The current very strong and the Rapids frightful in appearance but not dangerous,' wrote Amherst.[14] At first all the 800 boats, laden with men and stores, successfully navigated one danger after another. But at the Cascades 'boat after boat rushed madly down the torrent, 46 were totally wrecked, 18 damaged, and 84 men were drowned'. On 6 September, after a fatiguing and dangerous voyage of two-and-a-half months, the boats glided into La Chine, about nine miles above Montreal.[15] Then Amherst marched his men to the city, where he encamped unopposed beneath the eastern walls, and received news from Murray and Haviland of their respective positions.

Next day Murray landed at Pointe aux Trembles, to be met by country men and women with pitchers of milk and water for the soldiers, and 'many courteous expressions of concern that they had not better liquor for the officers,' wrote Knox. Thus the junction of the three armies had been achieved, and 17,000 men concentrated around Montreal – a remarkable military feat of timing, considering Amherst had covered some 300 miles from Oswego, and Haviland and Murray 150 miles from Crown Point and Quebec respectively, over difficult terrain. Amherst wrote of this achievement:

> I believe never three Armys, setting out from different and distant Parts from each other, joyned in the Center, as was intended, better than we did, and it could not fail of having the effect of which I have just now seen the consequence.[16]

By now the whole of the Canadian militia had deserted the French colours, and nearly all the colonial regulars went with them, together with some of the

French troops who had Canadian wives. Most of the French allied Indians, quick to desert a lost cause, had vanished into the woods.[17] The Montreal garrison hardly amounted to 2,500 dispirited and demoralised men. Further resistance was hopeless, and negotiations for a capitulation were begun at once. Vaudreuil, the governor, drew up 55 articles and sent them by Bougainville to Amherst, hoping to bargain for the best terms possible. Amherst granted some, but peremptorily refused others. 'I am come to take Canada and I do not intend to take anything less. The whole garrison of Montreal, and all other French troops in Canada, must lay down their arms, and shall not serve during the present war.'[18] The main French request to be allowed to march out of the city with arms, guns and the honours of war, he sternly refused:

> I am fully resolved to show to all the world my detestation of the infamous part, taken by the troops of France, in exciting the savages to perpetrate the most horrid and unheard of barbarities in the whole course of the War, and for other open treacheries and flagrant breaches of faith, and my disapproval of their conduct.[19]

Vaudreuil asked that the allied British Indians should be sent away before the capitulation. Amherst proudly answered that no Frenchman, woman or child, surrendering under treaty, had ever yet suffered from outrage by Indians co-operating with a British army.[20] The articles, as dictated by Amherst, were signed the next day. Lévis, who had actively tried to limit the carnage at Fort William Henry, was furious at the dishonour to French arms; he ordered the ceremonial burning of the French regimental colours, and broke his own sword in protest.[21]

The French laid down their arms on 8 September 1760. Colonel Haldimand, as a compliment to the Royal Americans or because he was personally acceptable to the French at this bitter moment,[22] was sent by Amherst to take possession of the conquered city. Knox[23] found their citizens amazingly affluent – 'the gay and sprightly of both sexes, and almost of all ages, perambulating the streets from morning to night in silk robes, laced coats, and powdered heads'. The French regiments paraded one by one, laid down their arms, and marched back to camp on the ramparts, where Lévis inspected them for the last time. He returned to France with Madame Pénissault, a one-time mistress of Intendant Bigot. He died a duke and a marshal of France two years before the Revolution; his widow and two of his three daughters were guillotined during the Terror.

The capitulation terms required all the French regular troops in Canada, not only in Montreal but also in the small isolated garrisons, and all military officers and civil officials, to be transported to France in British ships.[24] The married were allowed to take their families with them, and all their servants and baggage. Bigot, for instance, was allowed to embark with 'his papers, which shall not be examined: his equipages, plate, baggage, and those of his suite.'[25] On 14 September the French regiments embarked on the transports. The Béarn Regiment, for example, was escorted to Quebec by the 15 Foot,[26] part of the 300 French officers, 76 sergeants and 3,168 soldiers, together with their women and children, who took advantage of the offer.[27] Two thousand of the French troops who had married in Canada preferred to remain in the colony (*filer à l'Anglais*) and become settlers.[28] The last of the French troops had sailed from Quebec by the end of October. New France went with them!

The Canadian militia were disarmed. Anyone who wished to leave the country was permitted to do so. Those who remained were allowed to retain their property and given complete religious freedom. France's Indian allies were sent back to their homes, complying fully with the conditions laid down. 'Now they found we were men,' they said, 'the British would be good friends to us.'[29]

Amherst, with Vaudreuil in attendance, paraded his victorious troops in the Place d'Armes for the formal surrender of Montreal. At the victory parade were many seasoned veterans who richly deserved their triumph.[30] Some of the chief actors in the past seven years of war, however – Monckton, Bouquet and George Washington – were absent on other duties. Wolfe, Prideaux, the elder Howe, Braddock, Forbes and many others were in their graves. On parade, too, were some, who would win far greater fame and some who would lose their present glory, in the still distant struggle upon the same battlegrounds: the American War of Independence (1775–83).

Murray and Haviland led their brigades on the parade ground: Ralph Burton, Thomas Gage and Malcom Fraser headed their respective regiments. Sir Guy Carleton would become a famous viceroy of Canada. Colonel Viscount William Howe, who had led the troops up the cliffs at Anse au Foulon, would be forgotten for his failure as commander-in-chief in the American War of Independence. Sir William Johnson and the fearless leader of the provincial rangers, Robert Rogers, were on parade, with the two colonial colonels, Schuyler and Lyman. Amherst's naval captain, Loring, and Patrick MacKeller, whose engineering skills had constructed so many forts and ramparts in the campaigns, were there, too.

Before giving up his military command, Amherst sent Robert Rogers to the Great Lakes to enforce the capitulation of the French outposts in the west – Miami, Detroit, MacKinac and St Joseph.[31] Then he made a tour of the battle areas.[32] On 1 October he arrived in Quebec and, after breakfasting with Governor Murray, walked over the town – a heap of ruins! He rode out to the Plains of Abraham to inspect the battlefield, and strode round the ramparts.[33] The next day he went to Beauport and the Montmorency lines, visited Wolfe's camp at the Falls, and saw the whole extent of the French entrenchments. Then he crossed over to Point Lévi to survey the area – the site of the British batteries and the British camp on the Isle of Orleans, chiefly used as a hospital and stores depot – and see Quebec from across the St Lawrence River, as Wolfe first saw it. Afterwards he set out for Pointe aux Trembles, Isle aux Noix, Crown Point, the Forts of Ticonderoga, George and Edward, and so on to Albany and New York, where he was immediately appointed governor general of British North America.[34]

In Britain, news of the capitulation was greeted by Pitt and the people with wild enthusiasm – three days of rejoicing in London, with bonfires, gun salvoes, the ringing of bells and services of thanksgiving.[35] Sir Jeffrey Amherst was recognised as the conqueror of Canada, received the thanks of parliament, and was made a Knight of the Bath and colonel of the Royal Americans. 'Though not a great man, he deserves a very honourable position amongst English soldiers and statesmen of the 18th century'. Fortescue called him 'the greatest military administrator produced by England, since the death of Marlborough, until the rise of Wellington'.[36]

Colonel Johnson, for his services in Canada, was granted by the king a tract of 100,000 acres, to be held in perpetuity, about three miles from Fort Johnson. There he spent the rest of his life in baronial style, entertaining, and writing his memoirs on the languages, customs and manners of the Indian Six Nations. He died in July 1774.

The French court was indignant at the ignoble surrender of Montreal 'without having fired a single shot'.[37] In accordance with the terms of the treaty, the chief civil officers of New France, most of the land-owning *noblesse* and the leading merchants had left for Quebec (13–22 September). A month later about 1,000 of them, including their families, departed for France. They left behind the Canadian traders and peasants, whose new masters promised them security of property and person.[38]

When Vaudreuil, Bigot, Cadet, Pénissault, Vergor, Péan and 40 others who had plundered the colony, entertained, gambled and womanised at their country's expense, reached France, they were imprisoned in the Bastille for fraud and official misconduct (malfeasance). In a trial which lasted 15 months and attracted European interest, they made a sorry spectacle with their mutual recriminations. Vaudreuil and seven others were acquitted. Vaudreuil retired to live 'in dignified poverty' on a small pension. The prosecution wanted Bigot beheaded after publicly acknowledging his guilt: instead, he was banished from France, heavily fined, and all his property confiscated. Cadet, blamed as the arch-criminal, was banished from Paris for nine years and also heavily fined. Later, having collected money due to him in Canada, he returned to France to live in comfort, marrying his daughters into some of the noblest families. Twenty others received appropriate sentences, 'their dishonesty in the end profiting them but little'. 'There was enough ability among them all,' wrote Wood, 'to have saved New France from, at least, ignominious ruin.'[39]

Until the peace settlement in 1763 which decided the political future of Canada, the country was governed by three military commanders – General James Murray in Quebec, Colonel Ralph Burton in Three Rivers (previously Trois Rivières), and General Thomas Gage in Montreal.[40] General Amherst, as commander-in-chief, was in New York, and technically head of the administration. In practice, he left the three district governors to act on their own initiative, but gave them clear instructions – 'Govern according to military laws, if you should find it necessary, until the King's pleasure shall be known. But let the *habitants* settle their differences, according to their own laws and customs.' By giving the utmost latitude to the Canadians in religious, social and administrative matters, the governors won over the mass of people and protected them from the conqueror's Indian allies. This fair and kindly treatment made the Canadians happier under British rule than under that of Louis XV.

Within a month Amherst reported to Pitt that British soldiers and Canadians were fraternising.[41] Invitations to the Friday night dances at the governor's residence in Quebec, for example, were greatly sought after by the local beauties, keen to meet and marry well-heeled British officers. Grand balls at the fort became as glamorous as those in the reign of Louis XIV. Amherst wrote to his friend, the Earl of Albermarle, 'Everything well, here and in Canada, where General Gage is increasing fast His Majesty's subjects: his American wife, Mrs Gage, being expected to bring forth another Canadian in two or three months.'

But Amherst had little time for amorous adventures and frivolities. His thoughts were of returning home to Riverhead and his beloved Jane. During his military service in America he wrote many tender and charming letters to his young wife, who scarcely survived his long absence. He had told her how much he looked forward to seeing her again, and resuming the life of a country gentleman. 'I would rather hold a plough at Riverhead, than take here in Canada all that can be given to me.'[42]

At home the general public were becoming concerned about the conditions under which the British army women were living in America. Large sums of money were subscribed for the relief of widows and children of the soldiers, who had died on active service.[43] Amherst asked regiments to submit a return showing the number of women and children considered 'proper objects of benevolence', and how they proposed to distribute the subscriptions. Some units submitted 'Nil returns'; others showed up to 12 widows and 26 children in their regiment needing assistance. The 47 Foot (North Lancashire Regiment), the 17 Foot (Leicestershire Regiment) and 35 Foot (Royal Sussex) laid out their money 'for the benefit of those children, whose fathers had been killed in action'. The 2/60 Foot, the Royal Americans, donated ten dollars each towards the payment of fees at a school for soldiers' children founded at Quebec by

General Murray. They spent the remainder on clothing and feeding six orphans. The 42 Foot (Black Watch) supported a charity school place for each child admitted.

This early example of the public's concern for the welfare of its human casualties of war would be a feature of the 19th century. Although most regiments began to establish funds for the assistance of soldiers' widows and children, the first official help was not provided until 1881. Until then 'the soldier's widow gets no pension, his orphan children no allowance: he may have given his life for his King and country in some pestilential foreign station, but if he has not saved his miserable pay, there is no resource for his widow or his orphans but the workhouse or the road,' wrote the *United Services Gazette*.[44]

24

THE PEACE TREATY
1763

Before Amherst was allowed to return home to wife and grateful nation,
Pitt made one more demand on him. With the successful completion
of operations against Quebec and Montreal, Pitt decided Amherst could
spare troops to attack the French possessions in the West Indies. France, Spain
and Britain had huge economic interests in the 'Sugar Islands', and in the
African slave trade, which supplied the labour for the sugar and tobacco
plantations in the Caribbean and southern colonies. With superior naval forces
at his disposal, Pitt seized his opportunity to cripple the French sugar trade,
based on the islands of Martinique, Guadeloupe and St Dominique. (In 1697
the French had renamed the western part of the island of Hispaniola, St
Dominique; the other two-thirds is called Dominica.)

In 1759 an expedition had successfully captured Guadeloupe. Now Pitt
instructed Amherst to send 2,000 troops to reinforce Guadeloupe, and another
6,000 under General Monckton to attack Martinique and the other West Indian
islands still in French hands.[1] The expedition, which assembled in August 1761
on Staten Island, New York, sailed for Barbados and the naval bases at Port
Royal in Jamaica and English Harbour in Antigua. France had no such permanent
dockyards and provisioning bases. Dominica was easily captured, and an
augmented force of 19 regiments[2] sailed for Martinique. The enemy was taken
entirely by surprise and capitulated on 3 February 1762, together with the
islands of Grenada, St Vincent and St Lucia. France had lost her entire West
Indian empire, except Haiti.

Suddenly, in 1760, George II died at Kensington Palace, and the 21-year-
old George III ascended the throne. He quickly made it clear that he found
Pitt's warlike plans 'bloody and expensive'. War weariness was evident among
the combatants, and the financial costs of the war were soaring. Pitt was at the
peak of his power, adored by the nation. But the King wanted an end to Pitt
and the Whig supremacy; he wanted, too, to recover control of royal patronage,
and the power to select his own ministers.[3]

Pitt was to be replaced by a minister who wanted peace, John Stuart,
third Earl of Bute and George II's grandson, an inexperienced youth of 21 –
'twin babes in the dangerous world of politics', the historian Dorothy Marshall

called King and Minister.[4] The long years of Whig supremacy were over, as young Tories and office-seekers gathered around the new monarch and a new government. Within a fortnight of Pitt's resignation, Bute was seeking peace overtures with Choiseul – with only the King aware of the secret approaches.

Bute (1713–92) was a contemporary of Horace Walpole at Eton, and early in his life became a favourite of the young Frederick, Prince of Wales, and his wife, which laid the foundation for his future political career. He was the leader of 'the pleasures of their little, idle, frivolous and dissipated court', and one of the lords of the bedchamber (1750).[5] When Frederick died the following year, Bute became the constant companion and tutor of his son, the future George III. His intimate relations with the Princess of Wales gave rise to much scandal, and his elopement with Mary, daughter of Edward Wortley, did little to improve his public image.

On George III's accession Bute became the power behind the throne, and in practice the Prime Minister, 'through whom alone, the King's intentions were made known'. He followed the King's policy of ending 'the bloody and expensive war' with France, and severing England's connections with German politics. He strove, too, to make the King supreme over parliament. Handsome, proud and pompous, and married to one of the greatest fortunes in the kingdom, nevertheless 'he was utterly unfit to direct the destinies of a great nation'. His chief aim would be to restore the popularity and credit of his royal master – seen at a low ebb when, on 9 November, the King drove to the Lord Mayor's banquet at the Guildhall and the mob shouted for Pitt![6]

Few ministers have ever been so unpopular. Bute was constantly mobbed, lampooned and caricatured. A jackboot and a petticoat – the popular emblems of Bute and the Princess – were frequently burned by excited mobs, and his London house was the object of attack, whenever there was a riot. For corruption and financial incapacity, he was unlikely to be surpassed.

During 1762, without the knowledge of his cabinet, Bute secretly carried on peace negotiations with the court at Versailles. He found a willing ally in the Duc de Choiseul, the French Foreign Minister, who had gained and retained power by courting the favour of Madame de Pompadour. Choiseul hoped to disengage France from her disastrous war without the complete loss of her overseas' empire. He also wanted peace to gain time for his plan to mature, a Family Compact (*Pacte de Famille*, 1761) between the rulers of France, Spain, Parma and Naples, which would draw Spain into France's struggle with England. This secret alliance, once made public, was the reason for Pitt's resignation in October 1761, when the cabinet refused to accept his demand for immediate measures to be taken against the threatened attack. Now, so ill that he had to be carried into the House of Commons, Pitt fought bitterly against making any concessions to France for a peace. Bute was forced to declare war on Spain (4 January 1762), proving Pitt had been right! By the end of the year, Spain had lost Havana, Manila and the Philippines to Britain.

In Britain, the choice of restoring Canada or the West Indies to France at a peace conference was hotly disputed. The sugar trade of Guadeloupe and Martinique was many times more valuable than the commercial value (chiefly fur) of Canada or 'a few useless colonies on the Mississippi'. Britain's sugar islands were less efficient, and hence less prosperous, than the French plantations. It was recognised by some politicians and writers, on both sides of the Atlantic, that the removal of the French menace in Canada might bring in its train a revolt of the American colonies, but their growing population offered a valuable consumer market and kept English manufacturers busy. It was hoped Canada would contribute to the same end. Pitt backed this view, which would eventually win the debate and be incorporated in the peace settlement.[7] To have ceded Canada would have made a total nonsense of the French and Indian War.

The Peace of Paris was signed on 10 February 1763, after months of negotiations, on less favourable terms than they should have been. Tortured by gout, his legs and thighs wrapped in flannel, Pitt protested to the end, in a speech lasting three hours and 26 minutes, that the terms were too generous to France, and that Choiseul's negotiations had largely undone the military victories won by Great Britain. Our ally, Frederick of Prussia, had been abandoned. Pitt's arguments had little effect.

The Treaty redrew the map of North America. France ceded Canada, Nova Scotia and Cape Breton Island to Britain – in fact, all her North American possessions east of the Mississippi, except the city of New Orleans. France renounced her claims to Acadia but was granted fishing rights on the banks of Newfoundland and in the Gulf of St Lawrence. England restored the rich sugar islands of Guadeloupe, Martinique and St Lucia, and France gave up Grenada, St Vincent, Dominica and Tobago, two of which were the least fertile in the group. Minorca was regained in exchange for Belle Isle. France retained Goree as a necessary slaving-station; Britain received Senegal, and traded to Spain the island of Cuba in exchange for Florida. France ceded Louisiana and New Orleans to Spain, as some compensation for Spanish losses on her behalf. Five days after the Peace of Paris, Frederick II signed his own peace treaty with Maria Theresa, both pledging mutual friendship. The map of Europe remained exactly as it had been before the war.

So, French Canada was recognised as British, and became part of the growing British Empire. New France, founded when Richelieu was prime minister and for which Montcalm had given his life, passed into oblivion. Sixty thousand Catholic subjects of His Most Christian Majesty Louis XV became British nationals, under a British governor and administration. Some returned to France, for senior posts in government, commerce and the army were now denied to them. Those French Canadians who remained were allowed to keep their laws and language, in addition to their religion. 'Nothing is left to us,' wrote a nun in the Ursuline convent to her sister,[8] 'but to adore with submission the impenetrable decrees of the Almighty!'. In the West Indies, despite the British successes, Choiseul was the decisive winner, showing that in foreign affairs he had no peer but Kaunitz.

Pitt would have exacted harder terms, convinced that the territories gained were no equivalent for those surrendered. 'By restoring to France all the valuable West Indian islands, and by our concessions in the Newfoundland fishery, we have given to her the means of recovering her prodigious losses, and of becoming once more formidable to us at sea.'[9] He wanted France reduced to a second-rate power, and would have fought on, until he had captured every colony France possessed. For him the Seven Years' War was but another indecisive issue in the long struggle between France and Great Britain – a struggle still to be decided!

The Treaty of Paris did, however, mark the culmination of the fierce competition for sea power and colonial wealth, which had originated in the voyages of the early explorers seeking rich trade routes to India and Cathay. For 300 years five nations – Portugal, Spain, Holland, France and England – had engaged in that struggle. Portugal and Holland had dropped out: now, the French navy had been utterly ruined, and Spain's maritime resources were negligible. Britain had emerged from the contest the undisputed mistress of the seas, and laden with the spoils of empire.[10]

For America, the Peace saw the removal of the French threat from north of its borders, and of the Spanish from Florida. The colonists had been backward in defending their own territory, with Massachusetts and Connecticut perhaps honourable exceptions. In 1763 the 13 English colonies were separate states, each with rights of self-government in their internal affairs, but still divided by racial origin, religion, social ideals and material interest.[11] The war had carried thousands of young Americans across colonial boundaries and opened up to them a vast territory, which lay beyond their native plantation, town or village. They saw a land full of opportunities. In numbers they were no longer hopelessly inferior to the mother country, and if they did not yet constitute a nationality of their own, it was equally clear that they had ceased to be Englishmen of the type which now peopled the land of their birth.

The Seven Years' War, judged from its results, must be considered one of the greatest wars in military history. Britain took possession of an empire that circled the globe. No other war can compare with it in the magnitude of territory gained or surrendered (with India's fate also decided by the Peace). But its chief importance is that the war determined the pattern of the future civilisation of the North American continent. The native Indian culture was doomed, as the Americans expanded into their hunting grounds. An Indian chief, watching the English army marching towards Quebec, reflected:

There was a time when our ancestors were absolute lords of the woods and lakes, wherever the eye can reach or the foot can pass. They fished and hunted, feasted and danced, and, when they were weary, lay down under the first thicket, without danger and without fear... Then a new race of men entered our country from the great ocean, and ranged over the continent – to slaughter and deceive us.[12]

The English colonies, freed of their dangerous neighbours, became less dependent on the mother country. Furthermore, the war had trained a corps of American officers like George Washington, who learned from personal experience that the British were not invincible.

The preamble to the Treaty of Paris read:

It has pleased the Most High to diffuse the spirit of union and concord among the Princes, whose divisions had spread trouble in the four parts of the world, and to inspire them with the inclination to cause the comforts of peace to succeed the misfortunes of a long and bloody war.[13]

Pitt's sure vision told him that the treaty was but the prelude to new dangers for his country. The birth pangs of the United States of America were barely a dozen years away. The vast territory wrested from France during the French and Indian War was destined to become Canada, under Anglo-Saxon rather than French domination – though, as we today approach the millennium, the French in Quebec are once again on the political war-path!

No sooner was the ink dry on the Paris treaty than Britain's Bourbon enemy, with Choiseul at the helm, began to plot her revenge at 'the disgraceful peace'. 'England is, and always will be, the enemy of your power and your State,' Choiseul told Louis XV.[14] 'Her commercial greed, her arrogance, and her envy of your power should warn you that many years must pass, before we can make a lasting peace.' France would support the struggle of the thirteen colonies in the American War of Independence. Pitt would find a hero's resting place in Westminster Abbey, leaving the political destiny of his country in the capable hands of his son, Pitt the Younger.

But all that is another story!

APPENDIX A

BRITISH LAND FORCES AT LOUISBOURG 1758

[John Knox. *Journal of the Campaigns in North America.* 1914 Vol I. p 165 (Note)]

REGIMENTS				TOTALS	
NO	NAME	COMMANDER	MODERN NAME	ALL RANKS	ACTUAL[1]
1	Royals	Foster	Royal Scots (Lothian Regiment)	989	854
15	Amherst's	Murray	East Yorkshire Regiment	996	763
17	Forbes's	Morris	Leicestershire Regiment	775	660
22	Whitmore's	Lord Rollo	Cheshire Regiment	1,093	910
28	Bragg's	Walsh	1 Bn. Gloucestershire Regiment	766	627
35	Otway's	Fletcher	1 Bn. Royal Sussex Regiment	864	566
40	Hopson's	Handfield	Prince of Wales's Volunteers (South Lancashire Regiment)	948	550
45	Warburton's	Willmott	1 Bn. Sherwood Foresters (Derbyshire Regiment)	930	864
47	Lascelles's	Hale	Loyal North Lancashire Regiment (Wolfe's Own)	1029	857
48	Webb's	Burton	1 Bn. Northamptonshire Regiment	1072	932
58	Anstruther's	How	2nd Bn. Northamptonshire Regiment	785	615
60	Monckton's (2 Bn)	Prevost	King's Royal Rifle Corps (Royal Americans)	1,094	925
60	Lawrence (3 Bn)	Frazer	King's Royal Rifle Corps (Royal Americans)	1,083	814
78	Fraser's	Fraser		1,144	1,084
-	Three additional companies			317	-
-	Train of Artillery (officers included)			330	267
	Effective Total			14,215	11,288
	Rangers			600	499
	A company of carpenters			90	-
	Others			14,905[2]	13,142

NOTES

1. J S McLennan, *Louisbourg from its Foundation to its Fall (1713–58)*. Canada, 1957, p 262. The intended forces for the expedition (CO5/212) were 14,815.

2. Knox, I, p 166, for the year 1758 gives:

REGULARS	TOTAL	PROVINCIALS	TOTAL
Louisbourg	14,215	Rangers Carpenters	600 90
For Canada (27 Foot, 42 Foot, 44 Foot, 46 Foot) (55 Foot, 1/60 Foot, 4/60 Foot) (42 Foot (1 Coy) Artillery, NY Coys)	6,884	Not Yet raised	17,480
For Nova Scotia (35 det & 43 Foot)	989	-	-
For Fort Duquesne (60 det & 62 Foot + Others)	1,854	Provincials	5,000
	Total **23,942**		**Total** **23,170**
		Grand Total	**47,112**

Women

Official rate six per 100 regulars = 700 approximately.

Plus unknown number of 'unrecognised women' and camp followers.

Different commanders allowed different ratios at different times to accompany the various expeditions.

APPENDIX B

Admiral Boscawen's order (28 June 1758) for the fleet from Halifax to Louisbourg contained the following.

1. All arrears and sea pay for all the corps to be paid immediately 'as far as there is money to do it'.

2. The first body in Gabarus Bay to carry nothing in the boats but their arms and ammunition, with bread and cheese in their pockets for two days. All their tents and blankets to follow, after they have got a footing and beaten off the enemy.

3. Six days' provisions to be prepared at a proper time, in readiness to be sent ashore after the men.

4. The boats of the hospital ships to be used solely for that purpose.

5. Light boats will be provided to save any men who may fall into the sea by accident.

6. No women to be permitted to land until the men are all ashore and their tents, blankets, provisions and necessaries are likewise landed.

APPENDIX C

EMBARKATION RETURN 5 JUNE 1759

Regiment	Colonel	Officers	NCOs and Men
15	Amherst	34	560
28	Bragg	26	565
35	Otway	36	863
43	Kennedy	29	686
47	Lascelles	36	643
48	Webb	36	816
58	Anstruther	27	589
2/60	Monckton	27	554
3/60	Lawrence	29	578
78	Fraser	50	1,219
	Special Units		
3 companies of	LOUISBOURG		
22 Foot, 40 Foot	GRENADIERS	13	313
45 Foot	Alex Murray		
	{ Stark	3	92
Rangers	{ Brewer	3	82
Companies	{ Hazzan	3	86
(Major Scott)	{ Rogers	4	108
	{ Danks	3	90
Rangers	Goreham	7	88
Royal Artillery	Williamson	21	309
	TOTAL	387	8,241

HMS *NEPTUNE* 5 JUNE 1759 Signed: James Wolfe

Source: Major-General R H Mahon. *Life of General James Murray*. John Murray, 1921, p 95.

NOTES

Chapter 1

1. Cabot's *Charter*, dated 5 March 1496. See Thwaites, p 3 and H A L Fisher, *A History of Europe*. Arnold, 1957, p 476.

2. Samuel Sigmund, *The Seven Years' War in Canada (1756–63)*. 1934, p 1.

3. Arthur Lower, *Colony to Nation*. Longmans, 1953, p 8.

4. Lieutenant-Colonel F E Whitton, *Wolfe and North America*. Ernest Benn, 1929, pp 14–15.

5. Sir John W Fortescue, *History of the British Army*. Vol II, Macmillan, 1899, p 247.

6. Lower, p 11. Champlain is buried in the church of Notre-Dame de la Recouvrance.

7. M A Jones, *A Short Oxford History of the Modern World. The Limits of Liberty 1607–1980*. OUP, 1983, p 2.

8. *Dictionary of National Biography (DNB)*.

9. *The New Encyclopaedia Britannica*. University of Chicago, 18th edition, Vol 29 (USA), p 203. Samuel Morison, *History of the American Republic*. OUP, 1973, p 42. Louis B Wright and Elaine W Fowler, *English Colonisation of North America. Documents of Modern History*. Arnold, 1968, pp 149–50.

10. Parkman quoted Whitton, p 22.

11. Whitton, pp 23. Charles I married Henrietta Maria in 1626, when she was 15 years old.

12. Fortescue, II, p 248.

13. *English Historical Documents IX*. Eyre and Spottiswoode, 1958, p 24. In 17th century Europe the wearing of beaver fur hats became a status symbol.

14. Now the 19-mile Broadway crossing Manhattan.

15. Whitton, p 47.

16. *Ibid*, p 50.

17. O P Chitwood, *A History of Colonial America*. NY, Chapter 18.

18. Samuel E Morison, *Oxford History of the American People*. OUP, 1965. *English Historical Documents* IX, p 107. Chitwood, p 65. Wright and Fowler, p 150.

19. *English Historical Documents IX,* p 118.

20. *Ibid*, p 460. Frank McLynn, *Crime and Punishment in the 18th Century*. Routledge, 1989, p 286.

21. Edward Hyde, Earl of Clarendon; George Monck, Duke of Albermarle; The Earl of

Craven; Sir George Carteret; Sir John Colleton, a sugar planter from Barbados; Sir William Berkeley and his brother, John, of Virginia; Anthony Ashley Cooper, Earl of Shaftesbury.

22. Fortescue, II, pp 258–9.

23. *Ibid*, p 259 note I for details.

24. E H Docs, p 7. Lewis Butler, *Annals of the King's Royal Rifle Corps*. 1913, Vol I (*The Royal Americans*), pp 7–9.

25. Whitton, p 135. See also *Oxford History of the American West*. OUP, 1994, p 105.

26. Lower, p 26. Whitton, p 34.

27. James A Williamson, *A Short History of British Expansion*. Macmillan, 1947, p 354.

28. J M Burnsted, *Interpreting Canada's Past*. OUP, Toronto, 1993, Vol I, p 71. Quoted Whitton, p 57.

29. See Lower, Chapter IV.

30. Arthur G Bradley, *The Fight With France for North America*. London, 1902, p 31.

31. Colonel N T St John Williams, *Judy O'Grady and the Colonel's Lady*. Brassey's, 1988, p 42.

32. R Hargreaves, *The Bloodybacks. The British Servicemen in North America (1655–1783)*. Hart-Davies, 1968, p 74.

33. Whitton, p 30, and see Chitwood, p 337 and note. For 1666 census, see G M Wrong, *The Rise and Fall of New France*. Vol I, Macmillan, 1928, p 384.

34. Lower, p 51 and Wrong, II, p 740.

35. *The New Encyclopaedia Britannica*. Vol 29, 15th edition.

36. Lower, p 54. In the 18th century the population of the American colonies roughly doubled every 20 years (Williamson, 1922, p 327 note).

37. Whitton, p 44. The agreement was confirmed in 1722.

38. E H Docs, p 7.

39. Williamson, p 392.

40. Richard Middleton, *Colonial America*. Blackwell, 1996, Chapter 15.

41. See *New Encyclopaedia Britannica*, (USA), p 202 and *Concise Dictionary of American History*. Editor Wayne Andrews, New York, 1962.

42. Lower, p 20.

Chapter 2

1. E B Greene, *Provincial America (1690–1740)*. USA, 1905 (rep. 1964), p 165.

2. *American Colonial Documents to 1776*, IX. Eyre and Spottiswoode, 1955, p 28. Morison, pp 140–1. Theodore Draper, *A Struggle for Power*. Little, Brown, 1996, p 111. Richard Hofstadter, *America at 1750. A Social Portrait*. Cape, 1972, p 32.

3. J A Doyle, *The Colonies Under the House of Hanover.* Longman and Green, 1907, Chapter 1. Dorothy Marshall, *18th Century England.* Longmans, 1989, p 242. Williamson, pp 339–41.

4. Doyle, p 13. Charles M Andrews, *Colonial Folkways.* Yale University Press, 1919, Chapter 4. Carl Holliday, *Woman's Life in Colonial Days.* 1922, rep. Detroit 1970, p 162.

5. Quoted Morison, p 146.

6. John A Garraty, *The History of the USA.* Allan Lane, Penguin Press, 1968, p 48. Andrews, p 124.

7. Doyle, p 25.

8. Greene, p 321.

9. See Doyle, p 31. Norreys Jephson O'Conor, *A Servant of the Crown.* New York, 1938, p 50. 'We have Beef, Pork, Mutton, Poultry, Butter, Wild Fowl, Fish, roots and herbs of all kinds in their season,' wrote John Appy, Loudoun's secretary, p 49.

10. Quoted E J Eccles, 'The Social, Economic and Political Significance of the Military Establishment in New France', p 6. *Canadian Historical Review*, 1971, March, Vol LII, No 1.

11. Gottlieb Mittelberger, *Journey to Pennsylvania* (1756). Quoted Draper, p 120. Chitwood, p 255. Hofstadter, pp 66, 89.

12. Morison, p 149. Holliday, p 285. Doyle, p 43. Hofstadter, pp 51–2, 89. For 1718 Act see 4 GEO I, c11 and Blackstone, IV, p 370.

13. See Andrews, Chapter III and Morison, pp 147, 104–5.

14. See Chitwood, pp 495–7. Andrews, p 88. Holliday, p 189. Epitaph of Mary Randolph Keith, mother of Chief Justice John Marshall, Washington, Kentucky. Quoted Roger Thompson, *Women in Stuart England and America.* Routledge and Kegan Paul, 1974, p 11 and note.

15. A W Calhoun, *Social History of the American Family.* New York, 1917, Vol 1, pp 56, 67. Psalm 127. Richard Middleton, *Colonial America.* Blackwell, 1996, p 248.

16. See *Oxford English Dictionary.* Clarendon Press, 1989, 'To bundle with Yankee lasses' was regarded as an amusement in the 18th century. For Victorian England see Ronald Pearsall, *The Worm in the Bud.* Weidenfeld, 1970, p 275. Thompson, pp 127–8.

17. Calhoun, p 168. Middleton, pp 272–3.

18. Holliday, p 240. Daniel Defoe, *Moll Flanders* (1722). Panther Books, 1975, p 330 and original title page.

19. Thompson, p 39 and *DNB.*

20. Calhoun, p 248.

21. Holliday, p 262.

22. *Ibid*, p 240.

23. Calhoun, pp 332–4. Wrong, pp 477–8. The 'wooden horse' frequently caused rupture.

24. Greene, pp 253, 260.

25. Lower, p 56.

26. F Parkman, *Montcalm and Wolfe*. 1884, vol II, p 380.

27. See John Shy, *Towards Lexington. The Role of the British Army in the Coming of the American Revolution*. Princeton, 1965, p 87.

28. Williamson, p 359.

29. *The New Encyclopaedia Britannica,* vol 29, p 208.

30. Guy Frégault, *Canada. The War of Conquest*. Translated Margaret M Cameron, OUP, 1969, p 88.

31. Williamson, p 339. Middleton, p 366.

Chapter 3

1. Fisher, p 737.

2. *Ibid*, p 636. In 1652 the Duke of Condé entered Paris at the head of a Spanish army and 'a rout of idle nobles and smart ladies, street ruffians and enemy soldiers'. Louis was virtually a prisoner in the Louvre.

3. Nancy Mitford, *Madame de Pompadour*. Hamish Hamilton, 1968, p 12. *Duc et Pair. 'Celui auquel son titre de duc conférait les privilèges de la pairie (droit de siéger au Parlement etc)'. Grand Larousse.*

4. Guy Chaussinand-Nogaret, *The French Nobility in the 18th Century*. CUP, 1976, pp 43, 45–6, 62, 117.

5. M S Anderson, *Europe in the 18th Century*. Longmans, p 55. Chaussinand-Nogaret, p 66. William Doyle, *The Oxford History of the French Revolution*, Clarendon Press, 1989, p 28. *New Cambridge Modern History (NCMH)*. Vol VII, p 236.

6. Richard Cobb (editor), *The French Revolution*. Simon and Schuster, 1988, p 38. John Lough, *An Introduction to 18th Century France*. Longman, 1964, Chapter 1.

7. G P Gooch, *Louis XV*. Longmans, 1956, Preface. Has an excellent bibliography.

8. Alfred Cobham, *A History of Modern France*. Penguin Books, 1990, Vol I, 1715–99, p 52. *NCMH*, p 226.

9. H Noel Williams (HNW), *Madame de Pompadour*. Harper, 1925, p 3. Cobham, p 19. Tencin's sister, Claudine Alexandrine, the dissipated mistress of Philippe d'Orléans, ran one of the chief literary salons of the century.

10. Lough, pp 134, 136. *NCMH*, p 220.

11. *NCMH*, p 227.

12. Geoffrey Treasure, *The Making of Modern Europe (1648–1780)*. Routledge, 1985, p 313. Doyle, p 42.

13. E N Williams, *The Ancien Régime in Europe*. Penguin Books, 1972, p 233.

14. Margaret Trouncer, *The Pompadour*. Hutchinson, 1934 (rep. 1956), p 73.

15. Louise de Mailly (the eldest) (1733), Marquise de Vintimille (1739), and (the youngest) the Marquise de Châteauroux (1741). The fourth de Mailly sister was the Duchesse de Lauraguais.

16. Quoted Gooch, p 5.

17. *London Magazine*. October 1758, pp 511–13.

18. *Ibid*, p 511.

19. Mitford, p 85.

20. Jacques Levron, *Pompadour*. Allen and Unwin, 1963, p 20.

21. On 17 January 1747 Molière inaugurated the little theatre she had created in Versailles with a performance of *Tartuffe*, in which Pompadour played the leading role of Dorine. HNW, p 92.

22. Beckles Willson, *The Life and Letters of James Wolfe*. 1909, p 185.

23. *London Magazine*, p 512.

24. Gooch, p 153.

25. Parkman, II, p 15.

26. Levron, p 67. The Duc de Croÿ was a colonel in the Roussillon cavalry regiment and was more often to be found in the galleries of Versailles seeking promotion than on the battlefield. But he is one of the most valuable sources of the period.

27. Beckles Willson, p 185. Parkman, II, p 15.

28. *London Magazine*, p 513.

29. HNW, p 206. Walter L Dorn, *Competition for Empire (1740–63)*. Harper Torchbooks, New York, 1965, p 353.

30. Parkman, Introduction and II, p 44.

31. Frégault, p 15.

32. HRH Princess Michael of Kent, *Cupid and the King*. Harper Collins, 1991, p 216.

33. Levron, p 223.

34. T C W Blanning, *The Origins of the French Revolution*. Longmans, 1986, p 41. Gooch p. 161.

35. Built in 1748 and decorated by Falconet, Van Loo and Boucher, it was totally destroyed by the French Revolution mobs in 1789.

36. Quoted HNW, p 301.

37. Gooch, p. 166.

38. HNW, p 307, quoting E Goncourt, *Madame de Pompadour*, p 170. Levron, p 180.

39. Starhenberg to Kaunitz. Quoted Levron, p 179.

40. Basil Williams, *The Whig Supremacy, 1714–60*. OUP, 1982, p 233. HNW, p 399. General R H Mahon, *The Life of the Hon James Murray*. 1921, p 80. Lough, p 166.

41. Horace Walpole, *Memoirs of the Reign of George III*. 3 Vols, 1847, III, p 217.

42. Trouncer, p 186.

43. Joan Haslip, *Madame du Barry*. Weidenfeld and Nicolson, 1991, p 24.

44. Mitford, p 33. Levron, p 99.

Chapter 4

1. Fisher, p 737. Parkman, II, p 9.

2. Fisher, p 696 and I. WILL and MAR Session 2 Cap 2.

3. Basil Williams, pp 1–2.

4. *DNB*. King and Queen were buried side by side in Henry VII's Chapel in Westminster Abbey.

5. *English Historical Documents*. Vol X, 1714–83, editor D B Horn, Eyre and Spottiswoode, 1957, p 7.

6. *DNB*.

7. *DNB* (Caroline). Charles C Trench, *George II*, p 19. Marshall, p 149.

8. *DNB* (George II).

9. Stella Tillyard, *Aristocrats*. Chatto and Windus, 1994, p 43. Fisher, p 703.

10. *NCMH*. VII, p 253.

11. *English Historical Documents*, p 6.

12. Basil Williams, p 354 note. She was the niece of George I's mistress, Lady Darlington, and the great-niece of the elder Countess von Platen; her grandmother, sister of von Platen, was one of George I's early mistresses.

13. *DNB*.

14. E J Burford, *Royal St James's*. Hale, 1988 p 29. *DNB* (George II and Wallmoden).

15. John Carswell, *From Revolution to Revolution: England 1688–1766*. Routledge, 1973, p 34.

16. G E Mingay, *English Landed Society in the 18th Century*. Routledge and Kegan Paul, 1963, pp 3, 6.

17. E N Williams, *The Ancien Régime in Europe*. Penguin Books, 1972, pp 512–13.

18. Fisher, p 702. Parkman, I, p 8. George Rudé, *Europe in the 18th Century*. Weidenfeld and Nicolson, 1985, p 72. Defoe, p 108.

19. *NCMH*, p 58. Squire Western was Henry Fielding's fox-hunting squire in *Tom Jones* (1749).

20. Mingay, p 148.

21. Dorothy George, *London in the 18th Century*. Penguin, 1965, pp 380–1.

22. Roy Porter, *English Society in the 18th Century*. Revised edition, Penguin Books, 1990, p 125.

23. E N Williams, p 518. Daniel Defoe, *The Two Great Questions Considered* (1700), p 26.

24. Fisher, p 704. E N Williams, p 509.

25. *The Complete English Tradesman*. 1726–7, Vol 1, Letter 3. Defoe himself married not for love but to obtain the dowry of Mary, daughter of a wealthy merchant. Despite his frequent long absences travelling or in prison, she bore him eight children.

26. Daniel Defoe, *The True Born Englishman* (1701), Lines 15–19.

27. Fisher, p 704. Charles Wesley, *All Things Bright and Beautiful*.

> 'The rich man in his castle;
> The poor man at his gate;
> God made the high and lowly
> And ordered their estate.'

28. George Rudé, *The Crowd in History*, 1964. *Johnson's England*. Editor A S Turberville, Clarendon Press, 1952, p 12.

29. Five and a half million in England and Wales in 1700. Just over nine million in 1800. Marshall, p 7 note 1.

30. Porter, p 43.

31. Mingay, p 251.

32. Porter, p 38.

33. J B Macaulay, *The History of England*. 1850.

34. Horace Walpole, fourth son of Sir Robert Walpole.

35. Parkman, I, pp 6–7. Stella Margetson, *Leisure and Pleasure in the 18th Century*. Cassell, 1970, p 77.

36. George Rudé, *Hanoverian London*. Secker and Warburg, 1971, p 60.

'The simple dress of a woman of quality is often the product of a hundred climes', wrote Addison in *The Spectator* 69, 1711. 'The brocade petticoat rises out of the mines of Peru and the diamond necklace out of the bowels of Indostan.'

37. Rudé, *Hanoverian London*, p 72.

38. Now the Imperial War Museum.

39. See Hogarth's *The Rake's Progress Plate 3. The Tavern Scene* (1733).

40. John Gay, *The Beggar's Opera*. 1728. She married the third Duke of Bolton, colonel of the Horse Guards. He was said to have settled '£400 a year upon her during pleasure and upon disagreement £200 a year'.

41. J W Archenholtz, *A View of the British Constitution and of the Manners and Customs of the People of England.* 1794, p 119.

42. Marshall, p 36. Daniel Defoe, *A Weekly Review of the Affairs of France.* Vol 8, September 1711, pp 302–3.

43. Rudé, *Hanoverian London,* p 76.

44. John Fielding, *A Plan for the Asylum of Orphans and Other Deserted Girls of the Poor of the Metropolis.* 1758.

45. Peter Earle, *The Making of the English Middle Class.* Methuen, 1989, pp 119–20, 125. George, p 18. T E James, *Prostitution and the Law.* 1951.

46. Peter Earle, *The World of Defoe.* Weidenfeld, 1976, p 118.

47. Archenholtz, note 39. Defoe, *Moll Flanders,* p 26.

48. Sir William Blackstone, *Commentaries on the Laws of England* (1753). 1793, I, p 65.

49. Porter, p 25.

50. Earle, *World of Defoe,* p 249. Lawrence Stone, *Uncertain Unions. Marriage in England 1660–1753.* OUP, 1992, p 17.

51. George, p 305. About one-quarter of marriages at the Fleet 1700–10 were military marriages. They cost about one-third of legal marriages. Dorothy Marshall, *English Poor in the 18th Century.* 1926, p 206. W Lecky, *History of England in the 18th Century.* 1897, Vol 2, pp 115–16, R B Outhwaite, *Marriage and Society.* Europa Publishers, 1981, pp 123, 126. Six thousand marriages took place in the Fleet in 1740. Basil Williams, p 136. See also British Museum 1747 print, *Fleet Wedding.* Quoted E J Burford, *London, The Synfulle Citie.* Robert Hale, 1990, p 174.

> 'Jack, rich in Prizes, now the Knot is ty'd,
> Sits pleas'd by her he thinks his mayden Bride:
> But tho' a modest Look by Molly's shown
> She only longs for what she oft has known!'

52. N T St John Williams, p 16. Thomas Hardy, *The Mayor of Casterbridge.* 'And like a show of cattle lent on hire. Their points display to all who may desire.' Samuel Menafee, *Wives for Sale.* 1981, p 169.

53. Eliza Haywood, *Advice to a Serving Maid.* 1743.

54. N T St John Williams, Chapters 6 and 17 and pp 3, 14.

55. E N Williams, p 518.

56. Olwen Hufton, *The Prospect Before Her (1500–1800).* Harper Collins, 1995, Vol I, pp 322–3. 'In 18C Paris approximately one adult woman in 13 looked to prostitution for a whole or part of her income'. Erica Marie Benabou, *La Prostitution et la Police des Moeurs au XVIIIe siècle.* Paris, 1987.

57. J Black, *The Grand Tour.* Sutton, 1992, p 190. *London Magazine.* 1756, p 599. P D Brown, *William Pitt. Earl of Chatham.* Allen and Unwin, 1978, p 32.

58. Defoe, *True Born Englishman*, p 119.

59. Quoted Porter, p 7.

Chapter 5

1. Basil Williams, p 208. *DNB*.

2. Fisher, p 747.

    1689–97 King William's War.
    1701–13 War of the Spanish Succession – Queen Anne's War.
    1739–48 War of Jenkins's Ear. War of Austrian Succession. King George's War.
    1756–63 The Seven Years' War. French and Indian War.

3. Maurepas, *Mémoires,* cited Corwen, *American Historical Review*, Vol 21, p 45. Fisher, p 751. Williamson, p 385. For Châteauroux, see Gooch p 109.

4. Parkman, I, p 9.

5. Malcolm Fraser, *The Capture of Quebec. Journal. 8 May 1759–17 May 1760.* Lieutenant 78 Foot (Fraser's Highlanders). Editor R O Alexander. *Journal of the Society for Army Historical Research (JSAHR)* 18, 1939, p 273. Williamson, p 385. Fisher p 749.

6. Dorn, p 149. *DNB* (Pitt).

7. Peter Brown, *William Pitt, Earl of Chatham*. Allen and Unwin, 1978, p 77. *DNB* (Fox). Wrong, II, p 801. J H Plumb, *Sir Robert Walpole*. 1956 and 1950, I, p 203.

8. *DNB* (Fox). Brown pp 41, 66. Tillyard, pp 10, 46.

9. *DNB* (Shirley). Fortescue, II, p 264. The most volunteers came from Maine, New Hampshire and Connecticut.

10. Williamson, p 388. *NCMH*, Vol 7, p 533.

11. *DNB* (Shirley).

12. Wrong, II, pp 639–40, 665. Burnsted, *Interpreting Canada's Past*. OUP, Toronto, 1993. Vol 1, p 191.

13. The author's own regiment, the 45 Foot, later the Sherwood Foresters, served in Louisbourg 1746–9. It captured Fort Beauséjour in 1755, Louisbourg in 1758 and in 1759 two grenadier companies were at the capture of Quebec. In 1761 the 45 Foot recaptured St John's, Newfoundland. The 29 Foot left Louisbourg in 1749 for the founding of Halifax, and returned to Ireland in 1750.

14. Fortescue, II, pp 265–6.

15. Parkman, I, p 91.

16. Williamson, p 392.

17. Quoted *English Historical Documents 1714–83*. Editors D B Horn and Mary Ransome, Oxford, 1957, p 793.

18. *American Historical Review*. M P Clarke, *The Board of Trade at Work 1910–12*. Vol 17, p 39. Whitton, p 206.

19. Williamson, p 293.

20. Whitton, p 230. Frégault, p 167.

21. Fortescue, II, pp 268–9.

22. Williamson, p 393. Wrong, II, p 772.

23. Frégault, p 188.

24. *Ibid*, p 188.

25. Wrong, II, p 783. The lines are taken from Longfellow's *Evangeline*.

26. Levinge, *43 Foot*. 1868, p 15.

27. Samuel Johnson, *Tour to the Hebrides*. 23 September 1773.

28. Levinge, p 42.

29. *Ibid*, p 20.

30. *Ibid*, p 19. The wooden horse frequently injured the soldier and caused rupture, especially when muskets were tied to the soldier's feet to increase the punishment. It was abolished in 1780.

31. *Ibid*, pp 16, 21.

Chapter 6

1. Correlli Barnett, *Britain and her Army*. Allen Lane, 1970, p 195.

2. Marshall, pp 256–8. Derek McKay and H Scott, *The Rise of the Great Powers, 1648–1815*. Longmans, 1983, p 179.

3. Williamson, p 392.

4. Doyle, *Colonies Under Hanover*, p 549.

5. Bradley, p 68.

6. Doyle, *Colonies Under Hanover*, p 557. Whitton, p 213.

7. Fortescue, II, p 268. *DNB* (Newcastle).

8. L P Gipson, *The British Empire before the American Revolution*. 14 Vols, 1936, VI, p 54. Frégault, p 75.

9. Gipson, IV, p 289.

10. *DNB*.

11. Doyle, *Colonies Under Hanover*, p 560. Theodore Draper, *A Struggle for Power*. Little, Brown, 1996, p 177.

12. *Pennsylvania Gazette*. 9 May 1754. Quoted Frégault, p 38.

13. Wood, p 36. Wrong, II, p 755.

14. Clarke, p 42. Whitton, p 215.

15. Marshall, p 261.

16. Lieutenant-Colonel Russell Gurney, *History of the Northamptonshire Regiment (48 Foot), 1742–1934*. Gale and Polden, 1935.

17. Later the Essex and Northamptonshire Regiments respectively. In 1751 (Royal Warrant) British army regiments were identified by number instead of being called after the colonel's name.

18. *DNB*. Boscawen, letter to his wife, quoted N A M Rodger, *The Wooden World. An Anatomy of the Georgian Navy*. London, 1986, p 44.

19. Doyle, *Colonies Under Hanover*, p 568.

20. E J Burford, *Wits, Wenches and Wantons in the 18th Century*. Hale, 1986, p 176. Walter H Blumenthall, *Women Camp followers of the American Revolution*, Ayer Co. New Hampshire, p 46.

21. Gurney, p 6.

22. Henry Fielding, *Tom Jones*. 1749.

23. Barnett, p 141. George Farquhar, *The Recruiting Officer*. 1706.

24. *NCMH*, Vol 7, quoted p 184. M S Anderson, *War and Society in Europe of the Old Régime (1618–1789)*. Fontana, quoted p 121.

25. Stanley M Pargellis, *Lord Loudoun in North America*. OUP, 1933, pp 281–3 and notes. See also note 21.

26. Colonel N T St John Williams, *Redcoats and Courtesans. The Birth of the British Army (1660–90)*. Brassey's, 1994, p 107.

27. Fortescue, II, p 82.

Chapter 7

1. Pargellis, p 31. The 40 Foot was formed in 1717 from the four independent companies at Annapolis Royal and four at Placentia, Newfoundland, and served continuously at Annapolis and other centres in Newfoundland until 1760, from Louisbourg to Montreal. In 1764 the regiment left Canada for Ireland.

2. Whitton, p 218.

3. Marshall, p 262.

4. *NCMH*, p 170. Dorn, p 104.

5. Dorn, pp 108–9.

6. H A L Howell, 'Echoes from the Past'. *Journal of the Royal Army Medical Corps 1914*, Vol XXII, pp 326–7. M S Anderson, *War and Society*, p 165. C Lloyd, *British Seamen*. 1968, p 231.

7. Bradley, p 85.

8. Parkman, I, p 204. F. Anderson. *A People's Army.* University of North Carolina, 1949, p 50.

9. Ronald Wright, *Stolen Continents.* Murray, 1992, p 100. Richard Middleton, *Colonial America.* Blackwell, 1996, p 41.

10. Braddock's *Orderly Book.* 26 February – 17 June 1755. Published 1878. Quoted Blumenthall, p 45, p 46.

11. J F Findlay, *Wolfe in Scotland.* Longman Green, 1928, p 230. N T St John Williams, *Judy O'Grady,* p 12.

12. Williams, Chapter 2.

13. *Ibid,* pp 13–14. Army Order, 1 June 1685.

14. Williams, pp 42–43. Blumenthall, p 47.

15. Quoted Byron Farwell, *For Queen and Country.* Allen Lane, 1981, p 229.

16. St. John Williams, pp 43–4.

17. JSAHR, Vol 8, p 76, quoted Williams, p 43.

18. Paul E Kopperman, *The British Command and Service Wives in America (1775–83).* JSAHR, Summer 1982, p 17.

19. Anderson, p 119, notes

20. St. John Williams, pp 13–14. Fortescue, II, p 32.

21. William Wycherley (1640–1716), *The Plain Dealer* (1677), Act II. His masterpiece. *The Grand Duchess of Gérolstein* by Jacques Offenbach (1867) for the French quotation.

22. St. John Williams, p 10.

23. *Ibid,* p 16 and Walker, *History of the Northumberland Fusiliers.* Murray, 1919, pp 113–14.

24. Ernest Sanger, *Englishmen at War.* Sutton, 1993, p 156.

25. *DNB* (Boscawen).

26. N A M Rodger, *The Wooden World.* Fontana Press (HarperCollins), 1988, pp 75–6.

27. Warren Tute, *The True Glory.* Centurion Press, 1983, p 74.

Chapter 8

1. Parkman, I, p 193.

2. Doyle, *Colonies Under Hanover,* p 571.

3. Pargellis, p 37.

4. Doyle, *Colonies Under Hanover,* p 572. News from the colonies often reached the English newspapers weeks and months after the event.

5. Sir Winston Churchill, *Marlborough. His Life and Times*. Harrap, 1934, Vol II, p 112.

6. Michael Barthop, *The Northamptonshire Regiment (48/58 Foot)*. Famous Regiments Series. Leo Cooper, 1974, p 5.

7. *DNB*.

8. Barthop, p 6 and Doyle, p 574. Pargellis (see note 9) gives 1,319 rank and file: 906 (mostly raw recruits) and 100 sick were left behind with Dunbar.

9. Stanley M Pargellis, *Braddock's Defeat*. American Historical Review, 1936, Vol 41, p 257 note 14.

10. Barthop, p 6.

11. Pargellis, p 263. Lewis Butler, *The Annals of the King's Royal Rifle Corps*. 2 Vols, 1913, I, p 159.

12. Barthop, p 6.

13. Parkman, I, p 218.

14. Bradley, *The Fight with France*, p 100. George F Stanley, *New France. The Last Phase* (1744-60). OUP. 1968, p 100. (Contains an excellent bibliography.)

15. Williamson, p 394 gives nearly 800 casualties. Lt. Colonel Russell Gurney, *History of the Northamptonshire Regiment (48 Foot and 58 Foot) 1742-1934*. Gale and Polden, 1935, p 26.

16. Blumenthall, p 47.

17. Parkman, I, p 233. Dunbar was replaced in command of 48 Foot by Colonel Daniel Webb of the 7th Dragoon Guards, who arrived in June 1756.

18. *DNB*.

19. Lewis Butler, *The Annals of the King's Royal Rifle Corps (60F)*. Vol I, The *Royal Americans*, 1913, pp 2–3.

20. *Ibid*, p 3.

21. *Ibid*, p 4.

22. *Ibid*, p 25.

23. *DNB*.

24. Pargellis, pp 253, 269. Bradley, p 104. Stanley, p 99.

25. *Gentleman's Magazine*. September 1755, quoted Barthop, p 7.

26. 25 October 1755.

27. Fortescue, II, p 280. W.M. Thackeray, *The Virginians* (1857-9) tells the story of this campaign, some of his characters being imaginary member of the 48 Foot. Gurney, p 27

Chapter 9

1. *DNB.*

2. *Proceedings of the New York State Historical Association* (NYSHA). Vol XIII. 1914, p 92.

3. *Ibid.*

4. *DNB.*

5. Doyle, *Colonies under Hanover,* p 341 and Parkman, I, p 292.

6. Ian K Steele, *Betrayals. Fort William Henry and the Massacre.* OUP, 1990, p 35.

7. Cuneo, p 20.

8. Steele, p 6. Fortescue, II, p 281 for an account of the battle.

9. Bradley, p 115.

10. Steele, p 38. Anderson, p 118.

11. Steele. Quoting *The Papers of Sir William Johnson.* Editor James Sullivan. 14 Vols. Albany, NY, 1921–65. Vol 1, pp 783 and 861.

12. Doyle, *Colonies under Hanover,* p 587.

13. Brian Connell, *The Plains of Abraham.* Hodder and Stoughton, 1959, p 19.

14. NYSHA, p 108.

15. *DNB.*

16. Richard Dillon, *North American Indian Wars.* Arms and Armour Press, London, 1983, p 39.

17. Parkman, I, p 310.

18. Steele, p 57.

19. See Major W H Bertsch, *The Defence of Oswego,* in NYSHA. Vol XIII. 1914, p 112 ff.

20. *DNB.*

21. *Ibid.*

22. Today, the remains of the star-shaped fort, and much of the original earthwork, are preserved in the Beauséjour National Historic Site. There is also a museum, exhibiting the fort's early history, and that of the Acadians, who settled the region in the 1670's.

23. Parkman, I, p 330.

24. *Ibid,* I, p 350.

Chapter 10

1. Correlli Barnett, *Britain and Her Army.* Allen Lane, 1970, p 198.

2. Parkman, I, p 354 and Bradley, p 139.

3. Fisher, p 756. Frederick II was childless, and his marriage with Christina Elizabeth of Brunswick was probably never consummated.

4. T B Macaulay, *The History of England*. Geoffrey Treasure, *The Making of Modern Europe 1648–1780*. Routledge, 1985, p 585.

5. Trouncer, p 225. The Parc aux Cerfs was a private brothel near Versailles, where Louis XV kept in secret a series of 'lascivious little beauties', the most celebrated of whom was the 14 year old Louise O'Murphy, immortalised in a painting by Boucher, 'La Belle Morphise'.

6. Fisher, p 756. Dorothy Marshall, *18th Century England*. Longmans, 1962, p 268. Dorn, p 297. Treasure, p 418. E S Corwen, *French Objective in the American Revolution*. American Historical Review. Vol 21, p 48.

7. Voltaire, *Candide,* 1759. Levron, p 220. Corwen, p 49. Stanley, p 270.

8. William Wood, *The Fight for Canada*. Toronto, 1906, p 28.

9. *Burke's Complete Peerage*. Stanley Pargellis, *Lord Loudoun in North America*. 1933, Preface.

10. Parkman, I, p 358. See also Treasure, p 207. One officer to every 15 men on active service.

11. Wood, p. 57. Robin Reilly, *The Rest to Fortune*. 1960, p 231.

12. Wood, pp 56–60. G M Wrong, *The Conquest of New France*. The Textbook Edition. Yale University Press, 1918, pp 180–2.

13. *Ibid,* p 61.

14. Parkman, I, p 364.

15. Word, p 47. G M Wrong, *The Rise and Fall of New France*. Macmillan, 1928. Vol II, p 660.

16. Nothing to do with the sea. They were enlisted by the Marine Department, which was in charge of the French colonies.

17. Reilly, p 231 and Wrong, II, p 826.

18. Bernis to Choiseul. Quoted Mahon, p 84.

19. Wood, p 49. Wrong, II, p 827. The wealthy Duc de Richelieu bought many of these treasures after Bigot's trial.

20. Wood, pp 48–51. C P Stacey, *Quebec 1759*. Macmillan, 1959, p 10.

21. Stacey, p 11. Bradley, pp 206–7.

22. Mahon, p 86. Parkman, I, p 385 and II, p 18–23.

23. Wood, p 70. Stanley, p 209.

24. *Ibid,* pp 50–51.

25. *Ibid,* p 54.

26. Eccles, p 18 (See Chapter 2).

27. Bradley, p 143. Les Invalides had been opened in Paris by Louis XIV in 1674 for the care of French soldiers, aged, wounded or disabled in war.

28. *History of France*, XV, p 520. Quoted HNW, p 339. See also J F C Fuller, *The Decisive Battles of the Western World*. Eyre and Spottiswoode, II, p 201. A French army left behind ' pomades, perfumes, powdering and dressing gowns, bagwigs, umbrellas, parrots ... whining lackeys, cooks, friseurs, players and prostitutes'.

29. Bradley, p 143.

30. J W Archenholtz, *A View of the Constitution and Customs of England,* 1794.

31. Parkman, I, pp 12–13.

32. Fortescue, II, p 602.

33. Whitton, pp 245–6.

34. Parkman, I, p 370.

35. Frégault, p 62.

36. Wood, p 64.

37. Quoted Parkman, I, p 373.

38. Pargellis, p 302.

39. Parkman, I, p 389.

40. Whitton, p 248.

41. *Proceedings of the New York Historical Association. The Defence and Capture of Oswego,* p 113.

42. Parkman, I, p 397.

43. *Rogers's Journal*, p 19 quoted Peter Young, *The British Army 1642–1970*. William Kimber, 1967, p 104.

Chapter 11

1. John R Cuneo, *Robert Rogers of the Rangers*, 1959, p 49.

2. Stanley M Pargellis, *Lord Loudoun in North America*. London, 1933 (rep. 1969), p 162 and p 168.

3. Fortescue, II, p 302.

4. Parkman, I, p 410: Fortescue, II, p 303.

5. Pargellis, p 95.

6. Lieutenant General Sir Neil Cantlie, *A History of the Army Medical Department*. Vol I, 1974. Livingstone, p 112.

7. Lieutenant Colonel H A L Howell, *Echoes from the Past*. Journal of the Royal Army Medical Corps. 1914. Vol XXII, p 333.

8. *General Orders*, 19 September 1756. (Loudoun Papers).

9.   Parkman, I, p 500.

10. Cantlie, p 106. Beckles, p 367 (Letter dated 24 May 1758).

11. Cantlie, p 112.

12. Cuneo, p 33.

13. Cuneo, p 49.

14. Doyle, *Colonies under Hanover,* p 595, quoting Parkman.

15. Parkman, I, p 407.

16. *Ibid,* p 414.

17. Archibald Forbes, *The Black Watch (42 Foot).* 1896, p 46.

18. Frégault, p 131.

19. To maintain continuity in procedure the 52-62 Foot were renumbered as 50–60 Foot regiments.

20. The 42 Foot was formed on 25 October 1739 by John Crawford, 4th Earl of Lindsay.

21. Parkman, I, p 422.

22. Letter to Horace Mann, 14 Nov 1756, quoted NY. SHA, *The Defence and Capture of Oswego,* p 119.

23. George Stanley, *Canada's Soldiers.* Toronto, 1954, p 73.

24. *DNB* (Pitt).

25. Quoted Peter D Brown, *William Pitt, Earl of Chatham.* Allen & Unwin, 1978, p 123.

26. Fortescue, II, p 306.

27. Brown, p 130.

28. See Editor Tony Hayter, *An Eighteenth Century Secretary at War.* Bodley Head for the Army Records Society, 1988, p 71. *DNB* (Anson).

29. Richard Middleton, *Pitt, Anson and the Admiralty.* History, 1970, Part 55, p 197 and note 39. Dorn, p 110.

Chapter 12

1.   G M Wrong, *The Rise and Fall of New France.* Macmillan, 1928, Vol II, p 800. *DNB* (Pitt).

2.   Dorothy Marshall, *18th Century England,* Longmans, 1962, p 275. William Wood, *The Fight for Canada.* Constable, 1905, pp 15–16.

3.   See Stanley Pargellis, *Military Affairs in North America 1748-65.* 1936, p 229. *American Historical Review.* Vol 41. 19,000 Hessian and Hanoverian troops had been brought over to guard England, threatened with invasion.

4. Fortescue, II, p 305 and Adams, *History of the British Regular Army.* 1990, Vol 1. For letter Pitt to Loudoun, dated St James 23 December 1756, see *English Historical Review.* July 1902. Vol 17, p 168.

5. Fortescue, Adams and Wrong, II, p 808. Lord Stanhope, *History of England.* Vol 3, p 18. Basil Williams, *Life of William Pitt.* 1913, I, p 294. 77 Foot and 78 Foot were disbanded at the Peace of 1763, many remaining in America with land grants, the rest returning to Scotland.

6. John Dryden, *Cymon and Iphegenia* (1699).

7. Fortescue, II, p 307.

8. *DNB* (Pitt) and Basil Williams, *The Life of William Pitt.* 1913, pp 324–5.

9. See Mary Clarke, *The Board of Trade at Work,* p 43. American Historical Review. 1911–12.

10. See Pargellis, pp 229–30. Horace Walpole argued, 'Pitt kept aloof from all details, drew magnificent plans, and left others to find the magnificent means.' *Reign of George II.* Vol III, p 173 (1847).

11. Norrey's Jephson O'Conor, *A Servant of the Crown. The Papers of John Appy, Secretary and Judge Advocate of HM Forces.* NY, 1938, p 58.

12. Captain John Knox, *An Historical Journal of the Campaigns in North America (1769).* Edited A G Doughty. The Publications of the Champlain Society, 1914. Toronto, 3 Vols, I, p 16.

13. *Ibid,* Knox, I, p 18 and I, p 116 note.

14. See Williams, *Judy O'Grady,* p 17 and p 19. It was not until 29 October 1800 that the Army would pay for the lawful wives and children 'on the strength of the regiment', not permitted to accompany their husbands overseas, to return to their homes.

15. Knox, I, p 30.

16. Knox, I, p 34.

17. Lewis Butler, *The Annals of the King's Royal Rifle Corps (60 Foot).* 1913, pp 33–4.

18. Knox, 29 July 1757.

19. See Desmond Morton, *A Military History of Canada.* Hurtig Publishers, Edmonton, 1985, Chapter I.

20. Marc Lescarbot, *History of New France.* 1907, 3 Vols, III, Bk. 5, Chapter 7, p 8 and pp 268–9. Lescarbot sailed to Acadia c 1604. Volumes I & II. described the efforts of French explorers like Cartier, des Monts, Poutrincourt etc., to establish a foothold in the New World. Volume 3 is devoted to Indian customs.

21. Pargellis, pp 330–1. See G D Sheffield, *The Redcaps. A History of the Royal Military Police.* Brassey's, 1994.

22. *Ibid,* pp 332–3.

23. Williams, *Judy O'Grady,* pp 14–17. Col N T St. John Williams, *Tommy Atkins' Children. 1675–1970.* HMSO, 1971, pp 3–4. The bulk of the Army's recruits were

illiterate, so the Army appointed Regimental schoolmasters to teach the NCOs, soldiers and their children. In 1675 there were at least two in the garrison at Tangier. See also Colonel A C T White VC, *The Story of Army Education. 1643– 1963*. Harrap, 1963.

24. Fred Anderson, *A People's Army*. University of North Carolina Press, 1949, p. 132.

Chapter 13

1. See Brigadier Bernard Rigby, *Ever Glorious. The Story of the 22 (Cheshire) Regiment*, p 24. Sir Richard Augustus Levinge Bart, *Records of the 43 Foot 1868*, p 11.

2. *DNB*.

3. Archibald Forbes, *The Record of an Historic Regiment (The Black Watch)*. Cassell, 1896, p 45.

4. Ian K Steele, *Betrayals. Fort William Henry and the Massacre*. OUP, 1990, pp 81– 3 and letter quoted E P Hamilton, *The French Indian Wars*. NY, 1962, p 198.

5. Bradley, p 188.

6. G D Martineau, *A History of the Royal Sussex Regiment*, 1955.

7. Fortescue, II, p 312 and Pargellis, p 245 and notes.

8. Pargellis, p 247.

9. Knox, I, p 68.

10. Pargellis, 249 note 55.

11. Knox, I, p 68.

12. Steele, p 110.

13. Martineau, p 46.

14. Bradley, p 505.

15. Knox, I, p 69.

16. Steele, p 115. See also Hamilton, pp 203-5.

17. Steele, pp 112–3.

18. Knox, I, p 69.

19. Steele, pp 116–7.

20. Steele, p 122.

21. Steele, p 129. James Fenimore Cooper gives a literary account of the siege and massacre in *The Last of the Mohicans*.

22. Steele, p 138 gives 2308 paroled: 308 killed and missing, after 1763.

23. Knox, I, p 69 and Parkman, I, p 513.

24. Martineau, pp 46–7.

25. Steele, p 145.

26. Steele, p 183.

27. Williamson, p 399 and Hamilton, p 203.

28. George Stanley, *New France The Last Phase 1744-60*. OUP, 1968, p 161.

29. George Stanley, *Canada's Soldiers*. Macmillan, Toronto, 1954, pp 75–6. Williamson, 399.

30. 14, 22, 27, 35, 42, 44, 46, 48, 48 and 55 Foot regiments: Three Bns of the Royal Americans (60 Foot) and four Independent Companies. JSAHR. Vol XVI, p 352.

31. The Mutiny Act of 1703 allowed justices of the peace in England to billet troops in 'inns, livery stables and ale houses and in no private houses whatsoever'. Publicans were reimbursed for accommodation, victuals, candles and small beer, from deductions from the soldiers' subsistence money.

32. Doyle, *Colonies under Hanover,* p 599.

33. See Pargellis, pp 196–7 and O'Conor, p 57.

34. See Note 30 above.

35. Norrey's Jephson O'Conor, *A Servant of the Crown in England and in North America (1756–61)*. NY, 1938, p 80.

36. *Ibid,* pp 11–16.

37. *Ibid,* p 83. *DNB* (Woffington).

38. Bradley, p 206. Quebec's ration was four ounces of bread and a little salt pork per day, which would be halved by the next spring.

39. Stanley, *Canada's Soldiers,* p 143.

40. *Ibid,* p 76.

41. Bradley, p 177.

42. Lower, p 45.

43. *DNB* (Huck Saunders).

Chapter 14

1. Fortescue, II, p 321 and Rex Whitworth, *Field Marshal Lord Ligonier*. 1958, p 242 note 1. *DNB* (Ligonier). E J Burford, *Wits, Wenchers and Wantons*. Robert Hale, 1986, p 174.

2. *DNB* and J C Long, *Lord Jeffrey Amherst*. Macmillan, NY, 1933, p 44.

3. Major R H Barnes, *History of the Scottish Regiments of Britain and the Colonies*, 1956, p 64.

4. Brigadier Bernard Rigby, *Ever Glorious. History of the 22 Foot, the Cheshire Regiment,* p 26. Lewis Butler, *The Annals of the King's Royal Rifle Corps*. 1913, p 47.

5. Commanding 55 Foot and the Light Infantry.

6. Letter quoted William Wood, *The Fight for Canada*. Constable, 1905, p 41.

7. Beckles Willson, p 357 and Whitton, p 283. Reilly, p 175. Waugh, p 144.

8. H C Wylly, *The Loyal North Lancashire Regiment (47 Foot),* 1933.

9. Quoted J S McLennan, *Louisbourg. From its Foundation to its Fall 1713–58.* Fortress Press, Sydney, Nova Scotia Canada 1918 (2nd Edition 1957), p 239.

10. Bradley, *Fight with France for North America,* p 230.

11. Francis Parkman, *Montcalm and Wolfe.*

12. Amherst married Jane Dalison (3 May 1753), seven years younger than himself, in Gray's Inn chapel. She was the daughter of a wealthy Kentish family, and brought a substantial dowry. *Burke's Complete Peerage.*

13. Editor J C Webster, *The Journal of Jeffrey Amherst.* University of Chicago Press, 1931, p 43.

14. W T Waugh, *James Wolfe. Man and Soldier.* 1928, p 157.

Chapter 15

1. The Louisbourg Grenadiers of 1 Foot, 15 Foot, 17 Foot and 22 Foot Regiments, commanded by Colonel James Murray; a Light Infantry battalion, consisting of 550 selected marksmen from different regiments, formed at Halifax shortly before sailing, commanded by Major Scott of the 40 Foot: the 78 Foot (Fraser's Highlanders) and a company of New England Rangers. *London Gazette* of 15 August 1758.

2. Robert J Jones, *History of the 15th Foot (East Yorkshire).* 1958, p 139. Brigadier Bernard Rigby, *Ever Glorious. The History of the 22nd Cheshire Regiment.* 1994, p 28. G D Martineau, *A History of the Royal Sussex Regiment (35 Foot) 1701–1953.* Moore and Tiller, 1955, p 51. Colonel H C Wylly. *47th Regiment of Foot (The Loyal North Lancashire Regiment).* 1933, Vol I, pp 22–23.

3. Lieutenant Colonel Russell Gurney, *The Northamptonshire Regiment (48/58 Foot) 1742–1934.* 1935, p 23.

4. King's Royal Rifle Corps (KRRC), p 50. Gurney, p 32. Rigby, p 28. Fortescue, II, p 323.

5. Wylly, p 22.

6. KRRC, p 50.

7. Rigby, p 28 and Beckles Willson, p 381.

8. Fortescue, II, p 326 and KRRC, p 51.

9. Martineau, p 51. Gurney, p 33. Wylly, p 23 and Editor J Clarence Webster, *A J Amherst's Journal.* University of Chicago Press, 1931, p 65.

10. Beckles, p 370.

11. See Martineau, p 52 and Wylly, I, p 23.

12. Jones, p 140 and KRRC, p 52.

13. Jones, p 141. KRRC, p 53 and Clarence, p 70 (23 July).

14. Knox, p 249.

15. Anon, *Journal of the Siege of Louisbourg*. Canadian Archives. F173, p 274, C 11 V10–1.

16. Rigby, p 30.

17. McLennan, *Louisbourg*. 1957, p 281.

18. Parkman, II, p 75.

19. *Ibid,* p 72.

20. Fortescue, II, p 327. See Knox, I, pp 255-6 for capitulation terms.

21. Arthur R M Lower, *Colony to Nation*. 1946, p 60.

22. William Wood, *The Fight for Canada*. Toronto, 1906, p 141.

23. From the Regiments of Artois, Bourgogne, Cambise, Volontiers Etrangers and about 700 Canadians. See Note 66a, Major-General R H Mahon. *The Life of General James Murray*. John Murray, 1921.

24. Beckles Willson, p 382.

25. Wood, p 144.

26. *Ibid,* p 145.

27. Parkman, 76. *Historical Records of the 40th Regiment,* p 25 and note.

28. Clarence, p 63 note.

29. Knox, I, p 206.

30. *Records of 47 Foot* and *Amherst Journal,* p 73.

31. *Amherst Journal,* p 73 and Whitton, p 299 ff.

32. *Amherst Journal,* p 90.

33. *Ibid,* p 92. During the winter of 1758–9 the troops were quartered as follows:

    At Ford Edward: 2/60 Foot and 6 coys of Rangers.

    At Louisbourg Garrison: 22 Foot, 28 Foot, 40 Foot, 45 Foot and 1 coy of Rangers: 35 Foot mostly at Annapolis.

    At Halifax Garrison: 15 Foot, 58 Foot, 3/60 Foot, 4/60 Foot and 2 coys of Rangers.

    At Lunenburgh. Det of 3/60 Foot and one coy of Rangers.

    2/1 Foot (Albany) 17 Foot (Philadelphia) 27 Foot (West Jersey) 42 Foot (New York) 43 Foot (Fort Cumberland) 44 Foot (Long Island). 46 Foot (Schenectady) 47 Foot (East Jersey) 48 Foot (Connecticut) 55 Foot (below Albany on Hudson River) 1/60 Foot (Albany) 77 Foot (Lancaster) 78 Foot (Schenectady and Fort Stanwix). See *JSAHR*. Vol XVI, Notes 352).

34. *DNB.*

35. Theodore Draper, *A Struggle for Power*. Little, Brown and Co., 1996. Quoted, p 170.

36. John W Shy, *A New Look at Colonial Militia*. 1965, p 356. *DNB*.

37. Anderson, p. 119.

38. *Historical Records of 40 Foot*.

39. Knox, p 260.

40. Robin Reilly, *The Rest to Fortune. The Life of Major General James Wolfe*. Cassell, 1960, p 196 and W T Waugh, *James Wolfe. Man and Soldier*. 1928, p 184.

Chapter 16

1. Lewis Butler. KRRC, p 52 and Fortescue, II, p 328.

2. Fortescue, II, p 329.

3. *Memoirs of Anne Mac Vickor* quoted Norrey's Jephson O'Conor, *A Servant of the Crown in England and North America*. A Publication of the Society of Colonial Wars in the State of New York. 1938, p 94.

4. R F K Goldsmith, *The Records of the 32/46 Foot (The Duke of Cornwall's Light Infantry)*. Leo Cooper, 1970, p 6.

5. Fortescue, II, p 329.

6. Francis Parkman, *Montcalm and Wolfe* (1917). 2 Vols, II, p 96 and Fortescue, II, p 330.

7. *Ibid,* II, p 331.

8. George F G Stanley, *Canada's Soldiers (1604–1954)*. Macmillan, Toronto, 1954, p 80 and KRRC, p 57. Fortescue, II, p 334–5.

9. Fortescue, II, p 336.

10. Lieutenant William Grant of the Black Watch. Archibald Forbes, *The Record of an Historic Regiment 1896*.

11. Quoted KRRC, p 59.

12. Forbes, p 52. Also W Copeland Trimble, *The Historical Record of the 27 Inniskilling Regiment*. 1876, pp 33–4.

13. See Trimble, *Historic Records of the 27 Foot (Inniskilling's)*. 1876, p 33.

14. Forbes, p 53.

15. *Ibid,* p 55.

16. Stanley, p 81.

17. KRRC, p 60–1. Stanley quoted p 81 and see Hamilton, *The French and Indian Wars*. 1962, p 248. Knox, I, 265 note 2 for Bradstreet's report to Abercromby, dated Oswego 31 August 1758.

18. *Instructions to Amherst for the Campaigns of 1759.* Issued Whitehall 29 December 1758.

19. Dorothy Marshall, *18th Century England.* Longmans Paper Back, 2nd Edition, 1974, p 289.

20. Doyle, *Colonies under Hanover,* p 608.

21. John Shy, *Toward Lexington.* Princeton University Press, 1965, pp 15–16. Anderson, p 78.

22. Whitton, p 294 and KRRC, p 64. In 1755 Braddock had used the longer route via Alexandria (Washington) and Fort Cumberland.

23. Parkman, II, p 147.

24. KRRC, pp 64, 65, quoting Parkman, II, p 147.

25. *Ibid,* p 69.

26. Parkman, II, p 147.

27. KRRC, p 70.

28. Parkman, II, p 147.

29. Hamilton, p 99.

30. Fortescue, II, p 343. Reginald Hargreaves, *The Bloodybacks (British Servicemen in North America (1655–1783).* Hart-Davis, 1968, p 157. KRRC, p 70.

31. Correlli Barnett, *Britain and her Army.* Allen Lane. The Penguin Press, 1970, p 204.

32. Marshall, p 290.

33. Quoted American Historical Review. Vol 22, p 173.

Chapter 17

1. *DNB* (Wolfe).

2. Beckles Willson, *The Life and Letters of James Wolfe.* Heinemann, 1909. *Letter,* 24 February 1752, p 71.

3. Beckles, pp 144, 182 and 137.

4. William Wood, *The Fight for Canada.* 1905, p 122.

5. Lieutenant B Smyth, *History of the 20 Foot (Lancashire Fusiliers).* 1889, p 35.

6. W T Waugh, *James Wolfe. Man and Soldier.* Louis Carrier, NY, 1928, p 94.

7. Wood, p 129.

8. Wood, pp 133 and 120.

9. Fortescue, II, p 578.

10. Waugh, pp 108–9.

11. Beckles, pp 220, 227.

12. *DNB. Letter,* 17 October 1757.

13. *DNB. Letter,* 12 January 1758.

14. Beckles, p 339.

15. *Ibid,* pp 353 and 349. Stella Tillyard, *Aristocrats.* Chatto and Windus, 1994, p 36.

16. Williams, *Judy O'Grady and the Colonel's Lady.* Brassey's, 1988.

17. Beckles, p 202 and Williams, Chapter 17 (Modern Marriages).

18. See Chapter 4, p 12 and note 51.

    In 1720 196 soldiers and 385 sailors – 7.0% and 13.8% of *recorded* entries – married at the Fleet in 'clandestine marriages. In 1740 265 soldiers and 371 sailors – 5.4% and 7.6% of *recorded* entries.

    (See Outhwaite. *Studies in the Social History of Marriage.* 1981 p 123 ff).

19. Williams, p 13. J F Findlay, *Wolfe in Scotland.* Longman Green, 1928, p 106.

20. Findlay, p 232.

21. Williams, p 43.

22. Wood, pp 160 ff.

23. *DNB* (Monckton).

24. *DNB.*

25. General J F C Fuller, *The Decisive Battles of the Western World.* 3 Vols, 1957. II, p 265.

26. Wood, p 170. Beckles Willson, p 395.

27. Fortescue, II, p 367.

28. Wood, pp 166–7.

29. *DNB* (Saunders).

30. Bradley, p 288.

Chapter 18

1. *The Capture of Quebec.* Journal of the Society for Historical Research. 1939. Vol 18, pp 135–168.

2. Fraser's *Journal,* p 138.

3. Knox, I, p 334.

4. Fortescue, II, p 367.

5. A G Bradley, *The Fight with France for North America.* 1908, p 294.

Montcalm gave his strength at Quebec as: 2,900 regulars, 1100, 3800 and 3000 militia from Three Rivers, Montreal and Quebec respectively, making a total of 10,800, plus sailors and Indians. See Stanley, *New France,* p 294 note 19.

6. See Colonel N T St John Williams, *Judy O'Grady and the Colonel's Lady.* Brassey's, 1988, p 42 and p 19.

7. Now best remembered for giving his name to the tropical plant Bougainvillaea, and to the Bougainville Island in the South Pacific. He became a captain in the French navy and, like Captain Cook, circumnavigated the world.

8. *Peace is necessary or Canada is lost.* Fred E Whitton, *Wolfe and North America.* 1929, p 323.

9. R H Mahon, *Life of General the Hon. James Murray* (1921), p 89. Wrong, II, p 833.

10. Mahon, p 97.

11. Wood, p 80.

12. Whitton, p 326. American Historical Review. Vol 15, p 902.

13. Fortescue, II, p 369.

14. KRRC, p 74.

15. James Cook (1728–79) discovered Australia 1770. Killed by natives in the Pacific.

16. Bradley, p 290.

17. See Wood, p 177. Waugh, p 225 and Mahon.

18. Bradley, p 297.

19. Wood, p 151.

20. *DNB*.

21. Whitton, p 333.

22. KRRC, p 76 and Wood, pp 151–2.

23. Wood, p 156.

24. Whitton, p 341.

25. Beckles, p 439–40.

26. *Ibid,* p 440.

27. Knox, I, p 298.

28. Stacey, p 60.

29. *DNB* and Beckles, p 455.

30. Quoted Oliver Warner, *With Wolfe to Quebec.* Harper Collins, 1972, p 122.

31. Knox, II, p 49 note 1.

32. Mahon, p 118.

33. Wood, p 188.

34. Fortescue, II, p 373.

35. Fraser, p 144.

36. *Ibid,* p 143 note and Beckles, p 456.

37. Wood, p 196 (French Journal). Stanley, *New France,* p 226

38. Russell Gurney, *History of the Northamptonshire Regiment (48 Foot),* 1935. Quoted Sergeant Johnson of the 58 Foot (2nd Bn), p 39.

39. Fortescue, II, p 371.

40. Wolfe's Orders, 10 August 1759.

41. Fortescue, II, p 371.

42. Wood, p 191.

43. Robin Reilly, *The Rest to Fortune. The Life of James Wolfe.* Cassell, 1960, p 261.

44. Wood, p 191.

45. *DNB.* Beckles, pp 457, 459 and note. Whitton, p 351.

46. Quoted American Historical Review. Vol 15, p 903. *Historical Records of the 40th Regiment,* pp 27–8.

47. *DNB.* Beckles, pp (460), 458.

Chapter 19

1. Wolfe, *Letter to Rickson,* 5 November 1757. Quoted Reilly, p 161. Beckles, p 339.

2. Wood, p 198.

3. In 1690, Quebec and Montreal, defended by Frontenac, had been attacked by William Phips and a force of New Englanders.

4. Bradley, p 305.

5. Wood, p 200. Brian Connell, *The Plains of Abraham.* Hodder & Stoughton, 1959, p 214.

6. Major General R H Mahon, *The Life of the Hon. James Murray.* John Murray, 1921, p 124.

7. Bradley, p 313 and Fortescue, II, p 374.

8. Wood, p 198.

9. Fraser, pp 148–9.

10. Ward, *The Blessed Trade,* p 223.

11. *Ibid,* p 220.

12. Christopher Hibbert, *Wolfe at Quebec,* p 108.

13. Ward, p 220.

14. Wolfe's *General Orders, 17 August 1759.* See Hibbert, p 70.

15. Fortescue, II, p 378 and Bradley, p 314.

16. Quoted Connell, p 217.

17. Beckles, p 469 and Wood, pp 203–4.

18. Reilly, p 271.

19. Townsend's reply of 30 August and Wood, p 210.

20. Wood, p 213 and KRRC, p 85.

21. Fraser, p 150.

22. Fortescue, II, p 378.

23. William was the youngest of the three brilliant Howe brothers. The eldest was killed at Ticonderoga: the second, Richard, became an admiral and the first Earl Howe. William would become a general.

24. Bradley, p 315.

25. Fortescue, II, p 379. KRRC, p 86.

26. Fraser, p 150 and see Whitton, p 362.

27. Wood, p 215 and Reilly, p 288.

28. Wood, p 216.

29. See Reilly, p 291.

30. Beckles, p 473.

31. Beckles, pp 475–6.

32. Stacey, p 104.

33. Beckles, p 475 note 2 and Woods, p 218.

34. Wood, p 220.

35. *DNB*. Fortescue, p 279. KRRC, p 86.

36. Stobo had broken his parole and had been sent by Amherst to Wolfe, to whom he gave valuable information about Quebec and its defences. He left Quebec on 7 September – see Beckles, p 475 note 4 and Doughty, Vol II, p 114. A G Doughty and G W Parmelee, *The Siege of Quebec and Battle of the Plains of Abraham*. 6 Vols, 1902.

37. *DNB*. Parkman, II, p 276 and Reilly, p 295.

38. See Beckles, p 481. Townsend recorded in his diary on 10 September. 'By some intelligence the General has had, he has changed his mind, as to the place he intended to land: heard we had some deserters from the enemy's camp at Beauport.' Quoted Reilly, p 295. Saunders also sent to Wolfe urgent information he had obtained from a French deserter picked up by the Navy.

39. See Beckles, p 475 and Wood, p 216–17.

40. Major General R H Mahon, *Life of the Hon. James Murray*. London, 1921 and Wood, p 217.

41. Fraser, p 150. Bradley, p 316 and Beckles, p 480.

42. Knox, II, p 86–9.

43. G D Martineau, *A History of the Royal Sussex Regiment (35 Foot) 1701–1953.* Moore and Tiller, 1955, p 56. Details given Wood, p 337, Note 5.

44. Quoted Reilly, p 301.

45. Beckles, p 481 and *DNB.*

46. Townsend papers. Wood, pp 334–5, gives sources for Wolfe keeping his plans to himself, quoting Doughty.

47. Reilly, p 299 and Beckles, p 485.

48. Bradley, pp 316–7. *DNB.* Beckles, p 487 note I, and Wood, p 325.

49. Wood, pp 322–3 concludes. 'The story is probably true but not in its popular form.' Wolfe's own copy of the poem, given to him by Katherine Lowther, and annotated by him, was found in the papers he left. See *The Times* 15 January 1913.

50. See Stacey, p 122 and Beckles, p 487 note.

Chapter 20

1. Frederick George Scott. Quoted William Wood, *The Fight for Canada.* Constable, 1905. Preface.

2. W T Waugh, *James Wolfe. Man and Soldier.* 1928, p 284.

3. KRRC. Fortescue, p 380. Bradley, p 317.

4. Beckles, p 480. M Fraser, *Extracts from a Manuscript Journal relating to the Siege of Quebec 1759.* Literary and Historical Society of Quebec 1867, p 151, Note 54. Fortescue, II, p 380 notes 1 and 3.

5. Beckles, p 481, quoting Doughty, IV, p 296.

6. Stacey, p 106 and Mahon.

7. Wood, pp 230–1. Waugh, p 287.

8. Bradley, p 319. Knox, II, pp 94-7.

9. Bradley, p 320. Beckles, p 488.

10. Only one 6 pdr. was used in the battle: a second arrived at 11am and was used by Townsend against Bougainville [Wood 233]. For strengths of British force see Knox, II, p 298. Beckles, p 490. Wood, pp 236–7.

11. KRRC 88.

12. Colonel H C Wylly, *The Loyal North Lancashire Regiment (47 Foot).* 1933. 2 Vols. I, p 31. Captain R H Raymond Smithies, *The Historical Records of the 40th Regiment (2nd Somersetshire).* (Now South Lancashire Regiment). 1894, p 28.

13. Knox, II, p 68.

14. KRRC, p 89.

15. See note 10 above.

16. Waugh, p 289. Smithies (quoting Return in the PRO signed by Brigadier Townsend) gives **Total 4,441** all Ranks. Regimental Strengths:

LEFT	CENTRE	RIGHT
78 Foot – 662	43 Foot – 327	Louisbourg Grenadiers – 241
58 Foot – 335	47 Foot – 360	28 Foot – 421
L.I. – 400		35 Foot – 519
Total 3,265		

17. Beckles, p 489.

18. Frederick E Whitton, *Wolfe and North America*. 1929, p 368. Bradley, p 321.

19. R Reilly, *The Rest to Fortune*. 1960, p 308.

20. Parkman, II, p 292.

21. Bradley, p 322. Knox, II, p 101.

22. See Beckles, p 490 and C P Stacey, *The Siege and Battle of Quebec 1759*. Macmillan of Toronto, 1959, p 140.

23. Reilly, p 309.

24. See for account of Battle: Wood, pp 251–6. Beckles, pp 492–4 (based on Knox). Fortescue, II and regimental histories.

25. Wylly, p 32.

26. Fortescue, II, p 387.

27. For the death scene on the Battlefield – see Wood, p 324, Note 9. Fortescue, II, p 115 note. Bradley, p 326. Brigadier Bernard Rigby, *Ever Glorious. History of the 22 Foot. The Cheshire Regiment*, p 42 and note. The Regimental Colour of the 22 Foot allegedly used to wrap Wolfe's body is hanging in Chester Cathedral. The Colour was at Louisbourg.

28. Wood, p 257. Whitton, p 371. Parkman, II, p 297, quoting Knox who was nearby. James Henderson's letter is given in full in English Historical Review. 'The Death of General Wolfe'. Vol 12 (1897), p 119.

29. Wylly, p 34.

30. Knox, II, p 102. Stacey, p 152.

31. See Christopher Hibbert, *Wolfe at Quebec*. Longman, Green, 1959, p 162.

32. KRRC, p 93. Knox, II, p 118. Official figures from PRO.

33. Lieutenant M Fraser, p 157 and Wood, p 261.

34. Wood, pp 267–9.

35. Reilly, p 313.

36. Major General R H Mahon, *The Life of the Hon. James Murray*, John Murray, 1921. Stanley, *New France*, p 295 note 29.

37. NCMH. Vol 7, p 539.

38. Knox, II, p 102.

39. Bradley, p 328.

40. R Levinge, *Historical Records of Monmouthshire Light Infantry. 43 Foot*. 1868, p 35.

41. Parkman, II, p 309.

42. Knox, II, p 111 note.

43. Parkman, II, p 310.

44. Some of the British soldiers were buried in the garden next to the Convent. During excavations in 1912, a number of skeletons were found, some still buried in their uniforms.

45. Parkman, II, 307.

46. Bradley, p 329.

47. KRRC, p 93.

48. Letter of 30 October quoted Wood, p 278.

49. Tour Guide to Canada.

50. Stacey, p 158. Capitulation terms in Sigmund Samuel, *The Seven Years War in Canada*. 1934, p 121.

51. See Bradley, pp 330–1.

52. *DNB*.

53. Wylly, p 35. They also received a commemorative medal.

54. *Monitor*. 22 December 1759, quoted Dan E Clark, *News concerning America in English Newspapers 1754–63*. The Pacific Historical Review. 1941. Vol 10, p 80.

55. Williams, *Judy O'Grady*, p 23.

56. *DNB*.

57. Parkman, II, p 410.

Chapter 21

1. Appointed commander-in-chief in America, 9 November 1758.

2. Fortescue, II, p 375 note 1. 44 Foot, 46 Foot, 4/60 Foot and 2,500 New York Provincials.

3. Lewis Bulter, *The Annals of the King's Royal Rifle Corps. Vol I. The Royal Americans*. 1913, p 94.

4. Fortescue, II, p 376 note 2. 1st Brigade. Colonel Forster. 27, 55, 1st Bn, 1 Foot. 2nd Brigade. Colonel Grant. 17 Foot, 77 (Montgomery's Highlanders), 42 Foot (Black

Watch). The 80th Light Infantry. 5,000 Provincials, a body of Rangers, a detachment of Artillery.

5.   Jeffrey Amherst, *The Journals*. Edited J Clarence Webster. 1930, 16 May, p 109.

6.   Knox, II, p 458.

7.   Lieutenant General Cantlie, *The History of the Royal Army Medical Corps*. I, p 113.

8.   Amherst, p 115.

9.   *Ibid*, p 116. *Rogers's Island*. 9, 11 June. Colonel H C B Rogers, *The British Army of the 18th Century*. Allen and Unwin, 1977 p 138.

10. Knox, II, p 468.

11. *Ibid,* II, p 468.

12. Bradley, p 338.

13. KRRC, p 95. Ticonderoga, the best example of a colonial fort, has been beautifully reconstructed, and is now a museum. The museum houses an outstanding collection of 18th century military memorabilia, including articles in daily use in the garrison. One can relive the Fort's history with costumed guides, and tour Lake Champlain in *M/V Carillon*.

14. Guy Frégault, *Canada. The War of Conquest*. OUP, 1969, p 259.

15. Samuel, p 64 and Amherst, p 151 note.

16. Amherst, p 158.

17. KRRC, p 95.

18. Frégault, p 260.

19. Fortescue, II, p 375.

20. Bradley, p 48 and KRRC, p 96.

21. Fortescue, II, pp 375–6 and KRRC, p 97.

22. For capitulation terms see Samuel, p 79.

23. Bradley, p 352.

24. Bradley, p 342.

25. Bradley, p 342 and Parkman, II, p 253.

26. Amherst, p 168.

27. Bradley, p 343.

28. *Ibid,* p 345.

29. Amherst, p 188.

30. Parkman, II, p 257.

31. Bradley, p 346.

32. American Historical Review. Vol 22, p 171.

Chapter 22

1. Mahon, p 191.

2. Robert Jones, *History of the 15 Foot. The East Yorkshire Regiment.* 1958, p 164.

3. Knox, II, p 246 and KRRC, p 94.

4. Fortescue, II, p 395 note 1.

5. Parkman, *Montcalm and Wolfe.* Vol II, p 340.

6. Knox, II, pp 270–1, 280, 289.

7. 7lbs of bread or flour (1 pound = 0.45 kg), 2lbs of pork, 2lbs of beef, one pint and a half of pease, two pints of oatmeal, _lb of butter (or 1lb of cheese in lieu): half a pint of oil: 1_lbs of flour and half a pound of suet or fruit.

8. Knox, II, p 282.

9. Knox, II, p 271.

10. Parkman, II, pp 328–9.

11. *Ibid,* p 329 note.

12. Mahon, p 202.

13. Sir Richard George Augustus Levinge, *Historical Records of the 43rd Regiment (Monmouthshire Light Infantry).* 1868, p 37. Colonel H C Wylly, *The Loyal North Lancashire Regiment Vol I. (1741–1914).* The Royal United Service Institution. 1933, p 36.

14. Lieutenant M Fraser (later Colonel – 78 Foot), *Extracts from a Manuscript Journal relating to the Siege of Quebec.* 1759 (1867) Literary and Historical Society of Quebec, p 160. Published in the Journal of the Society for Army Historical Research 1939, Vol 18. The Regiment was disbanded in 1763, and a large number of both officers and men settled in the Province of Quebec, especially along the shores of the lower St Lawrence. Malcolm Fraser settled at Murray Bay, married Marie Allaire, a French-Canadian, and had between 25 and 30 grandchildren.

15. Knox, II, pp 292–7 and Fraser, p 161.

16. Knox, II, pp 306–7 and Fraser, p 161.

17. Fraser, p 161 note.

18. Knox, II, p 310.

19. *Ibid,* p 307.

20. Wylly (47 Foot), p 37.

21. W H Blumenthall, *Women Camp Followers of the American Revolution.* Philadelphia, 1952, p 51.

22. General Sir Neil Cantlie, *History of the Army Medical Department.* Vol I, p 115.

23. Knox, II, p 365.

24. Knox, II, p 367.

25. *Ibid,* p 330.

26. F E Whitton, *Wolfe and North America*. 1929, p 396. For Q M S Johnson see Lieutenant Colonel Russell Gurney, *History of the Northamptonshire Regiment. 48 Foot and 58 Foot. 1742–1934*. Gale and Polden, 1935, p 49.

27. Knox, II, p 351.

28. Fraser, p 168.

29. Michael Barthop, *48 Foot/58 Foot Northamptonshire Regiment*. Leo Cooper, 1974, p 15. Fortescue, II, p 578.

30. Knox, II, p 399 and Mahon, p 240.

31. Bradley, p 370.

32. KRRC, p 108.

33. Fraser, p 168.

34. KRRC, pp 108–9.

Chapter 23

1. Eight battalions of regulars, grenadiers, Light Infantry and a company of Rangers. Mahon, p 251 note.

2. 17 and 27 Foot and a contingent of militia from Massachusetts, Rhode Island and New Hampshire.

3. Whitton, p 401. Colonel Grant brought the 1st Foot (Royal Scots) with him. See Rigby, *Ever Glorious: The Story of the 22nd Foot*. Vol 1, Chapter 7 for an excellent account.

4. Frégault, p 280.

5. Dorothy Marshall, p 305.

6. Frégault, p 280.

7. Right Bde: 1 Bn (15 Foot and 48 Foot) 3 Bn (35 Foot and 3 Bn 60 Foot) 5 Bn (47 Foot and 78 Foot) under Colonel Ralph Burton: Left Bde 2 Bn (28 Foot and 58 Foot) 4 Bn (43 Foot and 2 Bn 60 Foot) under Colonel William Howe.

8. Fortescue, II, p 403.

9. KRRC, p 111.

10. *The Journal of Jeffrey Amherst*. Editor J C Webster. (Member of the Historic Sites and Monuments Board of Canada). University of Chicago, 1931, p 219. Fortescue, p 399 gives less than 6,000 regulars, 4,500 provincials and 700 Indians.

11. 1,000 savages of the Iroquois, the greatest number ever seen in arms in the cause of England. *Annual Register* 1760, quoted Samuel, p 180.

12. Wood, p 302.

13. *Journal,* p 240.

14. *Ibid,* 242.

15. Samuel, p 182 quoting *Annual Register* 1760, p 60.

16. Knox, II, p 521. Amherst – quoted Colonel H C B Rogers, *The British Army of the 18th Century*. Allen and Unwin, 1977, p 151.

17. Wood, p 304 and Whitton, p 402.

18. *Amherst's Journal* (7 September), p 246 and Parkman, II, p 373.

19. Knox, II, p 561.

20. Capitulation Article IX.

21. Ian K Steele, *Betrayals. Fort William Henry and the Massacre*. OUP, 1990, p 148 and see Wood, p 305.

22. KRRC, p 113.

23. Knox, III, p 605. (There were only 2,132 all ranks fit for duty).

24. Capitulation Article XVII and Stanley, p 96. Wood, p 306.

25. Samuel, p 193. Stanley, *New France,* p 258 quoting Bigot, Capitulation Terms (article 15).

26. Robert J Jones, *History of the 15 Foot (East Yorkshire)*. 1958, p 173 note.

27. Eccles, p 19. Amherst's *Journal,* p 250 gives 4,004, including women and children.

28. The Canadian historian, Benjamin Sulti. Quoted Stanley, *Canada's Soldiers,* p 96.

29. *General Orders 9 September 1760* – Samuel, p 205.

30. Bradley, p 390.

31. Thwaites, p 263.

32. Amherst, p 257.

33. It is easy to trace the whole course of the Siege and Battle in modern Quebec. The Tourist Office provides a walking tour booklet and a guide to the 'key' locations e.g. The Plains of Abraham (Champs de Bataille) and the Ursuline convent (Montcalm's skull).

34. *DNB.*

35. *DNB.*

36. *DNB* and Fortescue, II, p 405.

37. Frégault, p 288.

38. Thwaites, p 264 and Wrong, II, p 873.

39. Thwaites, p 264 quoting Parkman, *Montcalm and Wolfe,* II, p 385. Wood, p 56 and Wrong, II, p 882.

40. Stanley, Chapter 8.

41. Thwaites, p 265 quoting Amherst to Pitt, 18 October 1760.

42. J C Long, *Lord Jeffrey Amherst. A Soldier of the King*. Macmillan, NY, 1933. American

Historical Review. Vol 22, p 171. Amherst married twice and died without issue at 'Montreal', the house he built at Rivermead. He was buried at Sevenoaks.

43. Lieutenant Colonel Laws, *Welfare 1760*. Journal of the Royal United Services Institute. Vol CVI. February 1961, p 13. J C Long, p 159. See Mrs Gage, Chapter 15, p 6.

44. *United Services Gazette*. 30 March 1867, p 4. See Williams, *Judy O'Grady and the Colonel's Lady*, pp 138–40.

Chapter 24

1. See Fortescue, II, p 548 note. The 11 battalions were 17, 27, 28, 35, 40, 42 (two battalions) 43, 46 and 3/60 Foot regiments, escorted by a fleet under Admiral George Rodney *(DNB)*.

2. Fortescue, II, p 550 note. 4, 22, 38, 48, 65, 6 Foot Regiments, two companies of American Rangers, and ten companies of Barbados volunteers.

3. Dorothy Marshall, p 308 and Fisher, p 762. *DNB* (Pitt). Dorn, p 371.

4. Marshall, p 311.

5. *DNB* (Stuart). Peter Douglas Brown, *William Pitt, Earl of Chatham*. Allen and Unwin, 1978, p 256.

6. *Ibid*.

7. See Williamson, p 406. William L Grant, *Canada versus Guadeloupe*. American History Review. Vol 17. 1912, pp 735–43.

8. G.F. Stanley, *New France*, p 221, quoting *Scenes from the History of the Ursulines*. Quebec, 1897, p 289.

9. NCMH. Part VII. *The Old Regime (1713–63)*. Editor J O Lindsay. CUP, p 486. Parliamentary History XII, pp 1259–73.

10. Williamson, p 407.

11. *Ibid*, p 426.

12. Samuel Johnson, *The Idler*. No 81. 3 November 1759.

13. Dan E Clark, *News and Opinions concerning America in English Newspapers 1754–63*. The Pacific History Review 1941. Vol X, p 82.

14. Gooch, p 191.

INDEX I

INDEX II

British Army (1760)

42   1739   The 42nd Regt. of Foot (or Royal Highland Regt.) 101,105, 106,114,117,141,143,146,147, 198,217

*43   1741   The 43rd Regt. of Foot (Monmouthshire) (Light Infantry) 56,57,112,113,122,163, 164,176,179,180,185,187,210,223

*44   1741   The 44th Regt. of Foot (The East Essex) 63,64,71,75,77, 104,106,143,150,153,199,

*45   1741   The 45th Regt. of Foot (The Nottinghamshire) 52,55,67,115, 122,128,129,139

*46   1741   The 46th Regt. of Foot (The South Devonshire) 56,112, 114,143,199

*47   1741   The 47th Regt. of Foot (The Lancashire) 54,67,122,128,129, 139,164,180,185,187,189,190, 194,209,210,222

*48   1741   The 48th Regt. of Foot (The Northamptonshire) 63,64,71,75, 78,106,115,118,129, 135,139,164, 169,176,186,187,190,191,205,209,210

*Royal Warrant of 1 July 1751 renumbered regiments - instead of using the colonel's name, 54-59 were renumbered as 43-48 Foot respectively.

55   1755   The 55th Regt. of Foot (The Westmoreland) 112,115,143,146,

57   1755   The 57th Regt. of Foot (West Middlesex) 115

58   1755   The 58th Regiment of Foot (The Rutlandshire) 112,128,140,164, 170,171,180, 185,187,210

60   1755   The 60th (Royal American) Regt. of Foot 77,79,112,114,118, 128,135,136, 166,181,185,199, 200,217,219,221; 1Bn/60F 79,122,143,148,149; 2Bn/60F; 79,114,115,128,158,164,180,187,209,210,222; 3Bn/60F 128,140,164,169,186, 187,191,209,210; 4Bn/60F 122, 143,147,199

67   1758   The 67th Regt. of Foot (Raised 1756 as 2/20F) (The South Hampshire) 157,185

77   1757   The 77th (Montgomery's) Regt. of Foot (raised 1757 as 62F Reno. 1758, disb. 1763) 110,122,148,150,198

78   1757   The 78th (Simon Fraser's) Regt. of Foot (raised 1757 as 63F Reno. 1758, disb. 1763) 110, 122,128,139,163,164,169,176,180,185, 187,191,207-10,211

80   1758   The 80th (Gage's) Regt. of Foot (LI) 140,143,144,160,169,176,179, 180,185,186, 187,191,211,218

50   1745   Shirley's Regt. of Foot 52,63, 75,86,99,101,105

51   1745   Pepperell's Regt. of Foot 52,63, 75,86,101,104,105

(Note: Broken up 1748, reraised 1754 on the Irish Establishment, lost in action at Oswego 1756)

(Louisbourg) Grenadiers (22,40,45 Foot) 128, 129,135,138,160,176,187,189,190,193,217

Corps of Engineers (1716) 85,159,200

Provost 71,115,175,212

The Marine Regiments (1664) (Newly raised 1755 by the Admiralty) 51,71,108,160, 187,194

(Rogers's etc.) Rangers 57,71,87,98,104,106, 113,118,124,129,143,144,145,160,166,197, 205,210, 220

American Provincial Troops 5,8,23,24,51,52, 55,56,60,61,69,75,81,82,85,86,98,102,106,115, 118,122,129,143,145,147,148,150,159,163, 197,198,199,203,215,217

French Troops

Troupes de Terre (Regulars) 51,63,93,94,96, 104,106,117,118,119,120,130,145,164,166, 189,190, 191,211,219,220

Troupes de la Marine (Canadian Regulars) 51,52,94,97,98,130,145,164,188,190,211,218

Canadian Militia 23,84,94,97,104,105,106,117, 118,121,122,130,145,164,166,174,178,188,189, 190,191,193,200,207,211,216,217,218,220

Artois Regt. 67

Béarn Regt. 67,84,118,145,181,188,200,220

1st Berry Regt. 145

Bourgogne Regt. 67

Carignan-Salières Regt. 4,9

La Guienne Regt. 67,84,118,145,180,181,188

Languedoc Regt. 67,84,118,145,181,188

La Reine Regt. 67,84,118,145

Royal Roussillon 93,118,145,181,188

La Sarre 93,118,145,181,188

Artillery 95,104,118,130,189,212

Engineers 105